KU-244-848

Contents

CADOGAN

Cadogan Guides
West End House
11 Hills Place
London W1R 1AG
becky.kendall@morrispub.co.uk

The Globe Pequot Press
246 Goose Lane
PO Box 480
Guilford
Connecticut 06437–0480

Copyright © Helen Truszkowski 2000
Authors: Helen Truszkowski, Joseph Fullman

Editorial Director: Vicki Ingle
Series Editors: Catherine Charles, Matthew Tanner
Editing: Catherine Charles, Matthew Tanner
Series Administrator: Becky Kendall
Proofreading: Susannah Wight
Indexing: Isobel McLean
Production: Book Production Services
Series design: Animage
Book design: Kicca Tommasi
Maps © Cadogan Guides, drawn by Kingston
Presentation Graphics
Cover photographs
  front: Horacio Monteverde & Susannah Sayler
  back: French Picture Library
Original photography: Catherine Charles,
Ian Lazarus, Alex Robinson, Susannah Sayler,
Michael Wu

ISBN 1–86011–995–6
A catalogue record for this book
is available from the British Library
Printed and bound in Italy by Printer Trento srl.

Acknowledgments

Helen

Thanks go to Nicole Walsh and the
Disneyland Paris Press Office and PR teams;
to Roger Harrison at Eurostar; to Caroline
McDonagh and family for their input; and to
George for his unbridled enthusiasm.

Joseph

Merci beaucoup à Maman et Papa, Vicki,
Catherine, Mat, Caroline, Audrey, Sam et Beth,
Jean-Luc, Pascale, M. et Mme Delamotte et,
bien sur, Joanne, ma cherie amour.

About the series

Take the kids is the first guidebook series written specifically for people with children. Each guide draws on what is of particular interest to kids, and provides advice for carers on everything from tired legs to low boredom thresholds – enabling both grown-ups and their charges to have a great day out, or a fabulous holiday.

for Rose, an exceptional Mum and Granny

About the authors

Helen Truszkowski is an established travel writer and photographer. Over the past decade her journeys have taken her around the globe, including six months working in South Africa. She has contributed to a range of magazines worldwide, and is a former travel editor of *Executive Woman* magazine. Helen's four-year-old son, George, has accompanied her on her travels since he was a few weeks old, patiently awaiting his dream position as her research assistant for Disneyland® Paris. Helen is series sonsultant of Cadogan's *Take the Kids* series, and author of *Take the Kids Travelling*.

Joseph Fullman fell in love with Paris as an awe-struck six-year-old and has been returning regularly ever since. This guide is his chance to emulate his hero, Gene Kelly, and lead children singing and dancing through the streets of Paris. For Cadogan, he is author of *Take the Kids London*, *Going For Britain's Top Tourist Attractions*, *Going For London's Markets,* and a guide to Britain's preserved railways.

Specialist reader

Janet Mills is a highly experienced primary school teacher and mother of three who has worked in London since 1989.

Contents

Introduction

You probably think of Paris as a city strictly for grown-ups, and to a certain extent it is. If you know where to look, however, it's also great for kids. There are parks where they can take pony rides, sail model boats or have a picnic; funfairs with rides, games and candy floss galore; and museums stuffed full of weird and wonderful things. In particular, check out La Villette, a sort of science theme park with thousands of interactive exhibits. Make time for an evening trip on a *bateau mouche,* to see the riverside monuments picked out by spotlights. And don't forget the wonderful views – from the Eiffel Tower, Arc de Triomphe, Sacre Coeur and Grande Arche de la Défense.

You may find that your kids' greatest pleasure comes not from rides or sights or views, but just from seeing the little quirks of everyday living that make Paris different: cast-iron drinking fountains on cobbled pavements; driverless *métro* trains in which you can sit at the front and watch the tunnel rushing towards you; traders selling crêpes and roast sweetcorn on street corners; and accordion-players performing for crowded cafés.

Should the charms of Paris fade, just 20 miles (32km) east of the city is Disneyland® Paris, a fun-filled, child-centred palace of pleasure to rival that of the Sun King at Versailles. Here, kids of every age can loop-the-loop at blood-chilling speed, hurtle past stars and planets, spin gently round in gigantic tea cups, race through kooky mazes, clamber across swaying rope bridges, stare into the jaws of foul-smelling dragons, and come face to face with their Disney favourites, including the world's most famous rodent, Mickey Mouse.

Guide to the guide

Finding your way around this guide is easy. The opening sections contain all the practical information you need for living and travelling in Paris: essential details on trains, taxis, post offices, supermarkets, banks, policemen, and so on.

Next come the sights of Paris, divided into seven child-size areas. In each we have identified the primary sights, and secondary sights nearby; the best local shopping and places to eat; and other worthwhile attractions around and about.

For every attraction there is up-to-date information on how to get there, access, opening times and admission prices; as well as workshops and activities that have been specifically organized for kids. Some indication of appropriate age ranges is also given, as well as how long you should allow for your visit.

Next, we provide information on how to fill your days and evenings, with details of puppet theatres and circuses, shops and restaurants, a Paris calendar and a chapter on Paris for free.

The final section of the book is dedicated to Disneyland® Paris, with advice on how to book and what to expect, and tips on making the most of your visit: from which rides are suitable for younger children to the best places to stay.

Throughout, the text is sprinkled with questions and challenges for you and your children; the answers can be found at the end of the guide.

Finally, just in case that holiday villain, boredom, sets in, we suggest ways to keep you all amused – from toys to take along to games to play – which may, just may, prove to be lifesavers. Enjoy!

Symbols in the guide

☎	telephone
✉	fax
Ⓜ	métro

Map symbols

1	restaurant/café
Ⓜ	métro
Ⓡ	RER

getting there

Paris is not a difficult city to get to. It's one of the world's most popular destinations and is served by all the major air carriers. Intense competition on the transatlantic routes means there are always lots of cheap deals. Motorway and rail links with the rest of mainland Europe are good while, for Brits, it's never been easier to get to Paris. Now the Channel Tunnel is fully operational, London and Paris are just three hours apart by train.

Flights

Children under the age of two usually travel for just 10 per cent of the adult fare although they will not be entitled to either a seat or baggage allowance; between the age of three and eleven children cost between a half and two thirds of the adult fare. Children over twelve years are regarded as adults and must pay the full fare.

From the UK

Once you've taken into account check-in times and transfers from the airport, flying from London to Paris isn't much quicker than taking the train. It's only really worth considering if you can get a sizeable saving on the Eurostar fare. Scour the weekend newspapers for a bargain or, if you live in London, check the listings in *Time Out* and the *Evening Standard*.

Of the scheduled airlines, British Airways and Air France offer competitive packages which include accommodation; longhaul carriers sometimes offer a cheap stop-off deal to Paris en route to some far-flung destination. British Airways also operates flights from Edinburgh, Glasgow, Leeds, Manchester and Birmingham, while British Midland flies from Aberdeen, Edinburgh and Birmingham. Ryanair flies from Glasgow to Beauvais, 56km northwest of Paris.

Discounts are available to anyone under 26 and students aged 32 or under. There are also a multitude of cheap flight sites to be found on the web:

www.lowestfare.com
www.cheapflights.com
www.farebase.net
www.lastminute.com

Discount Agents

Campus Travel
52 Grosvenor Gardens, London SW1
✆ (020) 7730 3402
Branches at most UK universities.

STA
86 Old Brompton Rd, London SW7
✆ (020) 7938 4711
Branches across the UK.

Major Airlines

British Airways
✆ 0345 222 111
www.britishairways.com

Air France
✆ 0845 0845 111
www.airfrance.fr

British Midland
✆ 0345 554 554
www.iflybritishmidland.com

Ryanair
✆ (0541) 569 569
www.ryanair.ie

From North America

Competition on transatlantic routes is fierce and there are plenty of cheap deals to be found. The best value tickets offered by the major airlines are Apex and Super Apex, which must be booked 14–21 days before departure and involve a stay of at least 7 nights. Charter flights are usually the cheapest; or try the consolidators, companies which buy blocks of unsold tickets from major airlines and sell them at a discount.

Many of the larger airlines provide special on-board services for families: designated flight attendants, children's TV channels, play packs and seat-back computer games.

Flight Times to Paris from North America

New York: 7–8 hours

Miami: 5–6 hours

Los Angeles: 10–11 hours

Hawaii: 19 hours

Montreal: 7 hours

Toronto: 8 hours

Major Airlines

Air Canada
Canada: toll free ✆ 800 555 1212
US: toll free ✆ 800 776 3000
www.aircanada.com

American Airlines
toll free ✆ 800 433 7300
www.americanair.com

British Airways
toll free ✆ 800 247 9297
www.britishairways.com

Canadian Airlines
toll free ✆ 800 665 1177
www.cdnair.ca

**Delta Airlines
(now affiliated to Air France)**
toll free ✆ 800 221 1212
www.delta-air.com

United Airlines
toll free ✆ 800 538 2929
www.ual.com

Consolidators in North America

Air Brokers Travel
toll free ✆ 800 883 3273
www.airbrokers.com

Jetset
toll free ✆ 800 638 3273

Travac Tours & Charters
toll free ✆ 800 872 8800

UniTravel
toll free ✆ 800 325 2222

Arriving by plane

Roissy/Charles de Gaulle

23km north of central Paris
✆ 01 48 62 22 80

RER
Every 15 minutes 4.55am–11.55pm
Adult single 46F
Journey time: about 25mins to Gare du Nord
Line B to Ⓜ Gare du Nord, Châtelet-Les Halles, St Michel and Denfert Rochereau. Your RER ticket is valid on the métro to complete your journey.

Air France Bus
Every 12 minutes
Adult single 55F
Journey time: 45mins to the Arc de Triomphe
To the Arc de Triomphe via Porte Maillot.
Every 30 minutes
Adult single 65F
Journey time: about one hour
To Gare d'Austerlitz and Gare Montparnasse.

Roissy Bus
Every 15 minutes
Adult single 40F
Journey time: 45mins
To Opéra Garnier.

RATP Buses

Line 350
Every 20 minutes
Journey time: 50mins
The journey will use up 6 single tickets (*see* Tickets and Passes).
To Gare du Nord and Gard de l'Est

Line 351
Every 30 minutes
Journey time: 55mins
The journey will use up 6 single tickets.
To Porte de Bagnolet, Porte de Vincennes and Nation.

Taxi

By far the least stressful way of getting into the city centre from the airports, but also the most expensive; supplements will be added if more than three people are travelling or if you have a lot of luggage.
Fare from Roissy: 200 to 250F
Fare from Orly: 150 to 200F

Orly

14km south of Paris
☎ 01 49 75 52 52

RER: Line C or 'Orly Rail'
Every 15–30 minutes
Adult single 28.50 FF
Journey time: 40mins
To Gare d'Austerlitz and St Michel.

Orlyval
Every 4–8 minutes
Adult single 54F
Automatic métro to Antony on RER line B.

Air France Bus
Every 12 minutes
Adult single 40F
Journey time to Invalides: 30mins
Stops at Gare Montparnasse and Invalides.

Orlybus
Adult 30F
Every 12 minutes
Journey time: 30mins
Connects with RER B at Denfert-Rochereau.

Jetbus
Every 15 minutes
Adult single 21F
Journey time: 12mins
Connects with Ⓜ Villejuif-Louis Aragon.

On all public transport into the centre of Paris children aged between four and eleven pay half the adult fare and children younger than four go free, so long as they don't take up a seat.

Arriving by rail or ferry

By rail

Eurostar
☎ 0990 186 186
☎ 0870 167 6767 for a brochure
www.eurostar.com
20 times a day from London Waterloo International
Fares vary. An excursion return, which must involve a Saturday night away, can be bought for £89, child (4–11) £55, under 4s free
No baggage weight limit
Wheelchair-users need to inform Eurostar staff of their requirements when booking

Eurostar trains arrive at the Gare du Nord which has connections to two RER lines and two métro lines. It's a large station on several levels: taxis are down a level but are well signposted and not expensive. If you're going to continue your journey on the métro, it's a good idea to send the speediest member of your party sprinting off to buy tickets at the métro *guichet* (ticket office) before the rest of the train gets there.

Paris has five other mainline stations: Gare de l'Est (for services from northeast France, Switzerland, Austria, southern Germany), Gare de Lyon (southeast France, Switzerland and Italy), Gare d'Austerlitz (southwest France, Spain and Portugal), Gare

Don't miss the train!

Eurostar's service adheres to strict security codes. Much the same as when taking a scheduled flight, you are expected to check in (at least 20 minutes before the train is due to depart). Otherwise the gates are closed and your ticket is rendered useless.

Montparnasse (western France and Spain) and Gare St Lazare (UK and Normandy).

All have connections to the métro network. Call ✆ 08 36 35 35 35 for information on times and tickets.

By ferry

The completion of the Channel Tunnel in the early 1990s transformed the cross-channel travel industry. Decreasing passenger numbers have forced the ferries to make their fares highly competitive, and they now offer a range of deals in the hope of drawing some custom away from the Chunnel (under-4s usually travel free and there are discounts for under-14s). Most lines also boast good family facilities – restaurants, baby-changing rooms, children's play areas, video rooms, etc. The route between Dover and Calais is the quickest and most popular:

Dover–Calais
P&O Stena Line, ✆ 0870 600 9009
www.posl.com
35 sailings a day in high season
Journey time: 1 hour 15 minutes
Fares: A family of four travelling in a medium-sized car should expect to pay anything between £80–150 for a flexible return, depending on the time of year.

Other routes across the Channel:

Portsmouth–Roscoff and Poole–Cherbourg
Britanny Ferries, ✆ 0990 360 360

Portsmouth–Le Havre
P&O European Ferries, ✆ (0870) 600 0600

Hull–Zeebrugge
P&O North Sea Ferries, ✆ (01482) 377 177

Via the Channel Tunnel

Eurotunnel – Folkestone–Calais
✆ 0990 35 35 35
www.eurotunnel.com
Four departures an hour during peak times
Fares: flexible return tickets start at around £130 if you travel before 7am; the fare is for car space only, regardless of the number of passengers
Check in at least 25 minutes but no more than two hours before departure
No baggage weight limit
Wheelchair users need to inform Eurotunnel staff of their requirements when booking
British terminal: off junction 11a of the M20
French terminal: off junction 13 of the A16
Journey time: 35mins

Eurotunnel transports cars on purpose-built carriers through the Channel Tunnel between Folkestone and Calais. Most people choose to stay in their car although you can get out and stretch your legs and use the facilities if you wish. It is advisable to book in advance although it is possible just to turn up and wait. You will be put on a stand by list and given space on a first come, first served basis.

The drive from Calais to Paris on the A1/A16 motorway (*autoroute*) should cost around 105F in tolls and take approximately three hours. Alternatively, you could opt for a scenic (and free) cruise along the less congested D roads or green-signed *flèches vertes* (holiday routes) which avoid large towns. Michelin Map 911 details both motorways and *flèches vertes*.

Any car entering France must have its registration and insurance papers and should carry with it a hazard warning triangle which must be displayed 50m behind the vehicle in the event of an accident. If you're coming from the UK, remember to adjust the dip of your headlights for driving on the right. Drivers who hold a valid licence from an EU country, North America or Australia don't need an international licence. Seatbelts must be worn in the front seats of cars and in the back where fitted.

If you're thinking of hiring a car, bear in mind that rates in France are among the highest in Europe. Local firms usually offer much better deals than big name companies. If possible try to arrange a fly-drive or holiday package before you go. For more details, *see* **Getting Around**.

By bus

National Express/Eurolines

52 Grosvenor Gardens, London SW1
✆ 0990 808 080
Fares: from £44 return; discounts for under-25s;
under-16s half fare; under-5s free
Journey time London–Paris: about 8hrs

Paris' international coach station, the Gare Routière International Paris-Gallieni, is on the eastern edge of the city in the suburb of Bagnolet, Ⓜ Gallieni.

Travelling by coach is the cheapest but also the least comfortable way of getting to Paris.

Border formalities

From Europe

Visitors from the European Union can enter France for up to 90 days without a visa. If you plan to stay longer, you'll have to apply for a *carte de séjour*.

From elsewhere

Visitors from North America can enter France for up to 90 days without a visa. If you plan to stay longer, you'll have to apply for a *carte de séjour*. Other nationals should check on their particular entry requirements with their respective embassies.

Customs

EU nationals over the age of 17 are no longer required to make a declaration to customs upon entry into another EU country and so can now import a limitless amount of goods for personal use. Quantities defined as being for personal use are: 800 cigarettes, 400 small cigars, 200 cigars, 10 litres of spirits, 90 litres of wine and 110 litres of beer. For non-EU nationals the limits are 200 cigarettes, 1 litre of spirits, 2 litres of wine and 50g of perfume. Visitors can carry up to 50,000F in currency.

Detaxe refund scheme

If you are from a non EU country and have spent more than 120F in any one shop, you can claim a refund on any VAT paid (VAT currently stands at 20.6%) when you leave the country – so long as you don't stay longer than 90 days. Pick up a detaxe form at the shop, fill in the details, get the form stamped by customs and then send it back to the shop who will refund the money direct to your bank account or credit card.

getting around

Paris has one of the best public transport systems of any European city. The métro in particular is a godsend – fast, efficient and reliable – and kids who have never travelled on an underground train before will appreciate the novelty. On the newest line, the automatic Méteor between Madeleine and Bibliothèque, they can even sit at the front pretending to drive the train. There's also an extensive bus network and a train system, known as the RER, which you can use to zip quickly across town or take longer trips out into the Ile de France. Driving in Paris doesn't make much sense (too much congestion, too little parking), but walking does. Paris is a flat, safe, not to mention beautiful, city, best appreciated on foot. Do be aware, however, that the pavements in many of the older parts of town, such as the Marais and the Latin Quarter, are quite narrow (many with cobblestones) and can be tricky for buggies and wheelchairs.

By bus

Buses aren't nearly as speedy as métro trains – Paris' ongoing congestion problems have seen to that – but they do provide a more pleasant way of getting about the city. Métro tickets are also valid on the bus although, unlike on the métro, your ticket is valid only for one trip and not the entire journey and you'll have to use a new ticket each time you change buses or cross into a new fare zone. You must stamp your ticket (*oblitérer*) in the machine next to the driver as you enter. Drivers also sell individual tickets which can only be used on the bus.

Street maps (known as *Paris Par Arrondissements*) showing all the individual bus routes can be bought at most street kiosks and *papeteries*.

Buses run everyday between 5.30am and 12.30am, at which point the nightbus network Nactombus (*see* below) takes over. When the number displayed on the front of a bus has a slash through it, the bus will only run half its usual route. To get a bus to stop, press the red *arrêt demandé* button.

Nightbuses

The nightbus network, Nactombus, operates between 12.30am and 5.30am. There are 16 lines, most of which leave from the Châtelet-Hôtel de Ville area. The standard fare is 15F, double the daytime rate.

Sightseeing buses

Paris L'Open Tour
Tours: daily every hour 10–5; duration 2½ hours
Departs: Place de la Madeleine
Tickets are valid for two days; you can get on and off as often as you like.

Fares: adult 135F, child under 12 70F, child under 4 free
Recorded commentary in French and English. Run by the RATP, the tour takes in the Louvre, Notre Dame, the Jardin du Luxembourg, St Germain des Prés, the Musée d'Orsay, the Arc de Triomphe, the Eiffel Tower and Invalides, and there is a longer route out to Bercy or Montmartre.

Cityrama
✆ 01 44 55 61 00
Tours: summer daily 9.30–4.30; winter daily 9.30–1.30
Recorded commentary in English
Departs: Place des Pyramides, ✉ 75001
Fares: adult 150F, child under 12 free

Parisbus
✆ 01 42 88 69 50
Tours: daily 10–5; every 30 minutes aboard red London double decker buses
Recorded commentary in English
Departs: Eiffel Tower
Tickets are valid for two days; you can get on and off as often as you like
Fares: adult 125F, child under 12 60F

Paris Vision
✆ 01 42 60 30 01
Tours: daily 9.30–3.30
Multilingual commentary
Fares: adult 150F, child under 12 75F, under 4s free

By métro

The Paris underground system, the métro, is easily the most convenient way of moving around the city. The trains are fast, the service reliable, and the fares economical – and, with over 300 stations dotted through-

Tickets & Passes

Children aged 4–11 pay 50 per cent of the adult fare. Under 4s go free so long as they don't take up a seat.

Paris is organized into 5 concentric fare zones. The city proper consists of zones 1–2. A single ticket (adult 8F, child 4F) allows you to use as many different métro lines as you like within a single journey although you will have to buy/use a new ticket each time you change buses or cross into a new fare zone. Buying a *carnet* (10 single tickets sold together) is perhaps the best value option: adult 55F, child 27.5F, a saving of over 30%.

If you're planning to use public transport a lot (i.e. more than ten separate trips a day) you should get a Paris Visite card: 1 day adult 55F/child 30F; 2 days adult 90F/child 45F; 3 days adult 120F/child 60F; 5 days adult 175F/child 90F.

Hold on to your ticket until the end of your journey: failure to show your ticket to an inspector could result in a spot fine of between 85 and 230F.

out the capital, you're rarely more than 500 metres from a métro stop.

However, finding your way around the métro can be extremely confusing, as train directions are given by listing the station at the end of the line rather than the direction the trains are travelling. For instance; if travelling north on Line 4, which runs between Porte d'Orléans in the south of Paris and Porte de Clignancourt in the north, you should look for signs saying *Direction Porte de Clignancourt*. If travelling south on the

same line you must look for signs saying *Direction Porte d'Orléans*.

Direction signs are white, transfer (*correspondance*) signs are orange and exit signs (*sortie*) are blue. On the platform of every major métro station you'll find a map of the local neigbourhood (a *plan du quartier*).

There are now 14 métro lines. The 14th, known as the Météor, is the current pride and joy of the RATP: an automatic, electronically driven, rubber wheeled state-of-the-art service between Bibliothèque F. Mitterrand and the Gare St-Lazare. Try to get a seat in the front carriage with its head-on views of the on-rushing tunnel. Métro trains run from 5.30am to 12.50am every three to ten minutes, depending on the time of day.

If travelling with very small children, be aware that there are mainly stairs and only a few escalators in métro stations, while the heavy doors and tricky turnstiles require expert manoeuvring of pushchairs and buggies – if you can get hold of a baby backpack or quick-folding buggy your life will be much easier.

RATP

The *Régie Autonome des Transports Parisiens* controls Paris' buses and Métro system. For information in English call ✆ 08 36 68 41 14 (calls are charged at 2.23F per minute). Also check out their website: *www.ratp.fr*.

Lost Property
✆ 020 40 06 75 27

By RER

The high-speed RER (*Réseau Express Régional*) city-suburb network is run jointly by the national rail company SNCF (*Société Nationale des Chemins de Fer Français*) and the Parisian transport authority RATP (*see* above), and is best used for covering large stretches of town quckly and for day trips to places like Versailles, St Germain-en-Laye and (of course) Disneyland. For nipping about the city centre, however, stick to the métro.

There are four RER lines (A, B, C and D) which run approximately every 12 minutes between 5.30am and 12.30am. All trains stop at all central Paris stations and other destinations are indicated on a board on the platform; there are numerous points of connection to the métro network. Métro tickets are valid on the RER within the confines of the city.

By taxi

Paris' 15,000 licensed taxis are, on the whole, reliable, efficient and reasonably good value. Drivers are obliged by law to stop when hailed (if they're free), take you where you want to go (including the two airports) and follow whatever route *you* choose – although it doesn't follow that they always will.

Also be aware that drivers start their meters from the moment they set out to collect a fare so, if you call a cab from a distant rank, don't be surprised to see 20–30F already on the clock when it arrives. If you intend to use a lot of taxis, it will be worth finding out the number of the taxi stand closest to where you're staying.

A system of bulbs on the taxi's roof will tell you whether it's in service, driving to pick up a fare or free. When the taxi sign is fully lit, it's free. The minimum charge is 13F and there's a surcharge for luggage, more than three passengers (drivers are within their rights to refuse the fourth passenger) and after 10pm or before 6.30am. Taking a taxi to the suburbs can be particularly expensive: once the taxi crosses the *Périphérique* (the Paris ring road) the driver will immediately switch the meter over to a higher rate.

Taxi Companies:

Alpha
✆ 01 45 85 85 85

Artaxi
✆ 01 42 03 50 50

G7
✆ 01 47 39 47 39

Taxi Bleus
✆ 01 49 36 10 10

By car

24 hour emergency repair service
✆ 01 47 07 99 99
If your car breaks down in Paris.

Paris is a small city and has such a good public transport system that using a car doesn't make much sense – parking is nigh on impossible (few hotels have garages and parking meters can be hugely expensive), congestion is rising and, following the privatization of the tow firms, there's an increased risk of being towed away if you happen to park in the wrong place.

The speed limit in the centre of Paris is 50kph, on the Paris ring road 80kph, on country roads 90kph (80kph when wet) and on motorways (autoroutes) 130kph (110kph when wet). At intersections without signals, the car on your right has right of way. Seatbelts must be worn in the front seats of cars and in the back where fitted. Children under 10 are not allowed to travel in the front except in special rear-facing baby seats.

Rental rates in France are among the highest in Europe, so it's worth investigating fly-drive or holiday packages before you arrive. Otherwise, expect to pay around 300F a day for a small car. Local firms offer the best rates and most car rental companies can supply children's safety seats for a nominal cost:

Avis
5 Rue Bixio, 7th
✆ 01 45 50 32 31

City Loc
28 Rue Linois, 15th
✆ 01 45 79 40 40

Euro-Rent
42 Avenue de Saxe, 7th
✆ 01 44 38 55 50

Rual
78 Boulevard Soult, 12th
✆ 01 43 45 52 20

SNAC
118 Rue de la Croix-Nivert, 15th
✆ 01 48 56 11 11

By bike

Parts of Paris are extremely cycle-friendly, but on the whole you should avoid the centre of town, particularly during peak times. On Sundays, however, the *quais* beside the Seine are closed to traffic, allowing cyclists and pedestrians to meander along the riverbanks in peace.

There are two major cycle tracks in Paris: between the Bois de Vincennes and the Bois de Bolougne and between the Parc de Pantin and the Porte de Vincennes. There are also plans to open another 50km of lanes in the near future.

Bikes are not allowed on the métro but you can take your bicycle for free on some RER lines out into the Paris suburbs.

A.S.C.
88 Boulevard de la Villette, 14th
Ⓜ Colon Fabien
✆ 01 42 01 28 29
Bike hire from 1/2 day, day or week.

La Maison du Vélo
11 Rue Fénelon, 10th
Ⓜ Gare du Nord
✆ 01 42 81 24 72
Bike hire from 1/2 day, day or week.

Paris à Velo C'est Sympa!
37 Boulevard Bourdon, 4th
Ⓜ Bastille
✆ 01 48 87 60 01
Rentals and a variety of city bike tours.

Star Location
8 Rue des Ecouffes, 4th
Ⓜ St Paul
✆ 01 48 87 83 93
For scooters.

By riverboat

A trip aboard one of the famous *bateaux mouches* sightseeing boats is an excellent way to see the sights of Paris. On a hot summer day it's also one of the few ways to cool off with the breeze in your hair. Expect to pay 40–50F for a one hour tour. Most offer lunch and dinner cruises:

Bateaux Mouches de Paris

✆ 01 42 25 96 10
English language recording, ✆ 01 40 76 99 99
Departs: Pont de l'Alma (north side, 8th)
RER Pont de l'Alma
Night tours in summer; fancy dinner cruise (500F)
Lunch: Sat 300F, public holidays 350F

Bateaux Parisiens

Departs: Port de La Bourdonnais, 7th
Ⓜ Bir-Hakeim/Ⓜ Iéna.

Batobus

✆ 01 44 11 33 99.
Fares: adult 60F, child under 12 30F; 25% reduction with a Paris Visite pass
The boat bus also offers a passenger/sightseeing service up and down the Seine.
There are six stops: Eiffel Tower, Musée d'Orsay, St Germain des Prés, the Louvre, Notre Dame and Hôtel de Ville.

Canauxrama

✆ 01 42 39 15 00
Live commentary in English if there are enough English speakers to make it worthwhile
Reserve
3-hour tours of Canal St-Martin

Paris Canal

✆ 01 42 40 96 97
Departs: Musée d'Orsay
Live commentary in French (or English if there is sufficient demand)
Journeys up the Canal St-Martin to

La Villette, passing through old locks and under tunnels.

Vedettes du Pont Neuf

Departs: Sq du Vert Galant, Ile de la Cité, 1st
Ⓜ Pont-Neuf

Vedettes de Paris

From the Port de Suffren, 7th
Ⓜ Bir-Hakeim

On foot

Paris is a small, (mostly) flat city best explored on foot. Crossing Parisian roads, however, can be a tricky proposition for the uninitiated. Remember, French drivers are not obliged to stop at anything other than a red light and you should always cross at a designated crossing point. British visitors, in particular, need to be aware that French zebra crossings do not work in the same way as their British counterparts. A French zebra does not signify a pedestrian right of way but is simply a means of telling you that you're not allowed to cross anywhere else.

The following companies offer guided walking tours in English of all the major tourist attractions:

Anne Hervé

✆ 01 47 90 52 16
Tickets: 50F

Paris Contact

✆ 01 42 51 08 40
Tickets: 60F

Paris Walking Tours

✆ 01 48 09 21 40
Tickets: 60F, under 10s free
The tour takes you down into Paris' sewers, a particular favourite with children.

practicalities

New cultures can be frightening for children, who are often more deeply affected by changes to their familiar routine than adults, so it's good to know what's what: what temperatures to expect, where to buy medicine for common ailments, when you can expect to find things open, how to make a phone call, etc. In fact, once you've been in the city a few days you'll find that, language difficulties aside, there's little about Paris that is wholly unfamiliar. Also, despite its hustle and bustle, Paris is actually a good deal safer than most other cities of its size and stature.

Babysitters

If you fancy an evening out without the littl'uns in tow, finding a decent, reliable, trustworthy childminder in a strange city, can be a worrisome task. Thankfully, Paris has several reputable babysitting agencies. Most charge an agency fee (from 50 to 75F) in addition to the hourly rate (around 40F) that goes to the sitter. If you're out after the last métro, you'll be expected to drive the sitter home or pay for a taxi.

123 Babychou
✆ 01 42 79 80 02
Specializing in smaller children.

Ababa
✆ 01 45 49 46 46
Good for a pinch, usually able to get a sitter to you within an hour; has many English speakers.

Allô! Maman Poule
✆ 01 47 48 01 01
One of the biggest agencies, certain to have an English speaker available (3hrs minimum).

Avec Prositting
✆ 01 44 37 91 11
Excellent 24 hour service. Usually can get a sitter to you within two hours.

Baby Prestige
✆ 01 53 53 02 02
Another of the larger agencies with 24 hour service.

Baby-sitting Service
✆ 01 46 37 51 24

Grand-Mères Occasionnelles
✆ 01 46 33 28 45

Average temperatures

	F	C
Jan	48	9
Feb	47	8
Mar	50	10
April	60	16
May	62	17
June	74	24
July	77	25
Aug	78	26
Sep	69	20
Oct	62	17
Nov	54	12
Dec	45	8

Climate and when to go

With benefits and pitfalls to each season, there is no perfect time to visit. Springtime usually enjoys the best of the weather but the worst of the crowds. Summer can be sweltering and sticky and traffic fumes can reach alarming levels, but the city won't be as crowded; most Parisians take their annual holiday in late July and August. The downside of this migration is that many shops and businesses will be closed (look for the *congé annuel* sign in the window) although a number of children's attractions, including the fair in the Jardin des Tuileries, are only open in summer. Autumn, like Spring, tends to be a mixture of good weather and extreme congestion with a multitude of trade fairs putting hotel beds at a premium. Winter is as cold and gloomy as anywhere else in Northern Europe but the city's attractions, shops and restaurants will be much less busy and, more importantly, open. Take your pick.

Electricity

France's electricity supply is 220 volts. American visitors bringing electrical appliances will need a voltage convertor, while visitors from the UK will only require an adaptor in order to cope with the French-style round two-pronged plugs. If you need to stock up while you're in Paris, both convertors and plugs are sold at BHV, 52–64 Rue de Rivoli, 1st, Ⓜ Louvre.

Embassies in Paris

UK
36 Rue du Faubourg St Honoré
Ⓜ Concorde
✆ 01 44 51 31 02

Ireland
4 Rue Rude
Ⓜ Etoile
✆ 01 44 17 67 00

USA
2 Rue St Florentin
Ⓜ Concorde
✆ 01 36 70 14 88

Canada
35 Ave Montaigne
Ⓜ Franklin D. Roosevelt
✆ 01 44 43 29 86

Australia
4 Rue Jean Rey
Ⓜ Bir-Hakeim
✆ 01 40 59 33 00

New Zealand
7 Rue Léonard de Vinci
Ⓜ Victor Hugo
01 45 00 24 11

Families with special needs

Comité National Français de Liaison pour la Réadaptation des Handicapés (CNRH)
Service Publication
236bis Rue de Tolbiac
✉ 75013 Paris
✆ 01 53 80 66 66

Provides information on access and facilities throughout the city.

Association Valentin Haüy
Service des Ventes
AVH 5, Rue Duroc
✉ 75007 Paris

Publishes the 'Guide Métropolitan et du RER intégral en Braille', a braille métro and RER map, price 30F.

Disneyland® Paris Guest Communications
PO Box 305, Watford
Hertfordshire, WD1 8TP
England
or
BP 100, ✉ 77777
Marne-la-Vallée, Cedex 4
France
✆ 0990 03 03 03

Produces the *Disabled Guest Guide*.

Sadly, access to public transport is still less than ideal. Only bus nos. 20, 85 and 88 and the new line 14 of the métro are fully accessible, although the RATP and SNCF do offer a 'Compagnon de Voyage' service (for the hardly giveaway price of 60F per hour) whereby disabled passengers can be accompanied on their journeys on the métro, RER and buses. Taxis are required by law to accept disabled travellers.

National museums usually have good wheelchair access and offer free admission to disabled visitors. Detailed information is available by Minitel, 3614 HANDITEL.

In the UK

Council for Disabled Children
☏ (020) 7843 6000.
For information on travel health and further resources.

Disability Now
6 Markets Road, N7
☏ (020) 7383 4575
Produces a monthly newspaper with holiday ideas written by people with disabilities.

RADAR (Royal Association for Disability and Rehabilitation)
Unit 12 City Forum
250 City Road, London EC1V 8AF
☏ (020) 7250 3222
open Mon–Fri 8–5
Produces excellent guide books and information packs for disabled travellers.

Holiday Care Service
2nd Floor, Imperial Building,
Victoria Road, Horley, Surrey RH6 9HW
☏ (01293) 774 535
Provides information sheets for families with disabilities. All sites have been visited and assessed by Holiday Care representatives.

Mobility International
228 Borough High Street, London SE1
☏ (020) 7403 568
Issues a quarterly newsletter detailing developments in disabled travel.

Royal National Institute for the Blind
224 Great Portland Street, London W15 5TB
☏ (020) 7388 1266
Advises blind people on travel matters.

In the US

American Foundation for the Blind
15 West 16th Street, New York, NY 10011
☏ (212) 620 2000; toll free 800 232 5463.

Federation of the Handicapped
211 West 14th Street, New York, NY 10011
☏ (212) 747 4262
Organizes summer tours for members; there is a nominal annual fee.

Mobility International
PO Box 3551, Eugene, Oregon 97403, USA
☏ (503) 343 1284

SATH (Society for the Advancement of Travel for the Handicapped)
347 Fifth Avenue, Suite 610, New York 10016
☏ (212) 447 7284

In Australia

ACROD (Australian Council for the Rehabilitation of the Disabled)
55 Charles Street, Ryde, New South Wales
☏ (02) 9809 4488

Insurance

It's vital that you take out travel insurance before your trip. This should cover, at a bare minimum, cancellation due to illness, travel delays, accidents, lost luggage, lost passports, lost or stolen belongings, personal liability, legal expenses, emergency flights and medical cover. Remember, you are not obliged to buy insurance from the same travel company that sold you your holiday and it's well worth shopping around. The majority of insurance companies offer free insurance to children under the age of two as part of the parent's policy. Also bear in mind annual insurance policies which can be especially cost effective for families with two or more older children. Always keep the insurance company's 24-hour emergency number close to hand – if you have a mobile phone, it's worth storing it in the memory.

The most important aspect of any travel insurance policy is its medical cover. You should look for cover of around £5 million. If a resident of the European Union, Iceland, Liechtenstein or Norway, you are entitled to the same medical treatment as French citizens (*see* Medical Matters, below). In the US and Canada, you may find that your existing insurance policies give sufficient medical cover and you should always check these thoroughly before taking out a new one. Canadians, in particular, are usually covered by their provincial health plans. Few American or Canadian insurance companies will issue on-the-spot payments following a reported theft or loss.

Always report stolen or lost items to the police, however trivial, so that you can make a claim when you get back home. You will usually have to wait several weeks and engage in a hefty amount of correspondence with your insurance broker before any money is forthcoming.

In the UK

Association of British Insurers
✆ (020) 7600 3333

The Insurance Ombudsman Bureau
✆ 0845 600 6666
The government appointed regulator of the insurance industry

ABC Holiday Extras Travel Insurance
toll free ✆ 0800 171 000

Columbus Travel Insurance
✆ (020) 7375 0011

Endsleigh Insurance
✆ (020) 7436 4451

Medicover
✆ 0870 735 3600

World Cover Direct
toll free ✆ 0800 365 121

North America

Access America
US, ✆ 1-800 284 8300,
Canada, ✆ 1-800 654 1908

Carefree Travel Insurance
US & Canada, ✆ 1-800 323 3149

Travel Assistance International
US & Canada, ✆ 1-800 921 2828

MEDEX Assistance Corporation
US, ✆ 410 453 6300

The Internet

After some initial hesitation, the internet has now caught on in a major way in France, and both La Poste (the post office) and France Télécom are currently pulling out the stops in an effort to provide access. Soon you should be able to surf the net at any post office.

France Télécom has already set up several internet stations where people can come and learn how to use the internet, send email and access web information for an hourly fee (*c*. 30F). There's one at 35 Rue du Cherche Midi, 6th, ✆ 01 40 51 96 16, Ⓜ Sèvres Babylone.

There are endless internet sites with information about Paris, and a few official and unofficial sites about Disneyland® Paris. Here are a few we recommend:

Cybercafés

Café Orbital
13 Rue de Médecis, 6th
✆ 01 43 25 76 77
Ⓜ Luxembourg
www.orbital.fr
Open daily 10am–10pm

Hi Tech Café
10 Rue de Départ, 15th
✆ 01 45 38 67 61
Ⓜ Montparnasse
Open daily 12 noon–2am

Useful websites

French Government Tourist Office
www.francetourism.com

Travelling with children in Paris
travelwithkids.miningco.com/travel/travelwith-kids/msubparis.htm

Online Map
www.pageszoom.com/ruescommercants
Run by France Télécom, provides details of every street in Paris.

Paris Anglo
www.paris-anglo.com
English language guide for Francophiles.

Pariscope
www.pariscope.fr
Web version of the weekly entertainment guide, mostly in French.

Paris Free Voice
parisvoice.com
English Language magazine.

Paris Pages
www.paris.org

Paris Tourist Office
www.paris-touristoffice.com

Disneyland® Paris
www.disneylandparis.com
The official site.

The Ultimate Disney Links Page
www.magicnet.net/~tudlp/dlparis.html
Excellent source of Disney theme park information. Contains a list of links to other Disneyland Paris sites.

Lost property

Bureau des Objets Trouvés
36 Rue des Morillons, ✉ 75015
✆ 01 55 76 20 20.
Open: Mon–Fri 8.30am–7pm,
Tues and Thurs 8.30am–8pm.
You will need to visit in person in order to fill out a form stating when and where you lost your item.

Maps

Michelin's 'Paris Plan 14' is easily the best map of the city while their 'Environs de Paris 106' is equally good for day trips into the outskirts. Most stationery shops sell the Plan de Paris, the equivalent of the London A–Z, which details every single street, station and monument in the French capital. You can pick up bus, nightbus and métro route maps at any métro station.

WH Smith – The English Bookshop
248 Rue de Rivoli, 1st
✆ 01 44 77 88 99
whsmith.france@wanadoo.fr
Ⓜ Concorde
Open: Mon–Sat 9–7.30, Sun 1–7.30

Medical matters

Emergency Medical Service
✆ 15

24 hour call-out doctor
✆ 01 47 07 77 77

Dental Emergency
✆ 01 43 37 51 00

Anti-Poison Centre
✆ 01 40 37 04 04

First-aid kit

Whenever and wherever you're travelling, you should always carry a First Aid Kit with you. In Paris, this might contain:

- antiseptic cream and wipes
- Aspirin and Junior Aspirin
- calamine lotion and aloe vera gel (for soothing burns, bites and stings)
- decongestant
- diarrhoea remedy and oral rehydration sachets
- high factor, zinc-based sun screen
- lip salve
- paracetamol
- plasters (band aids) both fabric and waterproof
- pre-sterilized, disposable syringe and needle
- scissors
- sore-throat pastilles
- sterile wound dressings and bandages
- thermometer
- torch
- travel sickness preparations
- tweezers

English is spoken in the following hospitals:

The American Hospital in Paris
63 Boulevard Victor Hugo
Neuilly-sur-Seine Ⓜ Anatole France/Pont de Levallois
✆ 01 46 41 24 24

The Hertford British Hospital
3 Rue Barbès Levallois Perret
Ⓜ Anatole France
✆ 01 46 39 22 22

Visitors from the European Union, Iceland, Liechtenstein and Norway are entitled to the same medical treatment as French citizens so long as they carry with them the appropriate validated form. In the EU, this is the E111 form which covers families with dependent children up to the age of 16 (or 19, if in full-time education), and is available free of charge from post offices. Medical care, dental treatment and prescriptions (*ordonnances*) must be paid for up-front; 75–80 per cent will be reimbursed at a later date. It can be a time-consuming procedure, however, and you would be well advised to take out travel insurance with 100% medical cover before you go (*see* Insurance above).

Pharmacies

French pharmacists are highly trained and can prescribe a wide range of drugs and provide a good deal of medical advice. They can also provide a list of local doctors. French pharmacies are identified by a green neon cross.

24 hr Pharmacies
84 Avenue des Champs-Elysées, 8th
✆ 01 45 62 02 41

13 Place de la Nation, 11th
✆ 01 43 73 24 03

English is spoken in the following pharmacies:

Pharmacie Swann
6 Rue Castiglione, 1st
✆ 01 42 60 72 96

British and American Pharmacy
1 Rue Auber, 9th
✆ 01 47 42 49 40

Money and banks

The currency in France is the franc (abbreviated to F) which is divided into 100 centimes. There are nine coin denominations: 5, 10, 20 and 50 centimes, and 1, 2, 5, 10 and 20 francs; and five note denominations: 20, 50, 100, 200 and 500 francs.

Most shops and restaurants accept all the big name credit and debit cards – Visa, Delta, Mastercard, American Express, Barclaycard, etc. – and French automatic cash dispensers (known as DABs, *distributeurs automatiques de billets*) will normally dispense money on foreign bank cards linked to the international cirrus and maestro network, although you will normally have to pay a commission. Your bank's international banking department should be able to advise you on this.

Banks are generally open Mon–Fri 9am–5pm although some are also open on Saturday mornings. All are closed on public holidays. Travellers cheques can be changed at any bank or *bureau de change* for a commission. Le Banque de France usually gives the best rates, hotels and train stations the worst.

On 1 January 1999, France, along with 11 other European nations, signed up for European Monetary Union and bills in shops and restaurants are now given in euros as well as francs. You can ignore this for the time being, however. Although on 1 January 2002 the euro will replace the franc as the national currency, it will, until then, exist only as a sort of virtual currency, present on bills and statements but not in general circulation.

Carrying money around with you

Use a money belt fastened around your waist under a tucked-in shirt or T-shirt. Pickpocketing is rife in certain parts of Paris, especially busy shopping areas like Les Halles and around the major stations, but it is a very skilful pickpocket who is able to undress you without you noticing. Otherwise, always keep wallets in your trouser pockets and hold purses and bags close to your body.

Bureaux de Change

Chèque Point
150 Avenue des Champs-Elysées, 8th
✆ 01 49 53 02 51
Open: 24 hours a day

Thomas Cook
52 Avenue des Champs-Elysées, 8th
✆ 01 42 89 80 32
Open: 8.30am–11pm
There are also branches at all six Paris mainline railway stations.

Travelex
Roissy airport
✆ 01 48 64 37 26
Open: 6.30am–10.30pm

Orly airport
✆ 01 49 75 89 25
Open: 6.30am–10.30pm

Lost credit cards

American Express
✆ 01 47 77 70 00

Visa
✆ 08 36 69 08 80

Mastercard
toll free ✆ 0800 90 13 87

National holidays

There are 12 French national holidays. Banks, shops, museums and businesses all close, although the métro, cinemas and most restaurants stay open.

- 1 January
- Easter Sunday
- Easter Monday
- 1 May
- 8 May (VE Day)
- May (Ascension Day)
- June (Pentecost)
- 14 July (Bastille Day)
- 15 August (Assumption)
- 1 November (All Saints' Day)
- 11 November (First World War Armistice)
- 25 December (Christmas Day)

School holidays

- Autumn Half-term: end of Oct
- Christmas: about two weeks
- Spring Half-term: February
- Easter: April
- Summer: end of June until Sept

Diner's Club
✆ 01 49 06 17 90

Lost Travellers Cheques

American Express
toll free ✆ 0800 90 86 00.

National holidays

The French have a healthy attitude to public holidays, known as *'faire le pont'*: often when a holiday falls on a Wednesday they take the Thursday and Friday as holiday too to link it to the weekend. Watch out for this as it might mean that shops are closed.

School holidays

Bear in mind that the spring holidays in France revolve around the skiing season so they seem to last for weeks on end: the country is divided up into three zones and the holidays are staggered so that the resorts can cope with the invasion of future champions. The dates given in the box are a guideline.

Necessities

Wherever you're travelling with kids it is always worth taking a packet of wet wipes, a full change of clothing, toys to fiddle with, drinks and snacks, plus some empty, disposable bags for unforeseen eventualities, and a multi-blade pocket knife.

The bare necessities

- a torch
- matches
- a night light
- safety pins
- an extension cord
- needle and thread
- a roll of sticky tape
- a net shopping bag
- moisturizing cream
- travel socket converters
- mild soap and baby shampoo

Opening hours

The traditional opening hours for shops and businesses are from Tuesday to Saturday between 9 or 10am and 7 or 8pm, although there are various exceptions: large department stores tend to be open from 9.30am to 6.30pm, with a couple of days put aside for late opening till 9 or 10pm. Supermarkets (*supermarchés*) are usually open on Monday, and bakers (*boulangeries*) on Sunday morning and Monday.

Permanent street markets are open morning and afternoon (including Sunday morning but not Monday), while travelling food markets will normally begin winding down around noon. Most museums are closed on Monday, apart from national museums which are closed on Tuesdays.

Post offices

Main post office
52 Rue du Louvre, 1st
Open: 24 hours a day, 7 days a week

Most French post offices (ask for 'La Poste' or 'le bureau de poste') are open Monday to Friday between 8am and 7pm and on Saturday between 8am and 12 noon.

Because post offices handle such an array of tasks on top of their normal postal duties – including providing savings accounts, wire transfer of funds, retirement plans, investment plans and mortgages – queues are often very long, and performing a relatively simple task, such as posting a parcel, can sometimes take over half an hour. In fact, when you visit you may find that only a couple of windows (*guichets*) are being used for normal postal functions – and woe betide you if you join the wrong queue. Look for signs saying *Envoi de Lettres et Paquet* or *Toutes Opérations*.

There's no need to visit a post office just to send a letter or postcard, as stamps can be bought from any tobacconist (*tabac*) or supermarket. To send a letter or postcard up to 20g anywhere in France or the EU costs 3F, to America 4.40F.

French post codes are five digits long. In Paris the first two are 75, the department number for Seine-et-Loire, while the last two correspond to the appropriate *arrondissement* or district; so 75001 is the 1st arrondissement, 75019 the 19th, etc. All postcodes within Paris have been abbreviated in English to 1st, 2nd, etc. in this guide, but you will also see them abbreviated to the French equivalents: 1e, 2e, etc.

Safety and crime

Police
✆ 17

Fire Service
✆ 18

Paris, by today's standards, is a very safe city with little violent crime, few street muggings and a strong police presence (both visible and invisible; hordes of plain clothes policemen stalk the streets tackling everyone from drug dealers to fare dodgers). The crime you are most likely to fall victim to is petty thievery – of the pickpocketing, car breaking variety – and you should always take extra care with your valuables when in

The Golden Rules

⚠ Don't leave valuables in your hotel room.

⚠ Keep the majority of your money in travellers cheques.

⚠ Keep all your valuables in a money belt fastened around your waist under a tucked shirt or T-shirt.

⚠ Only keep small amounts of money in your wallet or purse. Keep your wallet in your trouser pocket and hold purses and bags close to your body with the flap facing towards you and the strap over your shoulder.

⚠ Steer clear of unfamiliar areas of the city late at night.

⚠ Avoid travelling alone on the métro late at night.

busy shopping districts (especially flea markets), on the métro or wherever crowds gather to watch performances by street artists. In particular, look out for groups of scruffy looking children who may be working the streets as part of a pickpocket gang. Never leave valuables in your car.

If you are a victim of a crime, you must report it to the nearest police station as soon as possible in order to get the form needed for your insurance claim. If your passport has been stolen, you will also need to contact your consulate who should be able to arrange emergency travel documents to tide you over.

Always carry your passport with you, preferably in a money belt or similar secure device. According to French law, French police can demand to see the ID of anyone they don't like the look of anytime they feel like it. The more hippyish or nonconformist you look, the less likely they are to like it.

Of course, when travelling with children, you need to be extra vigilant at all times. When on the streets or in a crowded place always keep your children in front of you and continually make a head count. In the event that you do get separated, encourage your children to remain in one place and wait for you to find them. It is a good idea to supply youngsters with a whistle to blow in case they lose sight of you in a crowd. A bright cap or jacket makes them much easier to spot. If you have more than one child, colour match their clothes so that you only have one thing to watch out for. Older children may be trusted enough to explore by themselves within bounds. Even so, always establish a central, easy-to-find meeting place. Ensure your children carry identification at all times (ID bracelets are a good idea) and make sure you have an up-to-date photograph of them too, just in case.

Smoking

Many restaurants and cafés will be smokier than you may feel is healthy for your children. The French tend to ignore laws they don't like or consider stupid and that includes much of the anti-smoking legislation passed in the early 1990s. Although some restaurants do have proper, sectioned off no-smoking areas, in many of the smaller eateries the no-smoking section may just be a single table located by the lavatory and (just in case) furnished with an ashtray. Eating al fresco is not just the groovier alternative, it can also be considerably healthier. Smoking is banned on public transport, in cinemas and theatres.

Telephones

Coin operated public phones are now few and far between in Paris which means investing in a *télécarte* (phonecard), available at any tobacconist, métro station, train station or post office. 40F buys you 50 units, 96F buys you 120. Mobile phone users can buy top-up cards in France-Télécom shops.

French phone numbers have ten digits – there are no area codes so you must dial all ten from anywhere in France. Paris and Ile de France numbers begin 01. If ringing Paris from abroad, dial the international code for France, 33, then the Paris number but omit the initial 0.

To make an international call from Paris, dial 00 followed by the country code (UK 44, US and Canada 1, Ireland 353, Australia 61, New Zealand 64, etc.), then the local code (minus the 0 for UK numbers) and finally the number.

Minitel

The recent split of the PTT (Postes Téléphones, Télégraphes) into La Poste (the post office) and France-Télécom has led to a rapid growth in France's telecommunication industry, the most significant development of which has been the invention of the proto-internet device Minitel. This mini domestic computer sends and accesses information across the telephone network and can be used as a telephone directory, research library, home shopping network, ticket reservation service and fax. Minitels are available for use at all post offices and most hotels.

Time

Paris is one hour ahead of London (GMT), six hours ahead of New York, nine hours ahead of California but nine hours *behind* Tokyo and Sydney. The French use the 24 hour clock when both writing and speaking.

Tipping

A 15 per cent service charge is usually added to the bill in restaurants and cafés and you need only tip above this if the service or food was particularly outstanding. Taxi drivers will be happy with a 10 per cent tip, cinema ushers with 2F.

Toilets

The famous holes in the ground, as featured in the nightmares of generation after generation of British schoolchildren, have now largely disappeared – although you'll still find the odd backstreet café and restaurant where you can indulge in a nostalgic squat (children, of course, are always convinced they're going to fall down the hole; some even do). Most museums, shops and restaurants have decent facilities and these days Paris' streets boast hitech superloos in place of the traditional sidewalk *urinoirs*. The new loos, the creation of the Decaux Company, cost 2F for 15 minutes and are automatically sanitized after each visit. Before you get too settled, however, do make sure that some delinquent hasn't run off with all the toilet paper.

Tourist information

French Tourist Board

127 Avenue des Champs-Elysées
✆ 01 49 52 53 54
✆ 01 49 52 53 56 for information in English on current cultural events
www.paris-touristoffice.com
Open: everyday 9am–8pm
The staff are bilingual and will provide you with a mountain of information on events, museums, restaurants, etc. They can also book you a hotel room.

There are smaller branch offices at:

Gare du Nord
✆ 01 45 26 94 82

Gare d'Austerlitz
✆ 01 45 84 91 70

Gare de l'Est
✆ 01 46 07 17 73

Gare de Lyon
✆ 01 43 43 33 24

Gare Montparnasse
✆ 01 43 22 19 19

Eiffel Tower
✆ 01 45 51 22 15

For information on the Ile de France, contact

Espace Régional du Tourisme Ile-de-France

Carrousel du Louvre
99 Rue de Rivoli, 1st
✆ 01 42 44 10 50.

In the UK

French Tourist Office

178 Piccadilly
London W1
✆ 0906 8244 123

In the USA

French Government Tourist Office

444 Madison Avenue, 16th Floor
New York
NY 10022
✆ (212) 838 7800

9454 Wiltshire Boulevard
Beverley Hills
CA 90212
✆ (310) 271 6665

the sights

Grand Axe

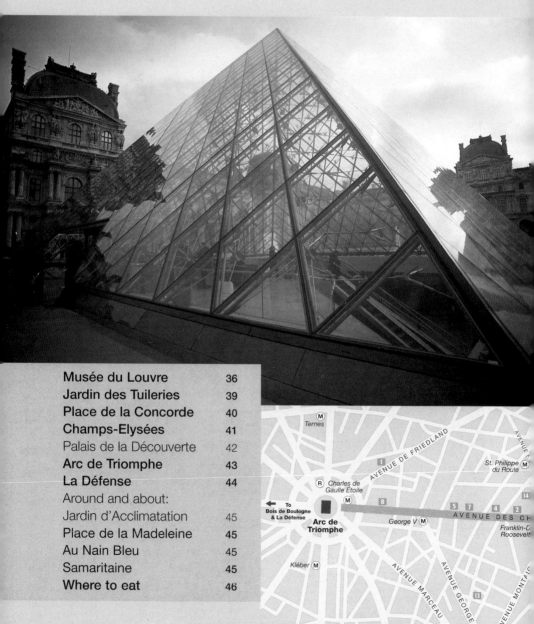

This great avenue is Paris' central axis, linking some of the city's most famous must-see attractions. It's a long straight line (about 8km or 5 miles), however, so plan your day carefully to cater to your family's particular tastes (and stamina). At one end is the Louvre, one of the world's great museums, crammed with seemingly endless galleries of pots and sculptures, and housing many wonderful artefacts that kids will find fascinating, including mummies, weapons, jewels and huge gory paintings. The Jardin des Tuileries links the Louvre to the Place de la Concorde, from where Paris' most famous street, the Champs-Elysées, stretches to the Arc de Triomphe, which offers fantastic views of the city. The Palais de la Découverte, a great hands-on science museum, and the Jardin des Tuileries, where in summer there's a funfair with a big wheel, give children ample opportunity to stretch their imaginations as well as their legs.

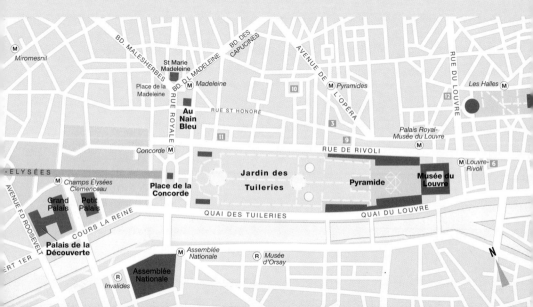

Musée du Louvre

This is one of the world's great museums, home of the *Mona Lisa* and the *Venus de Milo*, as well as countless other priceless historic artefacts and works of art. But that doesn't mean it has immediate appeal for children, and adults too are often daunted by the sheer size and scope of the collection. The Louvre is enormous, but don't be put off by its labyrinthine confines; every visitor gets lost at least once.

Palais du Louvre, Quai du Louvre, 1st
✆ 01 40 20 53 17
Infoline (in 5 languages): ✆ 01 40 20 51 51
Infoline for disabled visitors: ✆ 01 40 20 59 90
www.louvre.fr
Ⓜ Palais Royal-Musée du Louvre
Open: 9am–6pm (Wed until 9.45pm); closed Tues
Adm: adult 45F, child free; reduced adult rate of 26F applies after 3pm and all day Sunday; free admission for everyone on the first Sunday of each month
Carte Musées valid
Wheelchair access and adapted toilets
Suitable for all ages, particularly older children
Entrance via the pyramid in the courtyard or the Galerie du Carrousel (99 Rue de Rivoli) or the Passage Richelieu (for groups and visitors with museum passes)
Allow at least a couple of hours, if not the whole afternoon
The museum runs a wide range of activities for children throughout the year although these are primarily suitable for French speaking children

As with any major museum, it's best to treat your visit as a sort of treasure hunt. Pick out a few choice exhibits and plan your route accordingly – kids love being the first one to find each exhibit. The Louvre produces a good colour-coded map which you can pick up from the front desk (get in early before the English versions run out) along with a 'First Visit' leaflet which takes you to 50 of the most famous works of art. Audio guides (in English) are also available, as are guided tours – the museum organizes special storytelling tours (in French) for children. Otherwise, just follow the hordes making their way towards the *Mona Lisa*, a glazed hypnotic look in their eyes.

The museum is divided into three wings: Richelieu, Denon and Sully. Richelieu, which has the smallest number of headline exhibits, houses galleries dedicated to French, German and Dutch painting, a gallery of Middle Eastern Art featuring some very bloodthirsty pictures, and the sumptuous preserved apartments of Napoleon III.

Italian Renaissance art is housed in the Denon Wing. For most people this means just one thing – the *Mona Lisa*. Set behind bullet proof glass and permanently surrounded by a sea of furiously photographing tourists, it makes a peculiar spectacle. Indeed, should you manage to get a close look at it, you may find yourself wondering what all the fuss is about. It may be the world's most popular picture but does it deserve to be hailed as 'the greatest picture ever painted'? Indeed is it any better than the less crowded, less guarded canvases hanging along side it?

Denon also houses the Galerie d'Apollon, a vast royal dining room decorated with

Question 1

How is *La Joconde* better known?

answer on p.248

zodiac-themed frescoes and lashings of gilt. Its centrepiece is a jewel cabinet displaying Louis XV's lavish ceremonial crown. Covered in red, green and blue gems, and encrusted with diamonds, it could have been made by a small child unleashed on a jewel box with a pot of glue. This wing is also home to the Louvre's largest pictures – vast canvasses featuring life-size, and sometimes larger, figures. Look out for Delacroix's *Liberty Leading the People*, one of France's most beloved paintings.

The Sully Wing has several galleries devoted to classical antiquity where you'll find Greek statues, Roman mosaics and those perennial children's favourites, Egyptian mummies: there's an entire gallery stuffed full of ancient bandaged corpses – people, fish, birds and even cats. Sully's prized exhibit is, however, the *Venus de Milo*, a mysterious armless figure from Ancient Greece which is arguably the most famous statue in the world.

Whenever you feel yourself becoming overwhelmed by culture, remember you can always take refuge at the Carrousel du Louvre, a swish shopping centre built under the museum at the end of the 1980s. It can be accessed either from the entrance under the Pyramid in the central courtyard or from the less-crowded street entrance on the Rue de Rivoli. There's every chance that the Carrousel's shops will prove a bigger hit with the kids, particularly the younger ones, than the museum itself. **Nature et Découverte** is a strange but very popular chain which stocks an eclectic range of goods: aromatherapy kits, South American turquoise jewellery, iron weather vanes, pots made out of cinnamon, paper made from coffee beans, etc. The first floor is dedicated to kids: you'll find boxes of painted wooden toys, zoetrope lanterns, rocking horses, dinosaur model kits, mini hammocks, even mini accordions to get French youngsters started off on the right foot. Look out too for **Les Mineraux** with its wonderful window displays of brightly coloured fossilized minerals. Nearby stands a wooden model of the entire Louvre complex,

bisected to expose its subterranean levels. There are also a couple of good toy shops and various cafés and restaurants.

The History

The Louvre has been around for a while. Built as a fortress in 1190, it was demolished and rebuilt in the mid 16th century for use as a royal palace. In 1793, following the revolution, it was turned into a public museum to house the royal art collection.

President Mitterrand ordered its refurbishment in the 1980s as part of his 'Grand Projet' for restoring France's great buildings and monuments. He also commissioned the Louvre's most controversial feature, a huge glass and aluminium pyramid which now forms the main entrance to the museum. Designed by the Chinese-American architect I. M. Pei, the pyramid has divided French and world opinion down the middle. For everyone who considers it a futuristic masterpiece which neatly contrasts with the classical stone façade, there's someone else who considers it a horrible modern monstrosity. It's perhaps best viewed from below, with light streaming through it, or at night when the whole complex is beautifully illuminated.

A Carte Musées et Monuments (*see* p.107) gives access to 70 museums in Paris and the Ile de France and allows you to skip the queues. Queues for the Louvre are always shorter at the Rue de Rivoli entrance.

Can you spot?

The Pharaohs on Place du Palais Royal? Forget buskers, accordion-players, jugglers and other such overtalented wannabes. The only skill needed to be the favourite street performer of the younger generation is the ability to stand still. Dressed as a soldier, Charlie Chaplin, the Statue of Liberty or a bright gold Egyptian Pharaoh, these living statues are an endless source of fascination to children who will do anything in their power to make them move. A 10F coin usually does the trick.

Jardin des Tuileries

These grand formal gardens between the Place de la Concorde and the Louvre have long been one of Paris' most popular attractions for children. There's a playground, a carousel, two ponds where you can hire small wooden model sailing boats (10F each), pony rides and in summer a funfair with a big wheel. Remember, however, that the grassy areas of the park are out of bounds (or, as the signs say, *pelouse interdite*). The gardens were laid out in the 1560s on the site of a rubbish dump and tile works (hence the name Tuileries); they were only opened to the public in the 17th century after extensive reworking by Le Nôtre. In the 18th century the stately gravel pathways witnessed fashionable society promenades. It was also the site of Paris' first public toilets and its first newspaper kiosk, and it marked the spot where the world's first gas airship took to the skies. More recently, the gardens underwent a good deal of restoration work in the 1980s and 90s as part of the Grand Louvre project.

The two buildings overlooking the Place de la Concorde are the **Jeu de Paume**, which plays host to contemporary art exhibitions, and the **Orangerie** which has a permanent collection of Impressionist paintings including some of Monet's water lilies.

Rue de Rivoli, 1st
Ⓜ Tuileries, Concorde
Open: summer 7am–9pm,
winter 7.30am–7.30pm
Adm: free
Suitable for all ages
Entrances on Rue de Rivoli, Place de la Concorde and Avenue du Gal. Lemonnier
Allow at least an hour

Jeu de Paume
✆ 01 47 03 12 50
Open: Wed–Fri 12–7, Sat and Sun 10–7,
Tues 12–9.30pm
Adm: adult 38F, under 18 28F, under 13 free

Musée de l'Orangerie
✆ 01 42 97 48 16
Closed until end 2001 for reorganisation

Place de la Concorde

Question 2

Why was the head-chopping device used during the French Revolution called a *guillotine*?

answer on p.248

With its grand architecture, ornate fountains and great Egyptian obelisk, the Place de la Concorde was once Paris' most beautiful square. Its charms are now rather overshadowed by six lanes of fiercely speeding traffic, but it still offers some marvellous views. To the east are the Jardin des Tuileries and the Louvre; to the west the grand sweep of the Champs-Elysées and the imposing bulk of the Arc de Triomphe; while to the south you can see the neoclassical façade of the Assemblée Nationale (the home of the French parliament) on the other side of the Seine. The grand colonnaded buildings on the north side of the square are the Hôtel de la Marine (the French navy department since 1792), and the Crillon, one of Paris' most luxurious hotels. The square's corners are decorated with eight statues representing the largest cities in France outside Paris: Bordeaux, Nantes, Brest, Rouen, Lille, Strasbourg, Lyon and Marseille.

A tale of two obelisks

In the early 19th century Muhammad Ali, the viceroy of Egypt, presented the governments of France and Britain with an ancient Egyptian obelisk. Carved from pink Luxor granite in around 1250BC, and decorated from top to bottom with intricately carved hieroglyphics, these were extremely precious gifts and the two governments were suitably grateful. They were also a little overwhelmed – how were they supposed to get a 50ft, 225 tonne block of stone back home and, more importantly, what were they supposed to do with it once they got it there?

Britain would spend the best part of 59 years blundering from one mishap to another before the stone finally arrived in London. The journey of the French obelisk was, by contrast, serenity itself. Sailed up the Mediterranean in a specially designed open-backed boat, it was made the centrepiece of Paris' most beautiful square. The contribution of M. Lelais, who organized its transportation, is commemorated at the foot of the monument. You can see a three-stage 3D model of the hauling and despatch of the obelisk in the Musée de la Marine (*see* p.53).

On the spot where the Egyptian obelisk now stands there was once a guillotine where Louis XVI and Marie Antoinette were beheaded before a baying crowd.

Place de la Concorde, 1st
Ⓜ Concorde

Question 3

Who did France beat to win the 1998 football World Cup, and what was the score?

answer on p.248

The most famous road in France, and the main artery of Paris, this grand ornamental boulevard is divided into two contrasting sections. The lower section – from the Place de la Concorde to the Rond Point – is calm and serene, set in sculpted parkland and bordered on its southern side by the great fantasy constructions of the Grand and Petit Palais, while the recently renovated upper section – from the Rond Point to the Arc de Triomphe – is bustling and lively and lined with restaurants, pavement cafés, shops, banks and cinemas.

The Champs-Elysées' rise to prominence has been somewhat ad hoc. The lower section was laid out on parkland in the early 17th century by the great royal gardener André le Nôtre, and remained for over a century a quiet, tree-lined alleyway. During the 18th century the avenue was extended, and began to attract the fancy of society trendsetters who constructed well-to-do hotels and residences along the upper section and turned it into a fashionable promenade. By the mid 19th century it had been firmly established as Paris' most popular tourist attraction.

Its significance to the French people, however, goes much deeper than that. This, after all, is where Bismarck and Hitler made a point of marching their armies in 1870 and 1940, and where the French army led joyous national celebrations in 1945 following the Liberation. This is also where the nation came to celebrate victory in the 1998 football World Cup (an event which attracted the largest crowds since the Liberation), where the Tour de France finishes each year, and where the all-important 14 July celebrations are held.

The lower section of the Champs-Elysées will probably be of most interest to kids, with its parkland, fountains, buskers and marionette shows (every Wed, Sat and Sun on the corner of Avenue Matignon and Avenue Gabriel near the Rond Point). The upper section is good for shopping – there are branches of the Disney Store, Virgin Megastore, Planet Hollywood and Natalys – and a bite to eat, sitting at a pavement café watching the Parisian world go by. The area's principal attraction for kids, the Palais de la Découverte, is just south of the Rond Point.

Avenue des Champs-Elysées, 8th
Lower section: ⓜ Concorde,
Champs-Elysées-Clemenceau
Upper section: ⓜ Franklin D. Roosevelt,
George V, Charles de Gaulle-Etoile

Palais de la Découverte

Avenue Franklin D. Roosevelt, 1st
℡ 01 40 74 80 00
Ⓜ Franklin D. Roosevelt
Open: Tues–Sat 9.30am–6pm
Sun 10am–7pm
Adm: adult 30F, child 20F, family 80F; planetarium requires a 15F supplement
Wheelchair access
Suitable for all ages
Allow at least a couple of hours

The Palais de la Découverte tackles the problem of interesting children in science by mixing theory with as much interaction and fun as possible. The museum is a major resource of the Parisian education authority and whenever you visit you'll find yourself accompanied by at least half a dozen school parties.

Its galleries are full of buttons to press and levers to pull: you can charge some magnets to make a metal egg spin on its end, play a note on a keyboard and watch the sound transformed into waves on an oscilloscope, control the movements of a plastic spinning solar system, or make sparks fly through the air between two electrodes. Since every label, every description and every video presentation is in French, it's best to whizz through the galleries pressing any button that takes your fancy rather than getting too hung up on the intricacies of scientific theory.

There are a number of demonstration areas: in the electrostatics gallery you can watch a Van de Graaf generator creating 'mini' lightning, or members of the audience being charged with electricity so that their hair stands on end and sparks fly from their finger tips.

Although it has recently been revamped, the museum has a rather old fashioned feel to it with many of its exhibits displayed in old wooden cabinets. However, in contrast, it has an absolutely up-to-date 200-seat planetarium which uses a new projector and fibre optics to represent the starscape and planetary movement.

The museum shop is run by Nature et Découverte (see p.123), and is filled with dinosaur models, astronomy charts, kaleidoscopes and telescopes, some of which are for serious astronomers: the most powerful go for a touch under 40,000F.

Question 4

Which town gave its name to the French national anthem?

answer on p.248

Arc de Triomphe

This is one of the world's most recognizable landmarks, commissioned in 1806 by Napoleon to celebrate his own military achievements. Originally he wanted the arch to stand in the Place de la Bastille, but was eventually convinced by his advisors that its current location would be more prominent and more fashionable. The monument was only partially complete at the time of the his final defeat at Waterloo in 1815, whereupon work on it, unsurprisingly, stopped. On its eventual completion in 1836 it was dedicated instead to the revolutionary armies.

The Arc de Triomphe is decorated with relief panels depicting battle scenes, the most famous of which is Rude's *Le Départ des Voluntaires* or, as it's more commonly known, *La Marseillaise* (also the name of the French national anthem). It stands in

Can you spot?

The enormous 7.5m statue of a thumb, just to the right of the arch?

line with two of Paris' other great monuments, the Arc du Carrousel, in front of the Louvre, and the Grande Arche de la Défense, on the western edge of the city, both of which can be seen from the top of the arch (50m up). Looking down, the 12 ornamental boulevards radiate out from the Place Charles de Gaulle – explaining the square's popular nickname, *L'Etoile* (the star). Originally there were just five of these boulevards; Haussman added seven more – one of which, Avenue Foch, is still the widest street in Paris. There is a small museum in the base of the arch.

The Tomb of the Unknown Soldier was incorporated into the arch's base in 1920. A flame is lit every evening at 6.30pm to the memory of the victims of the First and Second World Wars.

Place Charles de Gaulle, 8th
℡ 01 55 37 73 77
Ⓜ/RER: Charles de Gaulle-Etoile
Open: summer 9.30am–11pm,
winter 10am–10.30pm
Adm: adult 35F, under 25 23F, under 12s free
Wheelchair access
Suitable for all ages
Allow at least an hour

La Défense

La Défense is a strange, otherworldly place of vast sealed buildings, enclosed walkways and indoor shopping centres. A mini Manhattan, neatly tucked away on the western edge of town, its landscape is almost entirely made up of concrete and glass. There are no gardens here, and what greenery there is sits in large imported plant pots, but the area still holds some attractions, and is worth an excursion from the city centre.

The area's focal point is the Grande Arche: vast, angular and undeniably impressive. It was completed in 1989 for the bicentenary of the Revolution, and officially opened according to plan on 14 July by the then President Mitterand. The left side contains the entire Ministry of Transport and Public Works, the right side privately owned offices.

Question 5

In New York it's the subway, in London it's the tube. What is it in Paris?

answer on p.248

You can take a thrillingly fast glass lift to the top, some 110m up, where there's an art gallery, a restaurant and some truly spectacular views towards the Arc de Triomphe and, on clear days, even as far as the Louvre.

In front of the arch is a great concrete concourse, home to a few sweet stalls and a vintage carousel (but few buskers or street performers) while, to the left, is an IMAX 3-D cinema and a vast indoor shopping centre, Les Quatre Temps, where you'll find outlets of the Disney Store, Nature et Découverte and a huge branch of Toys 'R' Us.

Grande Arche de la Défense, ✉ 92044
✆ 01 49 07 27 57
Ⓜ/RER: La Défense
Open: daily 10am–7pm
(last ride to roof 6pm)
Adm: adult 40F, child 32F
Wheelchair access and adapted toilets
Suitable for all ages
Allow at least a couple of hours

Dôme IMAX, ✉ 92044
✆ 01 46 92 45 50
Métro/RER: La Défense
Tickets: one film 57F, two films 80F;
under 4s free
Wheelchair access and adapted toilets
Suitable for children aged 6 and over
Films last between 10 minutes and an hour

Around and about

Jardin d'Acclimatation

Bois de Boulogne

☎ 01 40 67 90 82

Ⓜ Porte Maillot, Sablons

Open: summer daily 10–7;
winter daily 10–6

Adm: adult 40F, under 16s 30F, under 4s free

Le Petit Train runs on Wed, Sat and Sun every 15 minutes 11–6 and everyday during the school holidays; single fare 6F

Le Petit Train, a jaunty mock-steam train, will take you from Porte Maillot to the Jardin d'Acclimatation, a 25-acre children's amusement park on the edge of the Bois de Boulogne. There's a small zoo (where kids can pet the long-suffering goats and sheep), a hall of mirrors, a marionette theatre, a mini golf course, dodgems, a couple of junior-size (albeit still rather hair-raising) roller coasters, a riverboat ride, a bowling alley, an archery range, a mini motorbike course and two children's museums. There's also lots of fast food, and a babysitting service is available in summer.

Place de la Madeleine

8th

Ⓜ Madeleine

Come here to browse the extravagant food halls of Hédiard (No.21) and Fauchon (No.26), the poshest grocers in town, and in particular to marvel at their lavish confectionery sections piled high with ornate chocolate sculptures, boxes of sweets and sugared fruits. Everything is reassuringly expensive and you should expect to pay in the region of 150F for six small but delicious (and exquisitely wrapped) chocolates.

Afterwards take a ride on *La Météor*, Paris' newest métro line (No.14), which is electronically operated so you can sit right at the front, where the driver would normally sit, watching the tunnels rushing towards you. Your kids may have to wait their turn for the prime spot.

Au Nain Bleu

406–410 Rue St Honoré, 8th

(on the corner with Rue Richepance, just north of the Place de la Concorde)

☎ 01 42 60 39 01

Ⓜ Concorde, Madeleine

Open: Mon–Sat 9.45–6.30

Wheelchair access to ground floor only; there are no lifts

Suitable for all ages

Paris' greatest toy shop will cater to all your giant teddy needs. Founded in 1836, it has a great awareness of its own illustrious history and can be a slightly stiff and stuffy place, although children are still enchanted by it and can happily lose themselves in amongst its vast vaults of toy cars, dolls houses and board games.

Samaritaine

19 Rue de la Monnaie, 1st

☎ 01 40 41 20 20

Ⓜ Pont Neuf, Châtelet

Open: Mon–Sun 9.30–7, Thurs until 10pm

Wheelchair access

Samaritaine, a huge department store on the banks of the Seine, boasts the best toy section of any store in Paris. There's even a carousel on hand for when your kids tire of browsing the vast hordes of teddies, remote-controlled cars and video games. Afterwards, have a coke in the roof top café and enjoy some truly spectacular views of the city.

Where to eat

1 Androuet
6 Rue Arsène Houssaye, 8th
✆ 01 42 89 95 00
Ⓜ Charles de Gaulle-Etoile
Open: Mon–Fri 12–3 and 6.30pm–1am,
Sat 6pm–1am
Fixed price menu: lunch 210F, dinner 230F
Step beyond the cheddar boundary at this
veritable temple of cheese, for fondues,
raclettes and green salads with hot goat's
cheese. Perhaps the best option is a
sampler platter laden with a dozen different
cheeses accompanied by some freshly
baked bread. It's not cheap but it will appeal
to older, more adventurous children.
Reserve.

2 Bistro Romain
26 Avenue des Champs-Elysées, 8th
✆ 01 43 59 93 31
Ⓜ Franklin D. Roosevelt
Open: daily 11.30am–1am
Fixed price menu: 59F, 79F, 99F, 149F
Children's menu: 45F
The Romain chain prides itself on its family
service with large tables and a menu full of
kiddies favourites – chips, burgers and
chocolate mousse – as well as a range of
simple pasta dishes. If you're particularly
ravenous, you could always take on the
challenge of the all-you-can-eat beef.

3 Cafés et Thés Verlet
256 Rue St Honoré, 1st
✆ 01 42 60 67 39
Ⓜ Palais Royal-Musée du Louvre, Tuileries
Open: daily 9am–7pm
The perfect place for afternoon tea: a family-
friendly teashop filled with the aroma of tea
and coffee which wafts from the open sacks
on the tables. There are baskets of glacé
fruits and sweets for the kids

4 Hippopotamus
42 Avenue des Champs-Elysées, 8th
✆ 01 53 83 94 50
Ⓜ Franklin D. Roosevelt
Open: daily 11.30–5am
Fixed price menu: 98F, 143F
Children's menu: 47F
This is one of the flagship branches of Paris'
most child-friendly chain. There are colouring books and games for the kiddies, and
the food is tasty but familiar – chips, baked
potatoes, hamburgers, kebabs, barbecue
ribs, hot fudge sundaes, etc.

5 Planet Hollywood
78 Avenue des Champs-Elysées, 8th
✆ 01 53 83 78 27
Ⓜ Franklin D. Roosevelt
Open: daily 11.30–1am
Fixed price menu: 89F
Surely we didn't come to Paris in order to
eat at Planet Hollywood, you'll be telling
yourself as you're dragged through the door.
Despite the chain's recent financial problems,
this branch is still doing well and there's no
doubt that its mix of burgers and movie
memorabilia really does appeal to children
(particularly older ones) who'll probably
demand an overpriced baseball cap.

6 Terrasse de la Samaritaine
Quai du Louvre, 1st
✆ 01 40 41 20 20
Ⓜ Pont Neuf, Châtelet
Open: Mon–Sun 9.30am–7pm, Thurs until 10pm
Fixed price menu: 80F, 105F
Have a sandwich and a Coke, settle back
and enjoy one of the best views in Paris. This
pleasant café is located on the roof of the
Samaritaine department store, next to the
Louvre on the banks of the Seine. The food
is good and reasonably priced but it's the
views that will linger longest in the memory.

7 **Virgin Café**
Virgin Megastore
52 Avenue des Champs-Elysées, 8th
☎ 01 49 53 50 00
Ⓜ Franklin D. Roosevelt, Charles de Gaulle-Etoile
Open: Mon–Sat 10am–12 midnight,
Sun 12 noon–12 midnight
Watch the bustle of the Champs-Elysées from a window table in the top floor café. The food is surprisingly good and relatively child-friendly – salmon on toast, hamburgers, etc. – and reasonably priced, considering the location.

There are branches of **McDonald's**, the fast-food joint that all Parisians profess to hate and yet all visit, at **8** 140 Avenue des Champs-Elysées, 8th, and **9** 184 Rue de Rivoli, 1st.

Food on the go

You can pick up some excellent sandwiches and baguettes from:

10 **Le Pain Quotidien**
18 Place du Marché St Honoré, 1st

Lina's sandwiches

11 4 Rue Cambon, 1st

12 15 Rue de Louvre, 1st

13 Rue Marbeuf, 8th

La Boutique des Sandwiches

14 12 Rue du Colisée, 8th

Eiffel Tower

This is postcard Paris, the spot where every tourist must come to pay homage to (and climb) France's greatest monument. While a trip to the Eiffel Tower is usually the highlight of any trip to Paris, there are plenty of other attractions in the area worth checking out. There's the Palais de Chaillot arts complex which houses a great museum of naval history; the Champ de Mars, a formal park laid out at the foot of the tower; and the Hôtel des Invalides where France's favourite tyrant, Napoleon Bonaparte, is buried. The Musée Rodin with its beautiful secluded garden and sandpit is also well worth a visit – adults with prams get in free.

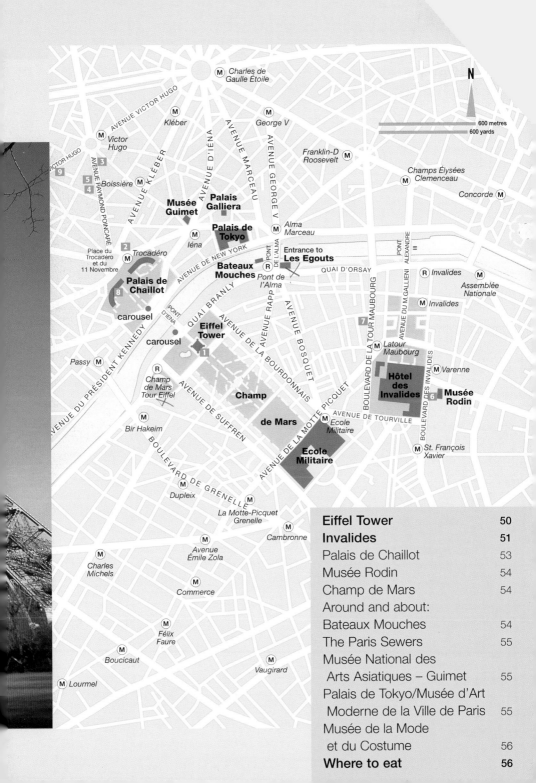

N

600 metres
600 yards

Charles de
Gaulle Étoile

AVENUE VICTOR HUGO

Kléber

George V

AVENUE VICTOR HUGO

Victor
Hugo

AVENUE D'IÉNA

AVENUE MARCEAU

AVENUE GEORGE V

Franklin-D
Roosevelt

Champs Élysées
Clemenceau

Concorde

AVENUE KLÉBER

Boissière

AVENUE RAYMOND POINCARÉ

9

5
4

3

Musée
Guimet

Palais
Galliera

Palais de
Tokyo

Iéna

Place du
Trocadéro
et du
11 Novembre

2

Trocadéro

AVENUE DE NEW YORK

Alma
Marceau

PONT DE L'ALMA

Entrance to
Les Egouts

QUAI D'ORSAY

PONT ALEXANDRE III

Invalides

Assemblée
Nationale

Bateaux
Mouches

Pont de
l'Alma

Invalides

Palais de
Chaillot

8

QUAI BRANLY

PONT D'IÉNA

carousel

carousel

Eiffel
Tower

1

AVENUE DE LA BOURDONNAIS

AVENUE RAPP

AVENUE BOSQUET

BOULEVARD DE LA TOUR MAUBOURG

AVENUE DE M GALLIENI

7

Latour
Maubourg

Hôtel
des
Invalides

BOULEVARD DES INVALIDES

Varenne

Musée
Rodin

6

Passy

Champ
de Mars
Tour Eiffel

AVENUE DU PRÉSIDENT KENNEDY

AVENUE DE SUFFREN

Champ

de Mars

AVENUE DE LA MOTTE PICQUET

AVENUE DE TOURVILLE

Ecole
Militaire

Bir Hakeim

St. François
Xavier

Ecole
Militaire

BOULEVARD DE GRENELLE

Dupleix

La Motte-Picquet
Grenelle

Cambronne

Charles
Michels

Avenue
Émile Zola

Commerce

Félix
Faure

Boucicaut

Vaugirard

Lourmel

ower

wer

You can't visit Paris and not climb the Eiffel Tower; it would be like going to New York and ignoring the Statue of Liberty or to Cairo and skipping the pyramids. Although Paris has plenty of other monuments with good views, none can match the splendour of the great iron flagpole. Even by today's skyscraperish standards it's impossibly huge, especially when seen against the low-rise Paris skyline. Try to imagine how it must have seemed one hundred years ago, when the 320m tower was officially the world's tallest structure.

Each of its three levels is accessible by lift or (for the super-fit) stairs – take heed that there are 1,710 of them on your way to the top. On your way up you'll find a restaurant, a gift shop, several boutiques and even a post office where your postcards can get that all-important 'Paris Tour Eiffel' post-mark. On a clear day you can see over 50 miles.

Approximately 16,000 people visit the tower every day so queues for the lifts can be very long – if you come mid-afternoon you can expect to wait at least an hour. Queues are shorter first thing in the morning and at night when the views of the illuminated city are even more magical. The lights are usually kept on until midnight. Every night from dusk until 1am during 2000 there is a special light show at the tower, including two long beams which light up the Paris skyline.

In time-honoured tradition, this most popular of monuments was actually largely reviled when first unveiled. Many members of Paris' artistic community, including Alexandre Dumas, signed a petition against It, while Guy de Maupassant actually

Champ de Mars, 7th
© 01 44 11 23 45
Infoline: © 01 44 11 23 23
Ⓜ Bir-Hakeim, Trocadéro
RER: Champ-de-Mars
Open: June–Aug daily 9am–12 midnight;
Sept–May daily 9am–11pm
Adm: by lift: First level adult 20F,
under 12s 11F, Second level adult 42F,
under 12s 21F, Third level adult 59F,
under 12s 30F, under 4s free;
by stairs: First and Second levels only 14F
Wheelchair access
Suitable for all ages
Allow at least a couple of hours

Question 6

At 320m, the Eiffel Tower was the tallest structure in the world until 1931. What surpassed it?

answer on p.248

Hôtel des Invalides

moved out of Paris so he wouldn't have to look at the 'metallic carcass' anymore. The government considered knocking the tower down in 1909 as it seemed to serve no useful purpose. Thankfully one was found for it: a meteorological station and wireless antennae were constructed on top of the tower in 1914, increasing its height by 20m.

Topped by a glittering gilded dome – one of Paris' most prominent landmarks – the Hôtel des Invalides was built in the 17th century for the wounded and retired soldiers of Louis XIV's numerous campaigns, its wards filled with 6,000-plus battle-scarred victims. Part of it is in fact still used as a hospital, but there are now only a handful of long-term patients.

The Invalides' greatest attraction is a shrine to one of France's secular saints: Napoleon, whose body was brought here from St Helena in 1840 to a hero's funeral. Since his final appearance on French soil 25 years earlier, Napoleon's reputation had grown to mythic proportions: no longer was he the power-crazed tyrant whose lust for military glory had almost destroyed France, instead he was the embodiment of France's true revolutionary spirit. His body lies beneath the dome in a blood red sarcophagus – within are a further six coffins made of mahogany, tin and lead; somebody wanted to make sure he wasn't going to get out.

The tower was designed by Gustave Eiffel (who also part-designed the Statue of Liberty) in 1889 for the centenary of the French Revolution. It cost a then staggering 8 million francs, weighs 9,700 tonnes, contains 2.5 million rivets and, to keep it looking spick and span, requires 40 tonnes of paint every seven years or so. Its lifts travel over 100,000km each year.

Esplanade des Invalides, 7th
℡ 01 44 42 37 72
Ⓜ Invalides
Open: summer 10am–5.45pm; winter 10am–4.45pm, in summer Napoleon's tomb is open until 7pm
Adm: adult 37F, under 18s 27F, under 12s free – this includes entry to the Musée de l'Armée, the Musée des Plans Relief and Napoleon's tomb
Wheelchair access
Suitable for children aged 6 and over
Allow at least a couple of hours

The complex also contains a couple of churches, St Louis and the Eglise du Dôme, built back to back (they originally shared an altar) – one for use by soldiers and staff, the other by the royal family. (The two congregations may have worshipped the same God, and may even have been regarded in His eyes as equal, but that was no reason why they should share the same pew.)

Musée de L'Armée

Napoleon's tomb aside, most people come to the Invalides in order to visit the Musée de L'Armée. Inside, the rooms are full of armour, uniforms (the museum contains over 100,000, but you get the general idea after the first 10,000 or so), weapons and paintings. There are sections devoted to the campaigns of Louix XIV, the First and Second World Wars and, of course, Napoleon – the last containing such singular items as a lock of his hair, his death mask and his stuffed pet dog. One curiosity worth looking out for is a 360° painting of the Battle of Rosaville. You can stand in the middle and follow the course of the battle around (and around and around).

The top floor is given over to the **Musée des Plans Relief** which holds a collection of scale models of France's fortified towns. The collection was begun in the 17th century under Louis XIV.

The Cannons

The complex seems to have inherited more cannons than it knows what to do with. They line the entrance, they line the central courtyard (known as the Cour d'Honneur), they line the colonnaded walkways.

If you look at the 18th-century cannons in the central courtyard (which bear such emotive names as 'Le Maniac') you'll see that these instruments of war are beautifully decorated with carved reliefs of lions and suns, and that they sport fish-shaped handles. The 19th-century cannons lining the walkways are much more austere and sombre in comparison.

If you look down the barrel of a cannon you'll see that the inside is slightly spiralled. This would help to spin the cannon ball as it was fired, thereby making it easier to aim. Also note that each cannon is helpfully marked with an arrow showing which end the cannonball was meant to come out.

Question 7

How did Napoleon die?
a) Shot by an Italian peasant
b) Blown up by a Russian bomb
c) Poisoned by the decorations in his home

answer on p.248

Palais de Chaillot

Place du Trocadéro, 16th
Ⓜ Trocadéro

Built for the 1937 World Exhibition, this rather imposing, creamy coloured authoritarian-looking complex sits atop a hill across the Seine from the Eiffel Tower. It's made up of two grand pavilions which envelop a central terrace decorated with monumental statues. The tiered Jardins du Trocadéro beneath it, stretching out towards the water's edge, contain a vintage carousel and several fountains, as well as a lively throng of souvenir sellers and skateboarders.

The complex contains four museums: the **Musée des Monuments Français** and the **Musée du Cinéma** (both currently closed for renovation), and the **Musée de la Marine** and the **Musée de l'Homme**.

Musée de la Marine

☎ 01 53 65 69 69
Open: Mon and Wed–Sun 10am–5.50pm
Adm: adult 38F, under 25s 25F, under 5s free
Wheelchair access
Suitable for all ages
Allow at least an hour

The Musée de la Marine is dedicated to French naval history. It displays hundreds of beautifully crafted model boats ranging from ancient Egyptian barges to medieval galleys, modern destroyers, submarines and aircraft carriers. There's even a model of the open-backed boat which brought the Egyptian obelisk all the way from Luxor to the Place de la Concorde. You can see the workshop where many of these models are created and watch the craftsmen at work.

Other exhibits include Napoleon's royal barge – powered by oarsmen instead of sails to make sure that Bonaparte looked as much like a Roman Emperor as possible – and a collection of lighthouse bulbs.

Musée de l'Homme

☎ 01 44 05 72 72
Open: summer Mon and Wed–Sun
9.45am–5.15pm
Adm: adult 30F, under 16s 20F, under 4s free
Wheelchair access
Suitable for all ages
Allow at least an hour

A museum of ethnography which will provide several hours of entertainment. Check out in particular the African tribal masks, the Mayan Temple and the collection of weird and wonderful musical instruments from around the world. It is currently being reorganized – a large part of the collection is earmarked to move to the Louvre – but it is still worth a visit.

Musée Rodin

Hôtel Biron, 77 Rue de Varenne, 7th
✆ 01 44 18 61 10
Ⓜ Varenne
Open: summer Tues–Sun 9.30am–5.45pm, winter
Tues–Sun 9.30am–4.45pm
Adm: adult 28F, under 25s 18F, under 18s and
adult with pushchair free
Partial wheelchair access
Suitable for all ages
Allow at least a couple of hours

Auguste Rodin, one of France's most influential and popular sculptors, lived in the Hôtel Biron for nearly 10 years before his death in 1917. His works and his collection are exhibited inside this beautifully preserved 18th-century house, with some sculptures scattered throughout the pretty, enclosed garden.

Rodin's sculptures often seem to appeal to the younger generation and many will already be familiar – *The Thinker* and *The Kiss*. They are sure to enjoy seeing sculpture outdoors, and when they've had enough there's a sandpit. A particular favourite with Parisian mothers.

Champ de Mars

7th
Ⓜ Bir-Hakeim, Ecole Militaire
RER: Champ de Mars

Today the Champ de Mars is a very grand, rather formal garden which provides the Eiffel Tower with a suitably elegant backdrop. If you had visited in 1900, however, you would have found it covered by an enormous iron pavilion, the Galerie des Machines, with a moving walkway running through the park's centre from the Ecole Militaire to the Tower.

Nowadays, the park does not welcome much in the way of uninhibited play within its carefully sculpted borders but there are marionette shows every Wednesday, Saturday and Sunday.

Around and about

Bateaux Mouches

Pont de l'Alma, 7th
✆ 01 42 25 96 10
Infoline: ✆ 01 40 76 99 99
www.bateaux-mouches.com
Ⓜ Alma Marceau
RER: Pont de l'Alma
Sailing times: summer daily every 30mins
10am–11pm; winter every hour 11am–9pm
Fares: adults 40F, under 15s 20F, under 5s free
Lunch *c.* 300–350F; dinner 500–700F

Wheelchair access
Suitable for all ages
The tour lasts one hour

Drifting down the Seine on board a sight-seeing boat is a great way to see Paris, particularly at night when many of the monuments are illuminated. The *bateaux mouches* ('fly boats') take you upriver from the Pont de l'Alma, just east of the Eiffel Tower, as far as the Ile St Louis, and then back again, past the Eiffel Tower, turning at the Pont de Grenelle (look out for Paris' own mini version of the Statue of Liberty) before returning to the Pont de l'Alma.

The recorded commentary is played through loudspeakers in four languages – French, English, Spanish and German (in that order). The only trouble is, once they've got round to pointing something out for the fourth time, you've usually passed whatever was being referred to.

The Paris Sewers

Entrance opposite 93 Quai d'Orsay
by Pont de l'Alma, 7th
✆ 01 53 68 27 81
Ⓜ Alma Marceau
RER: Pont de l'Alma
Open: Mon–Wed, Sat and Sun 11am–4pm
Adm: adult 25F, under 25 20F, under 12 15F,
under 5s free
Wheelchair assistance available (call in advance);
wheelchair hire
Suitable for all ages
Allow at least an hour

The smelliest tour in town, much loved by kids, the city's sewers (*égouts*) have become a strangely popular tourist attraction in recent years, and in high season the queues can be quite long. During the sewer 'experience' you are treated to a short film on the history of waste c ......un a quick tour of a section of the sewer network, laid out like some subterranean city. Every sewer has a sign stating the street it serves and every pipe bears the name of the building to which it is connected. Fear not, your kids will not be asked to wade through anything unpleasant, although the smell does tend to linger a bit.

Musée Nationale des Arts Asiatiques – Guimet

6 Place d'Iéna, 16th
✆ 01 45 05 00 98
Ⓜ Iéna
Open: Mon and Wed–Sun 9.45am–5.45pm
Adm: adult 16F (12F on Sun), under 18s free
Wheelchair access
Suitable for children aged 8 and over
Allow at least an hour

The Guimet holds one of the world's most important collections of Asian Art – Chinese ivories, Javanese shadow puppets, Indian lacquerware, Japanese ceramics and scores of big, fat smiling buddha sculptures from Japan and China. There's also a peaceful Japanese garden. Part of the collection is currently closed for restoration.

Palais de Tokyo/Musée d'Art Moderne de la Ville de Paris

11 Avenue Président Wilson, 16th
✆ 01 53 67 40 00
Ⓜ Iéna, Alma Marceau
Open: Tues–Sun 10am–5.40pm,
Sat and Sun until 7pm
Adm: adult 27F, under 25s 14.50F, under 18s free
Wheelchair access
Suitable for children aged 6 and over
Allow at least an hour

Another architectural tribute to the 1937 World Exhibition, the Palais de Tokyo was

Where to eat

originally called the Electricity Pavilion – inside, you can see Raoul Dufy's vast mural *La Fée Electricité* – and today it holds the city's small but impressive modern art collection. Picasso, Braque and Modigliani are all represented, and there's a room dedicated to Matisse featuring two versions of his most famous work, *La Danse*.

Musée de la Mode et du Costume

Palais Galliéra, 16th
✆ 01 47 20 85 23
Ⓜ Iéna, Alma Marceau
Open: Tues–Sun 10am–6pm
Adm: adult 45F, under 25s 32F, under 8s free
Wheelchair access
Suitable for all ages
Allow at least an hour

Housed in a 19th-century neo-Renaissance mansion, this 16,000-piece museum of fashion contains garments representing the last three centuries of Parisian *couture*. The collection is shown in rotation, usually according to a particular theme such as 'marriage' or 'town clothes'.

1 Altitude 95

First Level, Eiffel Tower, Champ de Mars, 7th
✆ 01 45 55 20 04
Ⓜ Bir-Hakeim
RER: Champ de Mars
Open: daily 11.30–3pm
Fixed price menu: 98F, 127F, 150F, 250F
Children's menu: 46F

Surely the best location in Paris: on the first level of the Eiffel Tower where the views are, as you would expect, spectacular – insist on a window table. The interior is deliberately unconventional (all struts and weird pieces of metal), the food is reasonable and they're very welcoming to families. One of the perks of dining here is that you get to use the private lift and don't have to stand in the lengthy queues below.

2 L' Ancien Trocadéro

2 Place du Trocadéro et 11 Novembre, 16th
✆ 01 47 04 94 71
Ⓜ Trocadéro
Open: daily 11.30–1am

Sit at a pavement table for good views of the Palais du Chaillot and, if you crane your neck, the Eiffel Tower. It's a bit touristy but the food is simple and reasonably priced.

3 Bistro Romain

6 Place Victor Hugo, 16th
✆ 01 45 00 65 03
Ⓜ Victor Hugo
Open: daily 11.30–1am
Fixed price menu: 59F, 79F, 99F, 149F
Children's menu: 45F

Relatively quiet branch of this family-friendly chain in a pleasant square in the heart of a very upmarket residential area. All the French staples are offered and there's a children's menu. The chocolate mousse is excellent and there's a huge selection of ice creams and sorbets.

4 Brasserie XVieme Poincaré

45 Avenue Raymond Poincaré, 16th
ⓒ 01 47 27 72 19
Ⓜ Trocadéro
Open: daily 12 noon–12 midnight
Simple, cheerful brasserie serving simple but tasty fare. The omelettes are excellent and nobody turns up their nose if you ask for ketchup.

5 Le Carré

47 Avenue Raymond Poincaré, 16th
ⓒ 01 44 05 05 44
Ⓜ Trocadéro
Open: 12 noon–2.30pm and 7.30pm–11.30pm
A small, cosy Italian restaurant serving excellent ravioli and dishes with pesto.

6 Café in the Musée Rodin

Hôtel Biron, 77 Rue de Varenne, 7th
ⓒ 01 44 18 61 10
Ⓜ Varenne
Open: summer Tues–Sun 9.30am–5.45pm, winter Tues–Sun 9.30am–4.45pm
A lovely quiet spot for a light snack and a think while your kids run amok in the secluded garden. Mothers with prams get in free.

7 Thoumieux

79 Rue St Dominique, 7th
ⓒ 01 47 05 49 75
Ⓜ Invalides, La Tour-Maubourg
Open: Mon–Sat 12 noon–3.30pm and 6.30–12 midnight, Sun 12 noon–12 midnight
Fixed price menu: 82F, 160F
A traditional bistro packed with local families at the weekend. Children are very welcome although good behaviour and smart dress are expected. The food is basic bistro classics – thick bean-heavy *cassoulets* and *crème caramel*.

8 Le Totem

Musée de l'Homme
17 Place du Trocadéro et 11 Novembre, 16th
ⓒ 01 47 27 28 29
Ⓜ Trocadéro
Open: daily 12 noon–2.30am
The Musée de l'Homme's extremely groovy café welcomes families and tourists for snacks and coffee during the day, although at night, when it reverts to full-on restaurant mode, it's a touch more exclusive.

The décor should interest children, particularly the two giant totem poles and an exhibition of American Indian art. When they tire of this they can always admire the magnificent views of the Eiffel Tower.

There's a branch of 9 **McDonald's** at 131 Avenue Victor Hugo, 16th.

Pompidou Centre and the Marais

The Marais is Paris' most cultured district, its narrow, elegant streets filled with mansions, antique shops and fashion boutiques – not to mention numerous toy shops and children's clothes stores. It's also home to several excellent museums. Les Halles, once the site of Paris' fruit and vegetable market, is now dominated by a vast underground shopping centre topped by a rather shabby park. Here too there are plenty of shops for children, but little of the Marais' charm. In between sits the Pompidou Centre, one of Paris' most child-friendly museums.

500 metres
500 yards

N

RUE RÉAUMUR
Sentier
Réaumur-Sébastopol
République
Place de la République
Temple
RUE DE TURBIGO
Arts et Métiers
BD. DU TEMPLE
Oberkampf
Filles du Calvaire
RUE DU LOUVRE
Etienne Marcel
St Eustache
3
La Bourse
5
Les Halles
Châtelet Les Halles
Jardin des Halles
BOULEVARD DE SÉBASTOPOL
Rambuteau
RUE RAMBUTEAU
Forum des Halles
Pompidou Centre
RUE BEAUBOURG
Musée de la Chasse et de la Nature
St. Sebastien Froissart
BOULEVARD BEAUMARCHAIS
Richard Lenoir
Musée Picasso
RUE DE RIVOLI
RUE DU RENARD
Musée Cognacq-Jay
Chemin Vert
Pont Neuf
Châtelet
Hôtel de Ville
8
Musée Carnavalet
RUE DES FRANCS BOURGEOIS
Bréguet Sabin
Hôtel de Ville
RUE DE RIVOLI
The Marais
7
Place des Vosges
6
Conciergerie
Sainte Chapelle
Cité
carousel
St. Paul
RUE ST ANTOINE
2
Place de la Bastille
Ile de la Cité
1
Musée de la Curiosité et de la Magie
RUE ST PAUL
St. Michel Notre-Dame
Pont Marie
Bastille
St. Michel
Notre Dame
BOULEVARD HENRI IV
La Sorbonne
Ile St Louis
Sully Morland
4

Pompidou Centre

The recently revamped Pompidou Centre (also known as Beaubourg) provides first class entertainment for its younger visitors. The fun starts in the courtyard in front of the centre where you'll find buskers, musicians, fire-eaters, sword-swallowers and performance artists entertaining the crowds.

The centre itself, created in the 1970s at the behest of the then president Georges Pompidou, was designed to become a 'department store for culture': an accessible, populist museum that would act as an antidote to other more elitist institutions. The building, the work of Richard Rogers and Renzo Piano, was designed to be as determinedly modern as possible and was initially pretty unpopular. Its technical infrastructure, its wires, tubes and tunnels, are displayed prominently on the outside of the structure and painted in gaudy colours: electrics are yellow, air conditioning is blue and ventilation ducts are white.

Despite the initial furore, the centre is now largely accepted and the majority of Parisians are actually rather fond of it. Kids usually respond favourably to its messy architecture and unfinished look – it's the sort of over-the-top construction they would probably come up with themselves.

A large part of the centre is given over to the **Musée Nationale d'Art Moderne** where you'll find works by all the great modern artists of the 20th century – Braque, Brandt, Chagall, Dali, Kandinsky, Klee, Matisse, Modigliani, Picasso, Pollock, *et al*. The front desk provides quizzes and trails for children. Also, look out for the **Atelier des Enfants**, an art workshop aimed at children aged 6–12.

On the top floor is a café with beautiful views of the city, best reached by the giant escalator that zigzags its way across the exterior. Come at twilight and watch the lights of the city gradually coming into view.

Can you spot?

The 'Stravinsky', the great fantasy fountain, just south of the centre on Rue du Cloître-St-Merri, featuring skeletons, dragons, an enormous pair of lips and water squirting every which way.

Rue Beaubourg, 4th
℡ 01 44 78 12 33
www. cnac.gp.fr
Ⓜ Hôtel de Ville, Rambuteau
RER: Châtelet-Les Halles
Open: centre: Mon, Wed–Sun 11am–10pm; musée: Mon, Wed–Sun 11am–9pm
Adm: centre: free; musée adults 30F, under 18s free
Wheelchair access and adapted toilets
Suitable for all ages
Allow at least a couple of hours

The Marais

The pace of life in the Marais is somehow more relaxed than in other parts of the city: this is the neighbourhood of choice for the well-to-do with time on their hands.

A historic enclave, extending from the Hôtel de Ville to the Place de la Bastille, the Marais is famed for its graceful architecture and elegant streets, and the whole area is dotted with mansions, art galleries, clothes shops, flower sellers, cafés and museums. Saunter through its narrow streets and you should find plenty of distractions to keep both you and the kids happy.

Once a small area of marshland (*marais* means 'marsh'), the Marais was drained and cultivated in the middle ages by the Knights Templar and began its rise to prominence in 1605 when Henry IV ordered the construction of the Place des Vosges. At a stroke the area was turned into one of the most desirable addresses in Paris. Numerous mansions and luxury residences went up over the next couple of centuries as the nobility poured in. The area's fortunes, however, went the same way as the nobility's following the revolution: its architecture went out of fashion, the monied classes moved away and the whole area became run down and dilapidated. This turned out to be something of a blessing, as the Marais escaped many of the modern architectural ravages that have blighted some of the surrounding areas.

Come the early 1960s and the Marais was once again back in vogue; its historic, unspoilt landscape appealing to trendsetters searching for an alternative to high-rise modernity. Today, the area is still a great place to soak up a little of old-time Paris' atmosphere and charm.

Place des Vosges

Square Louis XIII, 4th
Ⓜ Bastille, Chemin Vert

Paris' oldest square is a grand, formal open space lined with arcaded pavilions and covered in neatly sculpted grass lawns (which you are not allowed to walk on), fountains and gravel pathways and has long been a favourite stamping ground for school children (there's a sandpit) and *boules* players. Unlike many of Paris' other squares, it hasn't been turned into a traffic-filled roundabout and it still has a laid-back Sunday afternoon feel to it.

When first laid out in the early 17th century it was called the Place Royale. This was changed to the catchy Place d'Indivisibilité following the French Revolution when names with royal connotations were frowned upon. Napoleon gave it its present name in honour of its status as the first *département* in France to pay his new war taxes.

Musée de la Curiosité et de la Magie

11 Rue St Paul, 4th
℡ 01 42 72 13 26
Ⓜ St Paul, Sully Morland
Open: Wed, Sat and Sun 2–7
Adm: adult 45F, under 12s 30F, under 3s free
Wheelchair access
Suitable for all ages
Allow at least an hour
English-speaking guides
Magic courses for children during school holidays

This is a performance-based museum which kids just love: skilled magicians are on hand to perform conjuring shows, card tricks and optical illusions with lots of audience participation – kids fight for the right to be the one to pick the card. You can pick up equipment for your budding magicians – magic wands, trick card packs and demonstration videos – at the nearby Magasin de Magie on the Rue du Temple.

Musée Carnavalet

23 Rue de Sévigné, 3rd
℡ 01 42 72 21 13
Ⓜ St Paul, Chemin Vert
Open: Tues–Sun 10–5.40; the 19th- and 20th-century rooms open from 10–11.30am; the Louis XV period rooms don't open until 1.30pm.
Adm: adult 27F, under 18s free
Wheelchair access via entrance at
29 Rue de Sévigné
Suitable for children aged 6 and over
Allow at least a couple of hours

Set in one of the grandest mansions in the Marais, the museum tells the story of France

from prehistory to the present day through archaeological exhibits, personal effects, scale models and original house interiors – many recovered from mansions destroyed in the mid 19th century to make way for the grand boulevards. Kids will like the models and house interiors best. Highlights include a fantastically detailed paper model of Paris c. 1527, the glittering interior of a jeweller's shop c. 1902 and the opulent salons of the Hôtel d'Uzèz, Hôtel La Rivière and Hôtel Wendel. There are some delightful pieces of revolutionary memorabilia: a model guillotine carved in bone by French prisoners of war in England, Louis XIV's shaving kit and Napoleon's toothbrush.

The Marais' other museums

Musée Picasso

Hôtel Salé, 5 Rue De Thorigny, 3rd
℡ 01 42 71 25 21
Ⓜ Chemin Vert, St Sébastien Froissart
Open: summer 9.30–6, winter 9.30–5.30; closed Tues
Adm: adult 30F, under 25s 20F, under 18s free
Wheelchair access
Suitable for children aged 10 and over
Allow at least an hour

Dedicated to the 20th-century's greatest artist, the museum contains a lifetime of Picasso's works, displayed in chronological order, as well as his own private collection which contains works by Renoir, Cézanne, Rousseau and Braque.

Musée de la Chasse et de la Nature

Hôtel Guénégaud, 60 Rue des Archives, 3rd
✆ 01 53 01 82 40
Ⓜ Rambuteau
Open: Tues–Sun 11–6
Adm: adult 30F, under 25s 15F, under 5s free
Limited wheelchair access
Suitable for children aged 8 and over
Allow at least an hour

This small museum in a beautiful 17th-century mansion is dedicated to the history of hunting – in France as much a proletarian pastime as an aristocratic one – and has an eclectic range of exhibits: stone age axes, Persian helmets, ornate crossbows, swords once owned by medieval nobleman, and cases and cases of stuffed animals.

Musée Cognacq-Jay

Hôtel Denon, 8 Rue Elzévir, 3rd
✆ 01 40 27 07 21
Ⓜ St Paul
Open: Tues–Sun 10–5.40
Adm: adult 17.50F, under 25s 9F, under 18s free
Limited wheelchair access
Suitable for children aged 8 and over
Allow at least an hour
The museum organizes art workshops for children

A collection of 18th-century European art in yet another beautiful mansion, with works by Rembrandt, Watteau, Chardin, Fragonard, Rubens, Canaletto and La Tour. The collection was built up by Ernest Cognacq, founder of the Samaritaine.

Shopping in the Marais

Browsing the shops of the Marais is one of the great pleasures of Paris, and there's no need to leave the kids behind. In addition to its complement of antique shops, wine sellers, art galleries, cheese sellers and clothes boutiques, most streets also boast a toy shop and children's clothes store.

La Charrue et Les Etoiles
19 Rue des Francs Bourgeois, 4th
Huge collection of plastic and tin miniatures: international favourites such as the Simpsons, Spiderman, Wallace & Gromit and Tin Tin, alongside the sturdy French stalwarts, Asterix and Obélix.

L'Arbre de Vie Artisanat
21 Rue de Sévigné, 4th
Wide selection of Japanese toy robots.

Cath'Art
13 Rue Ste Croix de la Bretonnerie, 4th
Marionettes and inflatables.

Why!
14 Rue Bernard Palissy, 6th
A temple to tackiness: furry lava lamps, hummingbird-shaped key rings, glow-in-the-dark bags, gorilla-shaped staplers, etc.

Marais Plus
20 Rue des Francs Bourgeois, 3rd
Lots of educational toys and books, and a tea shop on the first floor.

Unishop Enfant, 4 Rue Rambuteau, 4th, **Catamini**, 6 Rue des Francs Bourgeois, 3rd, and **Croissant**, 5 Rue St Merri, 4th, are good for new and second-hand clothes; **Texaffaires**, 7 Rue du Temple, 4th, is good for nursery furniture and furnishings.

Question 8

Where else can you see the *Spirit of Liberty*?

answer on p.248

Place de la Bastille

11th
Ⓜ Bastille

This is where the French Revolution started. The Bastille was the royal prison, built in around 1370, where the nation's political prisoners were held – in other words, those people who had managed to annoy the monarch in some way or another. Many were kept under the terms of the notorious *lettres de cachet*, a device which allowed the king to imprison pretty much anyone he liked for as long as he liked without having to bother going through the courts.

Over the centuries the prison became a symbol of the corruption of royal power and was deeply hated by the Parisian lower orders. By the late 18th century, however, the Bastille had been in decline for some time. It was no longer the city's main prison, the *lettres de cachet* had been abolished, and the government was actually planning to demolish it. Indeed, when the revolution began in the summer of 1789, the Bastille held just seven people.

Nonetheless, its symbolic importance was great, and on 14 July the revolutionary forces stormed the fortress and released its prisoners. Of the seven, four were swindlers, one was an English madman and another an aristocrat accused of incest, while the final prisoner, a genuine political captive who had been sent to the Bastille some 30 years before for conspiring against the King, had become so used to his surroundings that he initially refused to leave. The prison's demolition began the very next day overseen by a young entrepreneur

named Palloy who would make his fortune creating instant souvenirs of the event; he had many of the Bastille's stones carved into models of the fortress which he then sold to each of the 83 *départements* of France (you can see one of the models in the Musée Carnavalet); the rest were used to build the Pont de la Concorde.

The outline of the fortress is still clearly visible on the paving stones covering the square. In the centre stands a 50m high column, *La Colonne de Juillet*, erected to the victims of the 1830 and 1848 revolutions, many of whom are buried beneath its base. The gold figure perched on top is meant to represent the Spirit of Liberty. The storming of the Bastille is celebrated on the square every 14 July with a lively street party.

On the southeast edge of the square is one of President Mitterand's controversial building projects, the vast, modernist Opéra National de Paris-Bastille. Although only a decade old, renovation had to be carried out recently to its geometric façade to stop chunks of it falling on passers by.

Question 9

What is a tumbril?

answer on p.248

The French Revolution

If there's one thing the French love, it's a revolution. They've had four so far: in 1789, 1830, 1848 and 1871. When people refer to the French Revolution, however, they're talking about the first one, the peasants vs Louis XVI. This is the key event in France's history, the moment when ordinary people decided for the first time to take a stand against cruelty and inequality. Both the national anthem, *La Marseillaise*, and the national flag, the *Tricolore*, were created at the time of the revolution.

14 July, the day the Bastille was stormed, is France's national day and is celebrated throughout the country with noisy street parties. For all the partying, however, it's worth remembering that the revolution itself was a thoroughly nasty, bloodthirsty affair, its history jam-packed with violence, murder and betrayal...

A brief history of the Revolution

1780s King Louis XVI is the absolute ruler of France; his word is law. The peasants and professionals (lawyers, doctors, magistrates, etc.) are becoming more and more unhappy with the situation, and are particularly upset at having to pay high taxes while the King and his nobles lead lives of luxury.

1788 The year's harvest fails. The peasants are starving but are still being forced to pay their taxes. The price of bread rises, and the nobles are accused of hoarding grain to keep the price high.

1789 The peasants and professionals, angered by Louis' refusal to cut their taxes, storm the Bastille. They set up a new parliament, the National Assembly, and insist that Louis listens to its views. Louis thinks of the enormous mob ready to leap on him if he refuses and, not surprisingly, agrees.

1792 Louis tries to leave France to raise an army and defeat the revolutionaries, but he is captured and brought back to Paris.

1793 The Kings of Prussia, Austria and Spain declare war on France. They are scared that if the revolutionaries are successful, their own people might revolt. Maximilien Robespierre, the leader of the revolutionaries, orders that Louis XVI be executed using a new fangled head-chopping device, a *guillotine*. He then orders that all enemies of the revolution be wiped out: at this point things get out of control, and nobles, clergy, criminals, madmen and anyone else who could possibly cause trouble, are murdered as Paris is turned into a bloodbath. This period becomes known as The Terror, during which some 30,000 people are killed.

1794 The people of Paris eventually turn on Robespierre in horror, accusing him of having become a tyrant, every bit as bad as King Louis. He is arrested and executed.

1795 The government starts raising taxes to pay for the new wars. Some people complain that they're no better off without a king and decide they want one again. They start a revolt in Paris hoping to install Louis' brother (also called Louis) on the throne, but they are defeated by a young army general, Napoleon Bonaparte, who takes control of the government. The revolution, he declares, is over. The time has come for Frenchmen to stop fighting one another, and start fighting everyone else instead.

1796 Napoleon begins the conquest of mainland Europe.

Les Halles

(pronounced 'Lay Al')
1st
Ⓜ Châtelet-Les Halles

For centuries this area was occupied by a lively sprawling food market, until a couple of decades ago when it was forced to move to the suburbs (not unlike London's Covent Garden). Now it is overrun by the Forum des Halles, a cavernous, rather shabby underground mall frequented mainly by teenage tourists and disreputable characters and, only grudgingly, by local residents.

Nevertheless, there are elements that make it worth visiting: it has several good children's clothes shops including branches of Catamini, Complices and Petit Bateau; a number of sweet shops, most notably the market themed La Guimauve en Folie with its baskets of sugar mushrooms, apples and fish; a huge underground swimming pool; a small version of the Musée Grevin waxwork museum; and a cinema multiplex Ciné Cité.

The Jardin des Halles, the park on top of the mall, lacks the liveliness or fun of most other Parisian parks. Its only saving grace is a very good supervised children's playground with various underground tunnels, swings, ropes and ball ponds.

Jardin des Enfants

105 Rue Rambuteau, 1st
☎ 01 45 08 07 18
RER Châtelet-Les Halles
Ⓜ Les Halles
Adm: 2.50F for a one hour session
Suitable for all ages

The hole at Les Halles

In 1969 when the French government decided the market should move, the

Can you spot?

The enormous head and hand sculpture that sits outside the Eglise St Eustache, the huge gothic church overlooking the Jardin des Halles.

market at Les Halles had been in existence for nearly 800 years and had seemed such a fundamental part of Paris – as timeless and vital as the river itself – that the ease and speed with which it was removed took most people by surprise – not least the traders themselves.

The government thought it would have to clear the spot quickly in order to make way for a rush of property speculation and development that would necessarily arise on such a prime piece of real estate. The beautiful market buildings were being sacrificed, they argued, for the greater economic good. But the rush never materialized. Every scheme earmarked for the site fell through and for over 10 years, until the mall appeared, it remained unused and deteriorating, the largest urban hole in Europe.

Where to eat

1 Aux Délices d'Asie
119 Rue St Antoine, 4th
✆ 01 42 72 94 81
Ⓜ St Paul
Open: daily 10am–10.30pm
Cheap good quality noodle house serving Chinese, Vietnamese or Thai dishes to different degrees of spiciness. The portions are generous and you can eat in or take away.

2 Bofinger
5–7 Rue de la Bastille, 4th
✆ 01 42 72 87 82
Ⓜ Bastille
Open: Mon–Fri 12 noon–3pm & 6.30pm–1am, Sun 12 noon–1am
Fixed price menu: 119F, 178F
Don't be intimidated by the reputation and luxurious Art Deco interior of this famous brasserie – as long as your children behave they'll be made very welcome. Try the vanilla and strawberry vacherin. A smaller, cheaper version, 'Le Petit Bofinger', is across the road.

3 Chicago Meatpackers
8 Rue Coquillière, 1st
✆ 01 40 28 02 33
Ⓜ Les Halles
Open: daily 11.30am–1am
Fixed price menu: 59F, 74F
Children's menu: 59F
Children's entertainment Wed and weekends.
Full-on American eaterie with line-dancing waiters and a model steam train that chugs its way around a track above your heads.

4 Dame Tartine
59 Rue de Lyon, 12th
✆ 01 44 68 96 95
Ⓜ Bastille
Open: daily 12 noon–11.30pm
Friendly popular café opposite the Stravinsky fountain – a good place for a quick sandwich or *croque monsieur*.

5 Le Frog & Rosbif
116 Rue St Denis, 2nd
✆ 01 42 36 34 73
Ⓜ Etienne Marcel
RER: Châtelet-Les Halles
Open: Mon–Fri 12–3pm and 7.30pm–10.30pm, Sat & Sun 12 noon–4pm and 7.30–10.30pm
The place to tuck into some traditional pub grub: shepherd's pie, toad-in-the-hole and chicken tikka marsala.

6 Hippopotamus
1 Boulevard Beaumarchais, 4th
✆ 01 44 61 90 40
Ⓜ Bastille
Open: daily 11.30am–5am
Fixed price menu: 98F, 143F
Children's menu: 47F
Straightforward menu – burgers, steaks, ribs, etc. – and the super-friendly staff will provide games and puzzles. A favourite spot for children's parties, especially at Christmas and Hallowe'en.

7 Le Loir dans la Théière
3 Rue des Rosiers, 4th
✆ 01 42 72 68 12
Ⓜ St Paul
Open: Mon–Fri 11am–7pm, Sat and Sun 10am–7pm
Super snazzy tea salon serving mouth-watering goodies: raspberry cheesecake, chocolate fondant and lemon pie.

8 Marais Plus
20 Rue des Francs Bourgeois, 4th
✆ 01 48 87 01 40
Ⓜ Rambuteau, Hôtel de Ville
Open: Mon–Fri 10am–7pm
Cheap café above a children's shop, serving tasty quiches and pastries.

Ile de la Cité
and the Left Bank

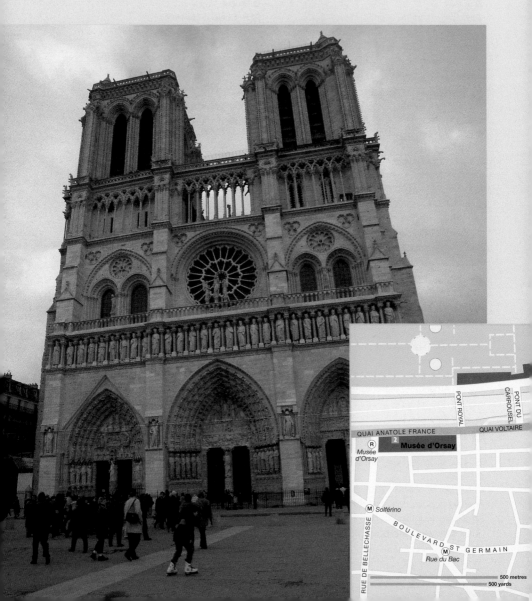

QUAI ANATOLE FRANCE

PONT ROYAL

PONT DU CARROUSEL

QUAI VOLTAIRE

R 2 **Musée d'Orsay**

Musée d'Orsay

M Solférino

BOULEVARD ST GERMAIN

RUE DE BELLECHASSE

M Rue du Bac

500 metres
500 yards

For the first thousand years or so of its existence, Paris was made up of small settlements on the left bank of the Seine and on the Ile de la Cité. This, then, is the acorn from which the mighty sprawling oak has grown. The area's focal point is the same today as it was in the Middle Ages: the great Gothic cathedral of Notre Dame, erstwhile home of the hunchbacked bell-ringer Quasimodo. Kids will love the gargoyles and the views from the top. Lurking nearby is the Conciergerie, a former prison full of grotesque memorabilia. The Left Bank is Paris' traditional centre of culture and learning and its *quais* are lined with booksellers and artists. The Musée d'Orsay, a wonderful museum of 19th-century art, stands in a converted railway station near the Pont Royal. You can pick up children's quizzes and trails at the front desk.

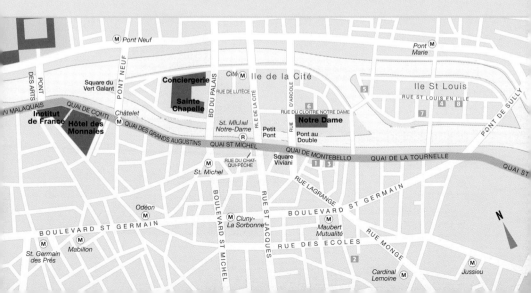

Notre Dame

When Victor Hugo penned his tale *The Hunchback of Notre Dame*, the cathedral had already been in existence some 700 years and its status as the city's most famous and important church had long since been assured. However, Disney's more recent version will no doubt strike a louder chord with your children, who will be hugely excited at the prospect of visiting the home of the movie's hunchbacked hero.

The cathedral appears to be in an almost non-stop cycle of restoration, but it is still one of Paris' must-see sights. The interior is certainly impressive, the gloom punctured by the glow from the beautiful stained glass windows. It is also worth the climb to the top of the lefthand tower for the dizzying views of the Ile de la Cité and the River Seine (beware the scary gargoyles), although only 50 people are allowed up at any one time and there is sure to be a queue. There are 238 steps to the top and there's no lift so it's not suitable for very young children (under 12s must be accompanied) or unfit adults. As you ascend you'll see the mighty bells once pulled by Quasimodo, each weighing over two tonnes, as well as a video presentation on the history of the cathedral.

Did you know?

That in the Middle Ages, churches were treated with much less reverence than they are today. Medieval Notre Dame was used as much as a meeting place as a house of worship: it was somewhere for people to come and chat, strike up a deal or eat some lunch in the company of friends. There were no seats, and the floor was strewn with rushes and straw. Furthermore, the statues inside the cathedral, which today seem rather faded and dull, would have been

Can you spot?

The market on nearby Place Louis Lépine where flowers are sold from Monday to Saturday and birds on Sunday.

Place du Parvis Notre Dame, 4th
℗ 01 42 34 56 10
Ⓜ Cité
RER: St-Michel-Notre-Dame
Open: daily 8am–6.45pm
Adm: free
Tower tours: adult 35F, under 25s 25F, under 18s 15F, under 12s free
Wheelchair access to church only
Suitable for all ages
Allow at least an hour

Musée d'Orsay

painted in bright, gaudy colours. Until 1785 a huge statue of St Christopher, the patron saint of travellers, stood over the front entrance. People used to touch it for good luck as they left.

The square in front of Notre Dame, the Place du Parvis Notre Dame, is also known as 'Kilomètre Zero', the official heart of Paris from where all distances from the capital are measured.

The most recent of Paris' trilogy of great art museums, the Musée d'Orsay covers the middle period from 1848 to 1914 (the Louvre tackles what came before, the Centre Pompidou what came after). While not quite matching the standards of the Centre Pompidou, the Musée d'Orsay is certainly more child-friendly than the Louvre. For one thing the collection is arranged on easily accessible levels beneath the single vast roof of this former railway station, and excellent quiz pamphlets for children (in both English and French) are also available from the information desk. These will direct you to many of the most famous works of art.

Before you enter the museum, be sure to point out the great clocks on its Seine-facing façade. Once inside, you can explore behind the clock faces and watch the huge clockwork mechanism in action.

1 Rue de Bellechasse, 7th
℗ 01 40 49 48 48
Infoline: ℗ 01 45 49 11 11
www.musee-orsay.fr
Ⓜ Solférino
RER: Musée d'Orsay
Open: Tues–Sat 10am–6pm,
Sun 9am–6pm
Adm: adult 40F, under 25s 30F,
under 18s free
Wheelchair access
Note – Visitors are not allowed to enter the museum with prams and back baby carriers. Folding strollers and wheelchairs can be borrowed from the cloakroom
Suitable for children aged 6 and over
Allow at least a couple of hours

If time is short, head to the Impressionist gallery on the upper level, where you'll find Renoir's *Les Baigneuses*, Van Gogh's *La Chambre* and, every little girl's favourite, Dégas' *Petite danseuse de quatorze ans*, a delicate statue of a young ballerina.

A scale model of Paris' Opera Quarter has been constructed underneath the ground floor, which you can tour on a glass ceiling as if you were floating above Paris.

If you and your kids start to get a little frazzled, there's a café on the upper level with an outdoor terrace and good views.

La Conciergerie

1 Quai de l'Horloge, 1st
✆ 01 53 73 78 50
Ⓜ Cité, Châtelet
Open: Tues–Sat 10am–6pm, Sun 9am–6pm
Adm: adult 35F, under 25s 323F, under 12s free
Some wheelchair access; call ahead for assistance
Suitable for children aged 6 and over
Allow at least an hour

After all the glorious architecture, magnificent vistas and beautiful bridges, it's time for a little gore. The Bastille may have achieved a more lasting fame but, in terms of lavish and unpleasant methods of incarceration and torture, the Conciergerie was where it was at. This was where the French Revolution's most illustrious victims – including Danton, Robespierre and Marie Antoinette – spent their final night before being marched to the public guillotine on the Place de la Concorde. You can visit Marie Antoinette's reconstructed cell.

Prisoners were accommodated in the Conciergerie according to their respective wealth. Rich nobles slept on comfortable beds and arranged for food to be brought in from outside, while the poor slept on straw and ate slops. Equality wasn't achieved until the guillotine blade fell. Non-celebrity prisoners were often executed using the *oubliette*, a box lined with vicious spikes into which the prisoner would be dropped through a trap door – their remains would then be washed away by the Seine.

As you walk through the huge 14th-century Gothic Salle des Gens d'Armes note the corridor separated by a grill on one side. This has been given the rather macabre name of the Rue de Paris in honour of the chief executioner, the 'Monsieur de Paris', who used it to move from one 'appointment' to another.

You can be sure that no one ever willingly booked an appointment at the Conciergerie's Salle de Toilette, where all prisoners came for a haircut before their execution – so the guillotine blade could be lined up properly with their necks.

Sainte Chapelle

4 Boulevard du Palais, 1st;
entrance through the Palais de Justice
✆ 01 53 73 78 50
Ⓜ Cité, Châtelet
Open: summer daily 9.30am–6.30pm,
winter daily 10am–5pm
Adm: adult 35F, under 25s 23F, under 12s free
Limited wheelchair access
Suitable for children aged 6 and over
Allow at least an hour

It's rare for a church or chapel to be rated highly by children. Unless it can offer gargoyles or views, they're usually not interested. Yet all kids seem to respond to the Sainte Chapelle despite the fact that it possesses neither, just a lot of stained glass. Of course, these are no ordinary stained glass windows but rather vast technicolour portals which on bright summer days bathe the church in a magical rainbow light – like stepping inside a kaleidoscope.

The chapel was built in the 13th century to provide a spectacular setting for Louis IX's rather dubious collection of holy relics – which included such authentic curios as Christ's crown of thorns, Moses' staff and the front half of John the Baptist's head; all of which are now in Notre Dame.

Square du Vert Galant

This tiny elegant park is a favourite spot for summer picnics under the shade of its weeping willow tree – traditionally the first tree in Paris to come into leaf. You can embark on a tour of the Seine aboard a Vedette du Pont Neuf (moored at the north end of the square; sailings summer daily every 30 mins 10–6.30, and floodlit sailings 9pm–10.30pm; winter on demand; adult 50F, under 12s 25F, under 4s).

The Left Bank *Quais*

There will be attractions along your route, but they needn't detain you; the fun of the *quais* comes from just walking about: browsing through the hundreds of bookstalls (where you can pick up all your DC and Marvel favourites in French), waving at the passengers in the passing *bateaux mouches*, and admiring the magnificent panoramic views. In 1992 the *quais* from the Pont d'Iéna, by the Eiffel Tower, to the Pont de Sully, at the tip of the Ile St-Louis, were inscribed on UNESCO's list of world heritage sites.

On your travels, see if you can spot the following:

- The Louvre. From this side of the river you can appreciate just how big it is.

- The Pont au Double, leading from the Quai de Montebello to the Ile de la Cité. So named because travellers had to pay twice to cross it, once to get on, once to get off.

- The Square Viviani, just off the Pont au Double where, supported on concrete crutches, you'll find Paris' oldest tree which was planted by the botanist Robin in 1602. It's an acacia.

- The Petit Pont, which spans the same stretch of river as Paris' first ever bridge, built in the 1st century BC at the time of Julius Caesar.

- The Rue du Chat qui Pêche, just off the Quai St Michel. At just 6ft wide, this is the narrowest street in Paris. It's also one of the oldest.

- The Quai des Grands Augustins. Built in 1313, this is Paris' oldest *quai*.

- The Hôtel des Monnaies, a vast building on the Quai de Conti. Until recently this was the national mint. France's francs are now produced in Bordeaux but the *hôtel* still produces the odd commemorative medal. You can take a tour of the medal workshops and find out about the history of money-making in the small museum (open Tues–Fri 11–5.30, Sat and Sun 12–5.30; adult 20F, under 16s free).

- The Palais de l'Institut de France, also on the Quai de Conti. Recognisable by its distinctive dome and handsome baroque wings, this is the seat of the Académie Française.

Ile St Louis

Paris' other island has little of note to fire the imagination of the younger generation. It's one of the most fashionable addresses in town, a quiet, expensive residential area full of beautiful architecture and exclusive shops. It's worth a detour, however, for a visit to Berthillon, to try one of their famed ice creams and sorbets.

Can you spot?

The Pont Neuf, the longest and oldest bridge in Paris. In the middle of the bridge is a statue of Henry IV riding a horse. Originally cast in the Middle Ages, the statue was destroyed by an anti-monarchical mob in 1792. When the royals came back into favour early in the next century, a new statue of Henry was forged from a melted-down likeness of the recently defeated Napoleon. The man who cast it, however, objected to desecrating the image of the former Emperor in this way, and made a tiny statue of Napoleon which he placed inside the belly of the horse.

Where to eat

1 La Bûcherie
41 Rue de la Bûcherie, 5th
℡ 01 43 54 78 06
Ⓜ Maubert Mutualité, St Michel
Open: 12 noon–2.30pm and 7.30pm–11pm
Quiet bistro with good views of Notre Dame, and a fire in winter.

2 Musée d'Orsay Café
1 Rue de Bellechasse, 7th
℡ 01 40 49 48 48
Ⓜ Solférino
RER: Musée d'Orsay
Open: Tues–Sat 10am–6pm,
Sun 9am–6pm
Adm: adult 40F, under 25s 30F, under 18s free
Excellent museum café offering soothing views of the river from its outdoor terrace.

3 Le Grenier de Notre Dame
18 Rue de la Bûcherie, 5th
℡ 01 43 29 98 29
Ⓜ St Michel, Maubert Mutualité
Open: daily 12 noon–2pm and 7.30pm–11.30pm
Fixed price menu: 75F, 78F, 105F
Excellent and cheap vegetarian restaurant. There's a children's menu and kids are invited to create their own non-alcoholic cocktails.

4 L'Ilot Vache
35 Rue St Louis en l'Ile, 4th
℡ 01 46 33 55 16
Ⓜ Pont Marie
Open: Tues–Sun 12 noon–3pm
and 7pm–12 midnight, Mon 7pm–12 midnight
Fixed price menu: 185F, 248F
Excellent, reasonably priced steaks and sea food, decorated to a suitably bovine theme.

5 Brasserie de l'Ile St Louis
55 Quai de Bourbon, 4th
℡ 01 43 54 02 59
Ⓜ Pont Marie
Open: 12 noon–3pm and 7pm–12 midnight
Fixed price menu: 150F

Mid-priced, good quality brasserie with views of Notre Dame and the Ile de la Cité.

6 Le Vieux Bistro
14 Rue du Cloître Notre Dame, 4th
℡ 01 43 54 18 95
Ⓜ Cité
RER: St Michel
Open: daily 12 noon–2pm & 7.30–11pm
Shadowy, traditional bistro just yards from Notre Dame. Good, old-style French cooking predominates: try the *tarte tatin*.

7 Café Floré-en-l'Ile
42 Quai d'Orleans, 4th
℡ 01 43 29 88 27
Ⓜ Cité, Sully Morland
Open: Mon–Sat 10am–10.30pm
The perfect place to sample French-style hot chocolate: one pot filled with chocolate and one with hot frothy milk – to be mixed at your leisure.

8 Berthillon
31 Rue St Louis en l'Ile, 4th
℡ 01 43 54 31 61
Open: Wed–Sun 10am–8pm
By far and away the best ice cream parlour in town, which means in summer you will have to queue for a good ten minutes before being served. It's worth it.

The Latin Quarter

Two of Paris' best parks for children lie on the Left Bank, south of the river: the Jardin des Plantes is a charming botanical garden near the Gare d'Austerlitz, with hothouses, a small zoo and awonderful museum of natural history; the Jardin du Luxembourg is a more

traditional Parisian park, still hugely popular with local youngsters. To get from one to the other, you'll cross the student district, or Latin Quarter, with its lively bars and multitude of ethnic restaurants. Past Boulevard St Michel, the area bleeds into St Germain des Prés, one of the most exclusive districts in Paris, where you'll pay upwards of 30F for a coke at a pavement café and where you can browse in such down to earth places as Baby Dior and Bonpoint.

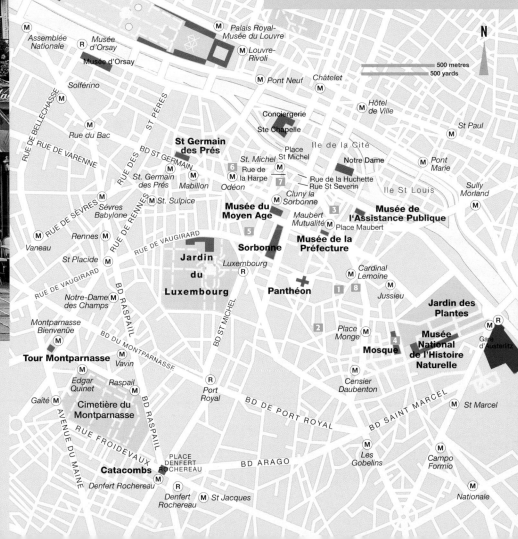

The Jardin des Plantes is always a big hit with children. The blooms may not be spectacular, the zoo may be rather small and old fashioned, and the hothouses may, often as not, be closed for renovation, yet the shady tree-lined pathways are perfect for a good old kick-about and there's a hill top labyrinth to whizz around and a dinosaur skeleton climbing frame to clamber over.

Kids don't usually make the keenest botanists, but they do seem to like old things, big things and strange things. Point them in the direction of the 250-year-old cedar tree from Lebanon, the enormous kiddie-size dahlias and the weird ironbark tree from Iran. The hothouses (when open) display an impressive collection of tropical plants including giant lillies, rubber plants and cacti.

Entrances on Place Valhubert,
Rue Buffon and Rue Cuvier, 5th
℡ 01 40 79 30 00
Ⓜ Gare d'Austerlitz, Jussieu

Musée National d'Histoire Naturelle

57 Rue Cuvier, 5th
℡ 01 40 79 30 00
Ⓜ Jussieu, Gare d'Austerlitz
Open: Mon, Wed–Sun 10–6,
Thurs until 10pm
Adm: *Grande Galerie*: adult 40F, under 16s 30F,
under 5s free
Other galleries: adult 30F, under 16s 20F,
under 5s free
Wheelchair access
Suitable for children aged 6 and over
Allow at least a couple of hours

The Musée National d'Histoire Naturelle (Natural History Museum) is split into three separate galleries. The Grande Galerie de l'Evolution (Evolution Gallery) is resolutely modern, with interactive consoles and state-of-the-art displays, the Galerie de Minéralogie (Mineralogy Gallery) is more traditional, and the Galerie d'Anatomie Comparée et Paléontologie (Gallery of Comparative Anatomy and Paleontology) is positively archaic. And yet it is the latter gallery, full of dusty wooden cabinets and Latin labels, and a grotesque collection of 19th-century medical specimens, that will perhaps leave the biggest impression.

Grand Galerie de l'Evolution

30 years in the making, this is an excellent museum which uses the most up-to-date technologies – interactive consoles, lighting and sound effects – along with some trusty old standbys like stuffed animals, fossils and mounted skeletons, to tell the story of the evolution of life on earth. There are lots

of things to marvel at, including the huge blue whale skeleton suspended from the gallery ceiling, the narwhal (a whale which sports a 6ft horn, a sort of aquatic unicorn) plus various recreated habitats – savannah, jungle, etc. – inhabited by a motley collection of fearsome-looking stuffed creatures.

Children, typically, seem to get almost as much enjoyment from the gallery's glass lifts which whizz between its three floors. A strong environmental message is pushed at every opportunity, with displays on endangered species and pollution, and there's a special Discovery Room for under-12s where nature workshops are held.

Galerie de Minéralogie

This is a gawpers' paradise, full of giant crystals, technicolour meteors and case upon case of precious gems. There's also a gallery of ancient plants, the Galerie de Paléobotanique, where you can see a 6ft cross section of a 2,000-year-old sequioa – a mere baby compared to the petrified stump of a 33 million-year-old fern nearby.

Galerie d'Anatomie Comparée et Paléontologie

Often overlooked by the crowds heading towards the Evolution Gallery, this gallery should be visited by anyone with an interest in the macabre (i.e. all children) for it holds what can only be described as the strangest, most bizzare collection of natural exhibits ever assembled. This is museum as freakshow.

The ground floor gallery, in particular, resembles nothing so much as a stage set from *The Elephant Man*. The gallery floor is lined with a huge herd of skeletal creatures – rhinos, hippos, giraffes, elephants, crocodiles, turtles – like some ghostly version of Noah's Ark, all mounted facing the main door to confront you as you enter. At its head stands a plastic model of a naked man; so naked, in fact, that he doesn't even have any skin, although he does sport a fig leaf to cover his modesty, a weirdly prudish touch considering the rest of the display. The glass cases surrounding the skeletons are filled with a ghastly collection of 19th-century 'medical' and 'scientific' exhibits including – wait for it – a pickled one-eyed cat (as in a 'cyclops' cat, with one big eye in the middle of its head), a pickled one-eyed 'cyclops' chicken, the skeletons of Siamese twins fused at the head, the skeletons of Siamese twins fused at the hip, the skeleton of a child with another child growing feet first out of its chest, a pickled rhino heart, various pickled human brains, several preserved monkeys nailed to boards (their vast gurgling intestines spilling out all over the place), and even a pickled human foetus, its skull sliced open to reveal its brain.

The menagerie was Paris' first zoo, founded during the Revolution from animals collected from the city's travelling circuses.

The general air of weirdness is further enhanced by the thick camphoric smell, the gnarly old wooden cabinets and the strange, archaic calligraphy labels, all in Latin. It's like stepping into a time warp: the collection has clearly been changed very little (if at all) since it was assembled in the 19th century. It shouldn't be changed: it's one of the few museums which portrays the natural world in something other than a cuddly, wholesome light, to remind you that the world can sometimes be a very odd and rather unsavoury place.

Be warned, however, that some of this stuff could leave you feeling rather queasy, although your kids will no doubt be absolutely fascinated, and running around asking question you don't even want to think about answering. The first floor gallery with its fearsome dinosaur skeletons and giant mammoths will come as something of a relief.

The Ménagerie

Open: summer 10–6, winter 10–5
Adm: adult 30F, under 16s 20F, under 4s free

The Ménagerie is a rather old-fashioned zoo, east of the rose gardens, with small cages and (mostly) small animals. It is, inevitably best liked by smaller children. There are llama, monkeys, deer and two bears, both called Martin.

Jardin du Luxembourg

Entrances on Place Auguste Comte, Place Edmond Rostand and Rue de Vaugirard, 6th
Ⓜ Odéon
RER: Luxembourg

A typically Parisian park with neat lawns, sculpted terraces and prim little wooden benches, which you could be forgiven for thinking would be a rather unwelcoming environment for children. Nothing, however, could be further from the truth. Whenever you visit you'll find it teeming with kiddies playing in the sandpit, clambering over the climbing frames in the adventure playground, sailing toy boats on the hexagonal pond or dashing madly around its gravel pathways. That, of course, is when they're not enjoying a pony ride or a puppet show. Older visitors are catered for with several *boules* pitches and tennis courts.

When the city was under siege by the Prussians in 1870, and meat was in short supply, some strange dishes began appearing on the menus of local restaurants: consomé d'éléphant, civet de kangarou and terrine d'antilope. In a few months the zoo's entire contents had been eaten (apart from the hippo, as nobody could meet the 80,000F asking price).

The Latin Quarter

This is the student district, site of the famous Sorbonne, where the streets are lined with cheap cafés, bars, academic bookstores and art house cinemas. It's always lively and bustling, and if you fancy a wander look out for:

- The cluster of roads immediately south of the Quai St Michel, including Rue de la Huchette, Rue de la Harpe and Rue St Severin, which are full of Greek, Turkish and Spanish restaurants, each sporting a more impressive sea food display than the last – great Busby Berkeley arrangements of crab and lobster surrounded by bowers of oysters and shrimps. Also note the Théâtre de la Huchette on the Rue de la Huchette, where Ionesco's play *The Bald Prima Donna* has been playing every night since 1957.

- The Boulevard St Michel, the area's main drag, and, in particular, the Place St Michel for the statue of St Michel slaying the serpent. In the 1968 student uprising at the Sorbonne, students used the cobblestones on Boulevard St Michel as missiles to hurl at the police.

- The Faculty of Medicine 13 Rue de la Bûcherie where, in the 19th century, students used to dissect and examine bodies stolen from local cemeteries – but only in winter when the cold helped to preserve the bodies.

- Place Maubert off the Boulevard St Germain where heretics (i.e. protestants) were hanged during the 16th century. Today it's home to a bustling market on Tuesdays, Thursdays and Saturdays.

- The Musée de la Préfecture, 1 Rue Basse des Carmes, which relates the history of the Paris police force from its formation in 1667 to the present day. Uniforms, confiscated bombs and various weapons and devices used by the criminal fraternity in centuries past make up much of the collection (open Mon–Fri 9–5, Sat 10–5; adm free).

- The Musée de l'Assistance Publique, Hôtel de Miramion, 47 Quai de la Tournelle, which focuses on the way the city has dealt with the poor over the centuries, revealing attitudes alternating between compassion and chastisement. You can find out about the history of the foundling hospitals and see some truly pitiful memorabilia, including bead name-bracelets that parents left with their child in case they ever found the money to take them back (open Wed–Sat 10–5, closed Mon, Tues and Aug; adm adult 20F, under 12s free).

- The Musée du Moyen Age – Thermes de Cluny, on Place Paul Painlevé, a well respected museum of medieval art, full of tapestries, alabaster and paintings. It also houses a Roman bath complex or Thermes, the best-preserved Roman remains in Paris (open Mon and Wed–Sun 9.15–5.45; adm adult 28F, under 25s 18F, under 18s free).

Note the statue of Montaigne outside which students traditionally rub for luck before exams.

Question 12

Why is it called the Latin Quarter?

answer on p.249

🌸 La Sorbonne, on Rue de la Sorbonne, one of the world's most famous universities, and a centre of learning since the late 13th century. The present buildings date from between 1885 and 1900.

🌸 The Panthéon, on the Place du Panthéon, just south of the Sorbonne. Intended as a church when building began in the late 18th century, it was converted into a 'Temple of Reason' and a tomb of great men following the Revolution: Voltaire, Victor Hugo, Emile Zola and Marie Curie are buried here. There are superb views from the top of its famous dome (open summer daily 9.30–6.30, winter daily 10–5.30; adm adult 35F, under 25s 23F, under 12s free).

St Germain des Prés

East of the Latin Quarter stands the church of St Germain des Prés, the oldest church in the city (parts of it date back to the 6th century) which is now at the very heart of the most exclusive district in Paris, the capital of café society. This was once the haunt of writers, poets and artists – Rimbaud, Sartre, Camus and Picasso among them – although its residents are now more *au fait* with high fashion than high art. Dior, Cartier and Armani all have branches in the area. Be sure to check out the classy street market on Rue de Buci.

Children's boutiques

St Germain's shops are nearly all a cut above the average: they're in the business of selling elegance, not convenience, retailing mini-*haute couture* to the most discerning of Parisian mothers.

Baby Dior
252 Boulevard St Germain, 7th
✆ 01 42 22 90 90
Ⓜ Solférino, Rue du Bac
The clothes may be smaller, but the prices are just as high as the adult version. You can pick up such toddler essentials as quilted fur-collared jackets, tailored sailor suits with gold buttons and a wide range of children's perfumes. The dishes of jelly beans are a nice touch.

Bonpoint
67 Rue de l'Université, 7th
✆ 01 45 55 63 70
The most exclusive name in town: the favourite establishment of parents whose children have balls and gala dinners to attend. Clients include Princess Caroline of Monaco, the Duchess of York and the Chirac family. The clothes are expensive but adorable: lots of velvet and frills for the girls, sharp suits and knickerbockers for the boys.

Petit Bateau
81 Rue de Sèvres, 6th,
✆ 01 45 49 48 38
Ⓜ Sèvres Babylone, Vaneau

161 Rue de Grenelle, 7th,
✆ 01 47 05 18 51

Ⓜ La Tour Maubourg

Petit Bateau is posh, but not too posh, and if you rummage hard enough you should be able to turn up something affordable. The twirly pyjamas are very reasonable, and there are lots of nice print T-shirts.

Petit Faune
33 Rue Jacob, 6th
Ⓒ 01 42 60 80 72
Ⓜ St Germain des Prés

Coordinated knitwear for babies and toddlers, patterned sweaters and smocks for older children.

Tartine et Chocolat
266 Bouevard St Germain, 7th
Ⓒ 01 45 56 10 45
Ⓜ Solférino

A wide range of formal, tasteful baby clothes and nursery furniture. Pastel shades predominate with lots of apple greens and an emphasis on natural fibres.

Jacadi
256 Boulevard St Germain, 7th
Ⓒ 01 42 84 30 40
Ⓜ Solférino

Ultra neat shop displays and the air thick with the sweet aroma of baby perfumes. Nothing too gaudy or controversial.

Du Pareil au Même
14 Rue St Placide, 6th

Ⓒ 01 45 44 04 40
Ⓜ Sèvres Babylone

A bit of a bargain: good, sturdy dungarees, thick coats, brightly coloured T-shirts and copies of designer labels at reasonable, department store prices.

Kerstin Adolphson
157 Boulevard St Germain, 6th
Ⓒ 01 45 48 00 14
Ⓜ St Germain des Prés

Welcoming shop, chaotically arranged, with great piles of clothes all over the place, a tile floor and wooden beams poking through the ceiling. These are the sorts of clothes kids will choose for themselves: patterned socks, bright jackets and painted wooden clogs.

Six Pieds Trois Pouces
223 Boulevard St Germain, 7th
Ⓒ 01 45 44 03 72
Ⓜ St Germain des Prés

Exquisitely crafted children's footwear: soft leather, Italian designs and high prices.

L'Oiseau de Paradis
211 Boulevard St Germain, 7th
Ⓒ 01 45 48 97 90

An activity shop for bored kids: plastic animals, toy drum kits, dolls, wooden forts, sailing boats and even little Red Riding Hood costumes.

Around and about

The Catacombs

1 Place Denfert Rochereau, 14th
℡ 01 43 22 47 63
Ⓜ Denfert Rochereau
Open: Tues–Fri 2–4,
Sat and Sun 9–11 and 2–4
Adm: adult 27F, under 18s 19F, under 7s free
No wheelchair access
Suitable for children aged 6 and over
Allow at least an hour

If you and your kids would like to see what six million skeletons look like, you should make your way south of Montparnasse cemetery and pay a visit to the catacombs – or the 'Empire of the Dead' as the rather frenzied marketing blurb puts it. Originally Roman stone quarries, these dark, damp subterranean passageways are filled with the former residents of Paris' numerous cemeteries, moved here as a result of graveyard 'overcrowding' in the 1780s. Every year, more than 50,000 people descend the 90 steps to explore a world of neatly arranged death: stack upon stack of ghoulish bones, and row upon row of scary skulls. Macabre but fascinating.

Tour Montparnasse

33 Avenue du Maine, 15th
℡ 01 45 38 52 56
Ⓜ Montparnasse Bienvenüe
Open: daily 9.30am–10.30pm
Adm: adult 46F, under 20s 34F, under 14s 30F, under 5s free
Wheelchair access
Suitable for all ages
Allow at least an hour

The 190m Tour Montparnasse was Paris' first skyscraper, and is still its tallest and (to be honest) ugliest. Until the construction of London's Canary Wharf in the early 1990s, it was the tallest building in Europe. Built in the early 1960s in what was then one of the most fashionable districts in town, it had the immediate effect of sending the trend-setters packing to the more northerly districts of St Germain des Prés and the Marais. Still largely unloved, it's worth visiting for the views alone. You can see for over 25 miles from the 59th-floor terrace, and there's a display of Paris views from the past showing how the city's skyline changed throughout the last century.

Where to eat

1 Chez Alexandre

39 Rue Descartes, 5th
✆ 01 40 46 82 20
Ⓜ Cardinal Lemoine, Place Monge
Open: Mon–Sat 12 noon–2.30pm and
6.30pm–12 midnight
Fixed price menu: 49F, 75F
Bustling eaterie near the Rue Mouffetard
market. Tasty tarragon chicken, grilled steak,
and superb desserts.

2 Chez Léna et Mamille

32 Rue Tournefort, 5th
✆ 01 47 07 72 47
Ⓜ Place Monge
Open: daily 12 noon–2pm and 7.30pm–11pm
Fixed price menu: 98F, 185F
Located in a narrow street south of the
Panthéon, this restaurant is worth a visit to
take on the all-you-can-eat chocolate
mousse. The terrace has views of a pretty
fountain and a park where kids can burn off
any excess calories.

3 Hippopotamus

9 Rue Lagrange, 5th
✆ 01 43 54 13 99
Ⓜ Maubert Mutualité
Open: daily 11.30–5am
Fixed price menu: 98F, 143F
Children's menu: 47F
Paris' top child-friendly chain: burgers,
steaks, chips, ice cream and games.

4 Le Mosque du Paris

1 Place du Puits de l'Ermite, 5th
✆ 01 45 35 97 33
Ⓜ Censier Daubenton
Open: daily 10am–midnight
The perfect pit stop after a morning in the
Jardin des Plantes. The café has been
designed as an architectural tribute to
Spain's Alhambra, and stands next to Paris'
largest mosque. Beautiful blue and white
tiles and graceful arches provide a wonderfully relaxed setting in which to enjoy a mint
tea and a fig-filled pastry.

5 Polidor

41 Rue Monsieur le Prince, 6th
✆ 01 43 26 95 34
Ⓜ Odéon
Open: Mon–Sat 12 noon–2.30pm and
7pm–12.30am,
Sun 12 noon–2.30pm & 7pm–11pm
Fixed price menu: 100F
A hugely popular traditional bistro near the
Jardin du Luxembourg, with great long
tables to accommodate the entire family.
The dishes are sturdy French staples such
as *boeuf bourgignon*, veal in white wine
sauce, and snails with garlic (for the adventurous). The chocolate tarts are particularly
recommended. And as a final treat for your
children – Turkish-style squat toilets.

Crêperies

The Latin Quarter has almost as many
crêperies as it does students. Try one of the
following:

6 Crêperie des Arts

27 Rue St André des Arts, 6th
Easily the best crêperie in town.

7 Crêperie Cluny

20 Rue de la Harpe, 5th

8 La Crêpe Carrée

42 Rue Monge, 5th

Montmartre

Montmartre, the village occupying the highest hill in Paris, was once Paris' funkiest address, the site of the Moulin Rouge where the capital's most determined hedonists came to paint the town red. These days it's a rather faded belle exuding a proud but slightly shabby elegance, and it's surprisingly child-friendly: kids love Sacre Coeur, the looming white basilica perched on the hill, almost as much as they love the funicular that takes them there. They'll also enjoy the vintage carousel on the Place St Pierre, the nearby Halle St Pierre with its dedicated children's exhibitions, and the Place du Tertre where hordes of pavement artists will fight for the right to draw their portrait.

N

↑ **Marché aux Puces**

RUE DU MONT CENIS

Marcadet
Poissonniers Ⓜ

BOULEVARD BARBÈS

5

Lamarck
Caulaincourt Ⓜ
3   RUE CAULAINCOURT

RUE CUSTINE

RUE DU MONT CENIS

Cimetière de
Montmartre

RUE DE CLIGNANCOURT

Ⓜ
Château
Rouge

RUE CAULAINCOURT

7 RUE LEPIC

4
Place
du Tertre

**Sacré
Coeur**

RUE DES ABBESSES

RUE DES TROIS FRÈRES

1

6
Place
des Abbesses

Abbesses Ⓜ

carousel ●

**Halle
St Pierre**

2

Place
St Pierre

RUE YVONNE-LE-TAC

**Moulin
Rouge**

Ⓜ
Blanche

BOULEVARD DE CLICHY

Pigalle
Ⓜ

Anvers Ⓜ

BOULEVARD DE ROCHECHOUART

Ⓜ
Barbès
Rochechouart

Sacre Coeur

Question 13

Which painter was famous for his pictures of girls performing the can-can at the Moulin Rouge?

answer on p.249

This shining white basilica perched high on a hill is Montmartre's dominant feature, visible from all over the city. It's a relatively modern monument by Parisian standards, commissioned in 1873 and completed in a little under 12 years. You can reach it either by clambering up a seemingly endless flight of steps or by taking the jaunty little funicular (métro tickets are valid).

The views from the steps in front of the church are pretty amazing, and from the dome they are truly spectacular: you can see the entire city spread out before you like a great 3D patchwork.

The basilica's interior will be of limited interest to children. It's suitably dark and spooky, and the stained glass produces some magical effects, but they won't insist on lingering long.

There is always someone praying inside Sacre Coeur. Every moment of every day since 1885 there has been someone on prayer duty within the basilica (not the same person, of course).

34 Rue du Chevalier-de-la-Barre, 18th
☎ 01 53 41 89 00
Ⓜ Abbesses, Anvers
Open: summer daily 9–7, wInter daily 9–6
Adm: church: free, dome: adult 15F, under 25s 8F, under 6s free
Wheelchair access to the church; call in advance for assistance
Suitable for all ages
Allow at least an hour

Place du Tertre

Lined with cafés and bars and permanently thronged with people, the Place du Tertre is not to everyone's taste. Some people cite it as an example of everything that's wrong with the modern Montmartre but, if you take it at face value, it's fun, it's lively, it doesn't take itself too seriously, and your kids will enjoy it.

Every inch of the square seems to be occupied by an artist in residence. Many have original works to sell, often as not featuring a major Paris landmark, although this is also the place to pick up cheap copies of works by great masters. Most of the artists are portrait-painters and silhouette-cutters, who will do a suitably flattering likeness of your child for between 100 and 150F.

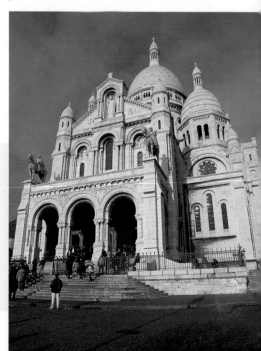

Around Montmartre

For a little more art (of the more serious kind, although kids will still enjoy it), check out the Espace Montmartre, 11 Rue Poulbot, just around the corner in the former wax museum. It now houses a permanent display of surrealist art, with exhibitions mostly focussing on the works of Salvador Dali.

Halle St Pierre

2 Rue Ronsard, 18th
℡ 01 42 58 72 89
Ⓜ Anvers, Abbesses
Open: Mon–Sat 10–6
Adm: 40F
Wheelchair access
Suitable for all ages
Allow at least an hou

Back in the 18th century Montmartre would have been covered in windmills in which the corn was ground to make the nation's daily bread.

At the foot of the hill leading to Sacre Coeur, just to the right of the vintage carousel, is the Halle St Pierre, a former market building that's been turned into a children's cultural centre where local mothers take their charges to watch puppet shows and take part in art workshops, eat child-friendly food in the child-friendly café, and wander through a gallery of naive art. The subjects on display are certain to be a hit with children: monkeys singing in a band; giant crabs catching people in their pincers; and lions roaring their way through the jungle, all rendered in bright gaudy colours. Special events are held at Christmas, Easter and Hallowe'en.

The Streets of Montmartre

As with the Marais, the district it most resembles, Montmartre is best appreciated on foot, strolling down its narrow lanes, popping in and out of boutiques and antique shops, and stopping here and there for a rest at a pavement café. Look out for the Monmartrain, a sightseeing bus made up to look like a train, that potters through the narrow streets.

There are also enough toy and sweet shops per street to keep the kids happy.

The Rue des Abbesses and the Rue Lepic have the most to offer window shoppers. Also, check out the fabric market on Place St Pierre.

For children head for the following:

Gaspard de la Butte
10 bis Rue Yvonne-le-Tac, 18th
Wide selection of handmade clothes for the under 6s: gorgeous dungarees and sweaters in ochres and reds.

Boudezan
24 Rue Yvonne-Le-Tac, 18th

Pylones
57 Rue Tardieu, 18th
Great range of toys, gadgets and gifts.

Question 14

There's something living on the Rue des Saules that can be found nowhere else in Paris. What is it?

answer on p.249

Can you spot?

The Chapelle du Martyr at 11 Rue Yvonne-le-Tac where, according to legend, St Denis was beheaded by the Romans in the 3rd century. St Denis had the last laugh, however. He picked up his newly severed head and marched off to found an abbey on the other side of town. Montmartre 'the hill of the martyr' was named in his honour.

Tête en l'Air

65 Rue des Abbesses, 18th
A collection of crazy, colourful hats.

Marché aux Puces

Near the Ⓜ Porte de Clignancourt, a few miles north of Montmartre
Open Mon, Sat and Sun 7am–6pm.

Some 3,000 stalls and shops combine to make this Paris', and indeed Europe's, largest flea market. You can turn up almost anything from antiques and memorabilia to vintage clothing and old toys. It's a huge rummage zone and a great place to soak up some real Parisian atmosphere.

Where to eat

1 Le Chinon

49 Rue des Abbesses, 18th
✆ 01 42 62 07 17
Ⓜ Abbesses
Open: daily 9am–midnight
Away from the crowds, this small café is a perfect afternoon pit stop. The omelettes are excellent and the service is friendly.

2 Café in Halle St Pierre

2 Rue Ronsard, 18th
✆ 01 42 58 72 89
Ⓜ Anvers, Abbesses
Open: Mon–Sat 10am–6pm
Just inside the entrance of the Halle St Pierre, Montmartre's dedicated cultural complex for children, this is a specialist family café serving coke and grenadine to hordes of small children throughout the day.

3 Le Maquis

69 Rue Caulaincourt, 18th
✆ 01 42 59 76 07
Ⓜ Lamarck Caulaincourt
Open: Mon–Sat 12 noon–2.30pm and 7pm–midnight
Fixed price menu: 100F, 159F
Montmartre's top choice, frequented by both culinary aficionados and local families. The 159F fixed price dinner is excellent value and consists of an entrée, main course, dessert, wine and coffee. The steaks come particularly recommended, as is the chocolate fondant.

4 Patachou

9 Place du Tertre, 18th
✆ 01 42 51 06 06
Ⓜ Anvers
Open: daily 12 noon–12 midnight
This pleasant, somewhat touristy, café is a
good vantage point from which to survey
the artistic bustle on the Place du Tertre
and, beyond, a view of the city towards the
Eiffel Tower.

5 Rendez-vous des Chauffeurs

11 Rue des Portes Blanches, 18th
✆ 01 42 64 04 17
Ⓜ Marcadet Poissoniers
Open: 12 noon–2.30pm and 7.30pm–11pm
Fixed price menu: 65F
Another good budget choice. The lunch
menu is just 65F for which you will get a
sturdy bistro meal worth twice the price. The
home-made apple pie with chocolate sauce
is a particular speciality.

6 Le Sancerre

35 Rue des Abbesses, 18th
✆ 01 42 58 08 20
Ⓜ Abbesses
Open: daily 7am–2am
It's kinda groovy and older kids will like it.
The food is decent and the atmosphere is
merry with live jazz musicians on weekends.

7 Au Virage Lepic

61 Rue Lepic, 18th
✆ 01 42 52 46 79
Ⓜ Blanche
Open: daily 12 noon–3pm and 6pm–2am
Fixed price menu: 98F
Popular with locals, this is a lovely back-
street bistro with an accordionist on hand to
entertain the diners at weekends.

La Villette

The sight of French school children dragging their parents off the train at **Ⓜ** Porte de la Villette should tell you all you need to know. After Disneyland, the great cultural complex at La Villette is Paris' top children's attraction. It's made up of several parts: the Cité des Sciences et de l'Industrie, a wonderful ultra-modern hands-on science museum; the Argonaute, a former French navy submarine which is now a naval museum and (unofficially) an indoor climbing frame for children; the Géode, an enormous sci-fi globe housing an IMAX 3D screen; a 35-acre park; a museum of music; and the Cité des Enfants, a sort of science themed adventure playground for 3–11 year olds. Kids will love them all.

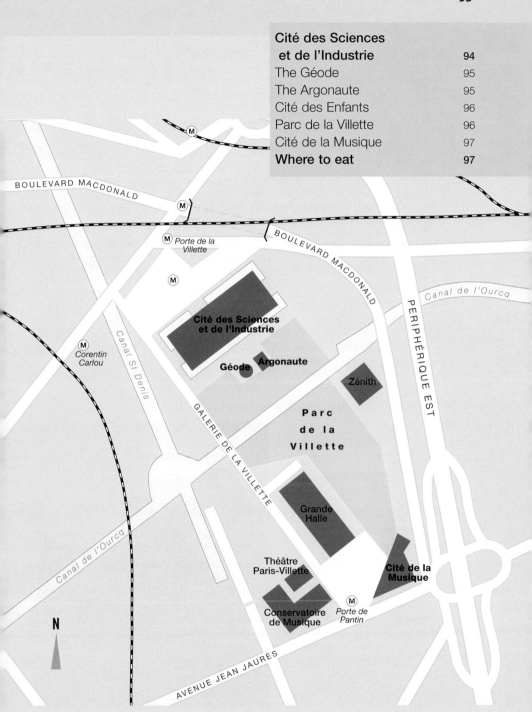

Cité des Sciences et de l'Industrie

The centrepiece and hub of La Villette's grand cultural complex, the Cité des Sciences et de l'Industrie is one of the most fun museums you could ever hope to visit. Unlike the rather dusty Palais de la Découverte in the centre of town, everything here is super modern and hi-tech (and that includes the building itself). Only the latest technologies are given houseroom.

Explora, the museum's permanent exhibition, is like a vast science playground covering two floors and over some 9,000m^2 of floor space. It's divided into no fewer than 18 sections: Space, Ocean, Images, the Garden of the Future, Environment, Automobiles, Aeronautics, Stars and Galaxies, Computer Science, Energy, Life and Health, Expression and Behaviour, Rocks and Volcanoes, Mathematics, Planetarium, Medicine, Sound, Biology and Light Games, each boasting magisterial displays of up-to-the minute hardware.

In Space you can see a full-size reconstruction of a moonwalk, complete with space station, satellite and a spaceman perched precariously on a telescopic arm; in Ocean you can examine a deep sea submarine capable of diving 600m below the ocean waves; while in Aeronautics you can walk beneath the wings and fuselage of a Mirage IV jet fighter.

Everywhere you go there are buttons to press, videos to see (many in English) experiments to perform and demonstrations to watch. This is museum as funfair. You can test your driving skills in a top-of-the-range driving simulator in Automobiles, don a stethoscope and examine a patient in

Parc de la Villette,
30 Avenue Corentin Cariou, 19th
℡ 01 40 05 80 00
www.cité-sciences.fr
Ⓜ Porte de la Villette
Open: Mon–Sat 10–6,
Sun 10–7
Adm: Cité des Sciences only: adult 50F,
under 16s 35F, under 7s free;
combined Cité des Sciences and
Géode ticket: adult 92F, under 16s 79F
Wheelchair access
The Louis Braille room at the
Mediatheque library offers translated
texts for visitors with visual disabilities
Film projections in sign language for
visitors with hearing disabilities
Suitable for all ages
Allow at least an hour

Medicine, pretend to be a weatherman in Images, examine yourself in a 'real' mirror in Expression and Behaviour – it reverses your image so that you can see yourself as others see you (not a pretty sight) – fire up a simple steam engine in Energy or have a whispered conversation with someone 17m away in Sound using the very technical-sounding parabolic sound reflectors (which are basically just a couple of enormous plastic dishes stood on their side). Light Games (Jeux de Lumière) is the museum's ultimate hands-on section, filled with various clever contraptions and devices designed to illustrate optical illusions and tricks of the light.

You can come and go through all these areas more or less as you please, although you will have to queue for the space shows, held on the hour in the Planetarium. The

During its term of operation, the Argonaute travelled over 210,400 miles, or ten times the circumference of the earth. It could dive to a maximum depth of 200m.

auditorium holds 300 and seats are allocated on a first come, first served basis. There are two shows on offer – both, as you would expect, as modern and with-it as they come. The first takes you on a tour of the night sky, exploring stars, planets and constellations, while the second, a much more scientific affair, attempts to unravel some of the mysteries of modern astronomy and astrophysics (it fails).

Surrounding the planetarium is an excellent astronomy gallery, Stars and Galaxies, where you can play with models of the solar system, weigh yourself to see how heavy you would be on Mars or Jupiter, and look through high powered telescopes.

This is the sort of museum in which you could easily spend your whole holiday without your kids uttering so much as a single word of complaint.

The Géode

Open: daily, hourly sessions from 10–9

The dazzling metal sphere is La Villette's one true architectural highlight. Inside, IMAX 3D films are shown on a huge curved screen which allows you to explore the beauty and wonder of the natural world while clutching a can of coke and a carton of popcorn.

The Argonaute

Open: Tues–Fri 10–5.30, Sat and Sun 10–6.30

Just outside the museum, next to the Géode, stands the Argonaute, a former French naval submarine built in the early 1950s. This is a 'hunter-killer' submarine, designed to track and destroy other submarines as well as surface craft although, during all its years of service, it was never called upon to fire a topedo in anger. Audio guides, distributed at the entrance, take you on a tour of its narrow decks to see its periscope, torpedo-launchers and sleeping quarters, where the sub's 50-man crew slept three to a bunk.

Question 15

What was this site originally intended for?

answer on p.249

fants

Open. minute visits on Tues, Thurs and Fri at 9.30, 11.30, 1.30 and 3.30, and on Wed, Sat, Sun and public hols at 10.30, 12.30, 2.30 and 4.30
Adm: 25F per person; children must be accompanied by an adult (max 2 adults per family)

A science and nature museum designed specifically for younger children, the Cité des Enfants is a must. Aimed at children aged 3 to 11, you'll find the *cité* filled with hyperactive youngsters enthusiastically making badges, experimenting with pumps, gears and robots, working on a mini construction site in plastic hard hats, arranging giant foam blocks into vaguely house-like shapes, and generally having a whale of a time – all in the name of science, of course. The nature exhibits include an ant farm, a butterfly farm and a greenhouse. On Wednesday and Saturday afternoons only, over 11s can visit Techno Cité which ups the ante in terms of theory and scientific techniques. You can see how racing bikes are made, how to programme a video game, how to crack a safe or take the controls of a helicopter simulator. Everything is carefully supervised and many of the instructors speak English, although these aren't the sort of exhibits which really require much explanation – just set them loose and watch them go.

The complex also contains the **Louis Lumière Cinema** which shows nature and science documentaries, including the occasional cartoon or 3D film; an **aquarium** which contains more than 200 species of fish, crustaceans, molluscs and seaweed

from Mediterranean coastal waters; and the **Cinaxe**, which is basically a rather good theme ride dressed up as a scientific experience. Using 3D visual technology and seats mounted on hydraulic jacks you can take a virtual trip to the bottom of the ocean.

Parc de la Villette

Plenty of non-scientific fun can be had in La Villette's 35-acre park between the Cité des Sciences et de l'Industrie and the Cité de la Musique. Ultra modern it may be, but it's still very French. A park just wouldn't be a park to Parisians if it wasn't hugely over-designed, with more lines, paths, enclosed

areas and other features than are strictly necessary. It's filled with extraordinary red pavilions or follies which serve a variety of purposes: some are climbing frames, others burger bars and first aid points, and a few are demonstration areas where art workshops for children are held throughout the year. The enormous Chinese dragon slide is a nice touch.

Cité de la Musique

This is the home of the Conservatoire National de Musique, a 1,000-seat auditorium and an excellent museum, the Musée de la Musique, which should appeal to older children.

Musée de la Musique

221 Avenue Jean Jaurès, 19th

📞 01 44 84 46 00

Ⓜ Porte de Pantin

Open: Tues–Thurs 12 noon–6pm,

Fri–Sat 12–7.30, Sun 10–6

Adm: adult 35F, under 25s 25F, under 18s 10F,

under 6s free

Wheelchair access

Suitable for ages 8 and up

Allow at least an hour

The audio guide (available at the entrance) demonstrates the sounds of some of the museum's 4,500-plus instruments (including Beethoven's very own clavichord). The interactive video screens only have information in French and may be of limited interest, although all kids will like the cutaway models of concert halls and opera houses – making them seem like hugely ornate doll's houses; every last detail, down to the scenery and backstage mechanics, is beautifully recreated.

Where to eat

There are several good food outlets within the complex including a self-service cafeteria, a fast-food restaurant, Croq Cité, and an ice cream parlour. There's also a café by Ⓜ La Villette. For something a touch more substantial, however, you'll have to head back into town.

days out

Paris is a city to last a lifetime,
but that doesn't mean you can't
pop out every now and then.
Here are four suggestions for
day trips outside the capital, all
less than an hour's drive away.

Chantilly

Château de Chantilly

☎ 03 44 62 62 62
Open: summer Mon and Wed–Sun 10–6;
winter Mon and Wed–Sun 10.30–12.45 and 2–5
Adm: adult 39F, under 18s 34F, under 11s 12F,
under 3s free
Facilities: gift shops, picnic areas
Wheelchair access and adapted toilets
Suitable for all ages

Standing proudly in the middle of a lake and surrounded by landscaped gardens, the Château de Chantilly is the fairy-tale castle of every child's dreams. However, despite its aged and romantic appearance, the château is a (mostly) late 19th-century con-struction. In fact, since the Middle Ages no fewer than five separate buildings have stood on this spot – and it was rebuilt twice in the 19th century alone. The château now contains the Musée Condé – a museum of Renaissance art with works by Raphael, Botticelli and Poussin – and a repository of rare manuscripts.

During the summer hot air balloon rides are given in the castle grounds offering spectacular views of the château and the surrounding area. The balloon, known as the Aerophile, is one of the largest in the world and can ascend to a height of 150m – it is connected to the ground via a rein-forced steel cable. Sightseeing boat rides are also available on the Grand Canal to the north of the château.

Musée Vivant du Cheval

☎ 03 44 57 13 13
Open: summer Mon and Wed–Sun 10.30–6.30;
winter Mon and Wed–Sun 2–5,

Sat and Sun 10.30–6.30
Adm: adult 50F, under 16s 35F, under 4s free
Dressage demonstrations daily at 3.30pm
Wheelchair access
Suitable for all ages

From a child's perspective, Chantilly is principally worth visiting for its wonderful stables, which have been turned into the Musée Vivant du Cheval (Living Museum of the Horse). Here you can meet and pet over 30 beautifully groomed horses, find out about the history of racing in France (Chantilly is the capital of the French horse racing industry) and watch dressage demonstrations every afternoon.

Around and about

To the south of the château lies the Forêt de Chantilly, a hugely popular picnic site with numerous pathways and nature trails run-ning throught it.

Further south, on the other side of the A1 motorway, is the Forêt d'Ermenonville where, deep within its confines (you'll need a car), you'll find the Mer de Sable a 50-acre sea of sand dunes which now boasts a chil-dren's entertainment complex themed very loosely on the Wild West, with various rides, games and shows.

Distance from Paris: 48km
By car: Chantilly exit of A1 motorway,
about 40km north of Paris
By rail: RER from Gare du Nord to Chantilly-Gouvieux
40 departures a day
the station is a short walk
or taxi ride from the castle

Versailles

The Château of Versailles is a proper, grand, over-the-top palace, worthy of any Disney hero. Kids will love its sheer excess, particularly the glittering Hall of Mirrors, the enormous gilt-covered Apollo Salon (or Throne Room) and the King's bedroom where Louis XIV (the Sun King) would arise each day watched by his entire court. The palace is far too vast to be explored in a single day, so pick up an orientation map at the information booth and let it guide you to all the best bits. Once you've had your fill of sumptuous fixtures and fittings, head for the beautiful gardens to stretch your legs and have a picnic overlooking the ornate fountains and flowerbeds. As with the palace, the gardens are much too big to be explored on foot, and you would be better off taking a ride aboard the glass-sided sightseeing train (recorded commentary in several languages including English). In summer you can hire rowing boats on the Grand Canal.

A firework spectacular, the Grandes Fêtes de Nuit, takes place twice a year (July and Sept), and if you are lucky you will catch the Grandes Eaux Musicales, when the fountains are set in motion to a musical accompaniment (May–Oct every Sun).

The château is extremely popular – it attracts over three million visitors a year (roughly 8,000 a day) – so aim to get there early to avoid the crowds.

A tribute to envy

Versailles was built in a fit of spite. In 1661 Louis XIV attended a party given by his finance minister, Nicholas Fouquet, to celebrate the completion of Fouquet's new home, the spectacular palace of Vaux-le-Vicomte. So majestic was this new palace, so ornate were its gardens and so splendid was the party (dishes were prepared by France's pre-eminent chef, Vatel, and served on gold and silver plates, entertainment was laid on by Molière, France's favourite playwright), that the young king became utterly consumed with jealousy, and decided there and then to build himself something even more opulent.

A small hunting lodge 20km southwest of Paris was chosen as the site for Louis' grand project, and 30,000 workers spent the next 20 years building the largest and

---

Distance from Paris: 20km

By car: Versailles-Château exit of A13 motorway, about 14 miles west of Paris towards Rouen; the drive should take about 30mins

Parking: Available (for a fee) in the Place d'Armes in front of the château

By rail: RER line C5 to Versailles-Rive Gauche; the station is 700m from the château; there are 60 trains a day, 35 on Sunday; all display a four letter code beginning with the letter 'V'.

Château de Versailles
✆ 01 30 84 74 00
www.chateauversailles.fr
Open: château: summer Tues–Sun 9–6;
winter Tues–Sun 9–5;
garden: daily dawn till dusk
Adm: château: adult 45F, under 25s 35F, under 18s free, after 3.30pm free to all; gardens: free
Tourist information office: l7 Rue des Réservoirs, at the north end of the château
Facilities: audio guides and guided tours in English, restaurant and snack bars in the gardens, shop
Some wheelchair access and adapted toilets
Suitable for all ages

most extravagant palace France had ever seen, capable of sleeping over 10,000 people (including 2,000 kitchen workers) and surrounded by the most lavish gardens in Europe. But this was more than just another big palace: it was a statement of royal power. Louis had been stung by Fouquet's presumption, and he built Versailles in order to reaffirm his standing, and to remind all who visited, including upstart finance ministers, just who was top dog.

Parc Asterix

Distance from Paris: 36km
By car: exit Parc Asterix from A1 motorway, 30km north of Paris
By rail: RER line 'B' Charles de Gaulle 1; from here Courriers Ile-de-France buses journey to the park every half-hour 9.30–1.30; buses return every half-hour from 4.30pm until half an hour after the park closes (adult return 35F, child return 25F)
✆ 08 36 68 30 10
Open: April–Oct Mon–Fri 10–7, Sat and Sun 9.30–8
Adm: adult 170F, under 12s 120F
Facilities: gift shops, fast food restaurants, picnic areas, pushchair rental
Wheelchair access and adapted toilets
Suitable for all ages

It may not have as many rides and attractions as Disneyland, but Parc Asterix is, at least, genuinely French. Asterix, the Roman-bashing Gaul, has long been France's most popular cartoon character and his adventures are one of its most successful literary exports – translated into over 40 languages. The theme park has, unsurprisingly, proved a big hit with both locals and tourists. The park is divided into themed areas, including a Gaulish village, a Roman city and Ancient Greece, each inhabited by rubber-suited cartoon characters. There are also lots of hair-raising rides, including the 'Tonnerre de Zeus', one of the most terrifying rollercoasters in Europe, capable of travelling at over 80kph. Elsewhere you can see live attractions such as a demonstration of swordplay and derring-do by 'musketeers'.

France Miniature

Distance from Paris: 25km
By car: exit France Miniature from A12 motorway; from Paris take the A13 to reach the A12
By rail: SNCF train from La Défense or Gare Montparnasse to La Verrière; then Sqybus no.411
✆ 08 36 68 53 35
www.franceminiature.com
Open: Mar–Nov daily 10–7
Adm: adult 75F, under 16s 50F, under 4s free
Facilities: fast food restaurants, audio guides, shop
Wheelchair access and adapted toilets
Suitable for all ages

This gallic Lilliput contains 150 miniature sites featuring 1/30th versions of some of France's most notable monuments, including the Eiffel Tower, Sacre Coeur and Notre Dame. The park took 53 architects and model-makers over two years to complete. Each model has been placed in its exact geographical context – every street, building, and landmark has been faithfully and painstakingly recreated, and model boats, trains and cars have been added (along with model passengers and pedestrians) to complete the overall effect. Firework displays (featuring proper life-size explosions) are held in summer.

kids in

Paris has more museums than it knows what to do with. Deciding which will most appeal to your children is usually a pretty straightforward process: the more interactive the exhibits, the more likely your kids are to enjoy it. Top of the interactive list are the Grande Galerie d'Evolution, the Palais de la Découverte and, above all, the Cité des Sciences et de l'Industrie, all of which boast a multitude of levers to pull, buttons to press and games to play. Of course, interactivity doesn't always come coated with a veneer of cultural and educational respectability. Paris is also home to several video game arcades, notably La Tête sous La Nuage on the Boulevard des Italiens which will no doubt prove to be just as big a hit with your children.

Museums in Central Paris

Cité des Enfants
Parc de la Villette, 30 Avenue Corentin Cariou, 19th
℡ 01 40 05 12 12
Ⓜ Porte de la Villette
Open: 90 minute visits Tues, Thurs and Fri 9.30, 11.30, 1.30 and 3.30, Wed, Sat, Sun and public hols 10.30, 12.30, 2.30 and 4.30
Adm: 25F per person; children must be accompanied by an adult (at most two adults per family)
For more information *see* p.96.

Cité des Sciences et de l'Industrie
Parc de la Villette, 30 Avenue Corentin Cariou, 19th
℡ 01 40 05 80 00
www.cité-sciences.fr
Ⓜ Porte de la Villette
Open: Mon–Sat 10–6, Sun 10–7
Adm: Cité des Sciences only: adult 50F, under 16s 35F, under 7s free; combined Cité des Sciences and Géode: adult 92F, under 16s 79F
For more information *see* pp.94-5.

La Conciergerie
1 Quai de l'Horloge, 1st
℡ 01 53 73 78 50
Ⓜ Cité, Châtelet
Open: Tues–Sat 10–6, Sun 9–6
Adm: adult 35F, under 25s 23F, under 12s free
For more information *see* p.72.

Espace Dali Montmartre
11 Rue Poulbot, 18th
℡ 01 42 64 40 10
Ⓜ Abbesses
Open: daily 10–6
Adm: adult 35F, under 25s 25F, under 8s free
For more information *see* p.89.

Hôtel des Invalides including the Musée de l'Armée, the Musée des Plans Relief and Napoleon's tomb
Esplanade des Invalides, 7th
℡ 01 44 42 37 72
Ⓜ Invalides
Open: summer 10–5.45, Napoleon's tomb 10–7; winter 10–4.45
Adm: adult 37F, under 18s 27F, under 12s free – covers entry to all of the above
For more information *see* pp.51–2.

Musée d'Art Moderne de la Ville de Paris
11 Avenue Président Wilson, 16th
℡ 01 53 67 40 00
Ⓜ Iéna, Alma Marceau
Open: Tues–Sun 10–5.40, Sat and Sun until 7
Adm: adult 27F, under 25s 14.50F, under 18s free
For more information *see* pp.55–6.

Musée d'Art Naif
Halle St Pierre
2 Rue Ronsard, 18th
℡ 01 42 58 72 89
Ⓜ Anvers, Abbesses
Open: Mon–Sat 10–6
Adm: adult 40F, under 26s 30F, under 4s free
For more information *see* p.89.

Musée de l'Assistance Publique
Hôtel de Miramion
47 Quai de la Tournelle, 5th
℡ 01 46 33 01 43
Ⓜ Maubert Mutualité
Open: Wed–Sat 10–5; closed Mon, Tues and Aug
Adm: adult 20F, under 12s free
For more information *see* p.81.

Musée Carnavalet
23 Rue de Sévigné, 3rd
℡ 01 42 72 21 13
Ⓜ St Paul, Chemin Vert
Open: Tues–Sun 10–5.40. The 19th- and 20th-century rooms are usually only open from 10–11.30, while the Louis XV period rooms don't open until 1.30
Adm: adult 27F, under 18s free
For more information *see* p.62.

Musée de la Chasse et de la Nature

Hôtel Guénégaud, 60 Rue des Archives, 3rd

✆ 01 53 01 82 40

Ⓜ Rambuteau

Open: Tues–Sun 11–6

Adm: adult 30F, under 25s 15F, under 5s free

For more information *see* p.63.

Musée Cognacq-Jay

Hôtel Denon, 8 Rue Elzévir, 3rd

✆ 01 40 27 07 21

Ⓜ St Paul

Open: Tues–Sun 10–5.40

Adm: adult 17.50F, under 25s 9F, under 18s free

For more information *see* p.63.

Musée de la Curiosité et de la Magie

11 Rue St Paul, 4th

✆ 01 42 72 13 26

Ⓜ St Paul, Sully Morland

Open: Wed, Sat and Sun 2–7

Adm: adult 45F, under 12s 30F, under 3s free

For more information *see* p.62.

Musée de l'Homme

Palais du Chaillot

Place du Trocadéro, 16th

Ⓜ Trocadero

✆ 01 44 05 72 72

Open: summer Mon and Wed–Sun 9.45–5.15

Adm: adult 30F, under 16s 20F, under 4s free

For more information *see* p.53.

Musée de la Marine

Palais du Chaillot

Place du Trocadéro, 16th

Ⓜ Trocadéro

✆ 01 53 65 69 69

Open: Mon and Wed–Sun 10–5.50

Adm: adult 38F, under 25s 25F, under 5s free

For more information *see* p.53.

Musée de la Mode et du Costume

Palais Galliéra, 16th

✆ 01 47 20 85 23

Ⓜ Iéna, Alma Marceau

Open: Tues–Sun 10–6

Adm: adult 45F, under 25s 32F, under 8s free

For more information *see* p.56.

Musée de la Monnaie de Paris

11 Quai de Conti

✆ 01 40 46 55 35

Ⓜ Pont Neuf

Open: Tues–Fri 11–5.30,

Sat and Sun 12–5.30

Adm adult 20F, under 16s free

For more information *see* p.74.

Musée de la Musique

221 Avenue Jean Jaurès, 19th

✆ 01 44 84 46 00

Ⓜ Porte de Pantin

Open: Tues–Thurs 12–6, Fri–Sat 12–7.30,

Sun 10–6

Adm: adult 35F, under 25s 25F, under 18s 10F,

under 6s free

For more information *see* p.97.

Musée Nationale des Arts Asiatiques – Guimet

6 Place d'Iéna, 16th

✆ 01 45 05 00 98

Ⓜ Iéna

Open: Mon and Wed–Sun 9.45–5.45

Adm: adult 16F (Sun 12F), under 18s free

For more information *see* p.55.

Musée National d'Histoire Naturelle

(Grand Galerie de l'Evolution, Galerie de Minéralogie and Galerie d'Anatomie Comparée et Paléontologie)

57 Rue Cuvier, 5th

✆ 01 40 79 30 00

Ⓜ Jussieu, Gare d'Austerlitz

Open: Mon, Wed–Sun 10–6, Thurs until 10

Adm: Grande Galerie adult 40F, under 16s 30F, under 5s free; other *galeries* adult 30F, under 16s 20F, under 5s free

For more information *see* pp.78–80.

Musée National du Louvre

Palais du Louvre, Quai du Louvre, 1st

© 01 40 20 53 17

www.louvre.fr

Ⓜ Palais Royal-Musée du Louvre

Open: daily 9–6 (Wed until 9.45pm);

closed Tues

Adm: adult 45F, child free; reduced adult rate 26F

after 3 and all day Sun

For more information *see* pp.36–8.

Musée National du Moyen Age

6 Place Paul Painlevé, 5th

© 01 53 73 78 00

Ⓜ Cluny-La Sorbonne

RER: St Michel

Open: Mon and Wed–Sun 9.15–5.45

Adm adult 28F, under 25s 18, under 18s free

For more information *see* p.81.

Musée d'Orsay

1 Rue de Bellechasse, 7th

© 01 40 49 48 48

Infoline: © 01 45 49 11 11

www.musee-orsay.fr

Ⓜ Solférino

RER: Musée d'Orsay

Open: Tues–Sat 10–6, Sun 9–6

Adm: adult 40F, under 25s 30F, under 18s free

For more information *see* pp.71–2.

Musée Picasso

Hôtel Salé, 5 Rue De Thorigny, 3rd

© 01 42 71 25 21

Ⓜ Chemin Vert, St Sébastien Froissart

Open: summer 9.30–6; winter 9.30–5.30;

closed Tues

Adm: adult 30F, under 25s 20F, under 18s free

For more information *see* pp.62–3.

Musée de la Préfecture

1bis Rue des Carmes, 5th

© 01 44 41 52 54

Ⓜ Maubert Mutualité

Open: Mon–Fri 9–5, Sat 10–5

Adm free

For more information *see* p.81.

Musée Rodin

Hôtel Biron, 77 Rue de Varenne, 7th

© 01 44 18 61 10

Ⓜ Varenne

Open: summer Tues–Sun 9.30–5.45,

winter Tues–Sun 9.30–4.45

Adm: adult 28F, under 25s 18F, under 18s free.

For more information *see* p.54.

Palais de la Découverte

Avenue Franklin D. Roosevelt, 1st

© 01 40 74 80 00

Ⓜ Franklin D. Roosevelt

Open: Tues–Sat 9.30–6, Sun 10–7

Adm: adult 30F, child 20F, family 80F; 15F supple-

ment for the Planetarium

For more information *see* p.42.

Pompidou Centre

Rue Beaubourg, 4th

© 01 44 78 12 33

www. cnac.gp.fr

Ⓜ Hôtel de Ville, Rambuteau

RER: Châtelet-Les Halles

Open: centre: Mon, Wed–Sun 11am–10pm;

musée: Mon, Wed–Sun 11am–9pm

Adm: centre: free; musée adults 30F,

under 18s free

For more information *see* p.60.

Museums outside the centre of town

Musée des Arts Forains

53 Avenue des Terroirs de France, 12th

© 01 43 40 16 22

Ⓜ Bercy

Open: groups only; call in advance

Adm: adult 75F, under 15s 25F

The museum of fairground art holds a

colourful collection of 19th-century

fairground exhibits, including some gaudily painted roundabouts, a tin can alley, a shooting range and a marionette theatre. Kids might get a bit frustrated since these are for display only and you're not allowed to ride them.

Musée Fragonard

9 Rue Scribe, 9th
✆ 01 47 42 93 40
Ⓜ Opéra
Open: Mon–Sat 9–5.30
Adm: free

The history of perfume-making from ancient Egyptian times to the present day. You are invited to sample many of the exclusive scents of the Fragonard Fragrance House.

Musée Grevin

10 Boulevard Montmartre, 9th
✆ 01 47 70 85 05
Ⓜ Grands Boulevards
Open: termtime daily 1–6.30;
school holidays daily 10–7
Adm: adult 55F, under 14s 36F, under 6s free

Paris' waxworks museum has a certain elegance and olde worlde charm. Wax versions of all the big international celebrities are here including Madonna, Michael Jackson and, for the domestic audience, Gérard Dépardieu. The most interesting waxworks have been arranged in scenes from French history: Josephine counselling Napoleon, the trial of Joan of Arc, Marie Antoinette in prison, Marat slumped dying in his bathtub (in the actual bathtub in which he died). Performances of magic and conjuring are given in the first floor theatre.

Musée National des Arts d'Afrique et d'Oceanie

293 Avenue Daumesnil, 12th
✆ 01 44 74 84 80
Infoline: ✆ 01 43 46 51 61
Ⓜ Porte Dorée
Open: Mon and Wed–Sun 10–6
Adm: adult 30F, under 25s 20F, under 18s free

Based on a collection of artefacts from France's colonial heyday, the museum contains a huge number of ethnology exhibits from Africa and the Pacific Islands, including Totem poles, sculptures, tribal masks and jewellery. The chief attraction, however, is the huge aquarium (one of Europe's largest) in the basement with its thousands of colourful, exotic fish and a pit of snapping crocodiles.

Musée Nissim de Camondo

63 Rue de Monceau, 8th
✆ 01 53 89 06 40
Ⓜ Monceau, Villiers
Open: Wed–Sun 10–5
Adm: adult 30F, under 25s 20F, under 18s free

This is the house of Count Moïse de Camondo, a wealthy banker, who, in the early 20th century, decided to build himself a palatial residence which he would furnish and decorate only with 18th-century artefacts. The opulent house interiors, full of elegant furniture and tapestries, will appeal to older children. The museum was named in honour of the count's son who died in an aerial dog fight in the First World War.

Underground fun

There are two subterranean attractions worth checking out, so long as you're not too squeamish: the Catacombs, near Montparnasse cemetery, a vast vault full of thousands of neatly arranged skeletons, and the Egouts, or Paris sewers, tours of which have become an increasingly popular (not to mention smelly) attraction.

The Paris Sewers
Entrance opposite 93 Quai d'Orsay
by Pont de l'Alma, 7th
✆ 01 53 68 27 81
Ⓜ Alma Marceau
RER: Pont de l'Alma
Open: Mon–Wed, Sat and Sun 11–4
Adm: adult 25F, under 25 20F, under 12 15F,
under 5s free
For more information *see* p.55.

The Catacombs
1 Place Denfert Rochereau, 14th
✆ 01 43 22 47 63
Ⓜ Denfert Rochereau
Open: Open Tues–Fri 2–4,
Sat and Sun 9–11 and 2–4
Adm: adult 27F, under 18s 19F, under 7s free
For more information *see* p.84.

Amusement arcades

La Tête sous la Nuage
5 Boulevard des Italiens, 2nd
✆ 01 53 57 31 31
Ⓜ Richelieu Drouot
Open: daily 10am–12 midnight

For a collection of exhibits that's guaranteed to appeal, join the truants at the Boulevard des Italiens' video game mecca, La Tête sous la Nuage, full of shoot 'em ups, fighting games, racing games and virtual reality hook-up points, as well a few more traditional games like table hockey and pool. You pay for the games using pre-bought tokens – each game costs 50–100F. There's also a branch of McDonald's.

Carte Musées et Monuments

1 day - 80F, 3 days - 160F, 5 days - 240F

Many of Paris' museums and monuments are free for children, but for adults it is worth buying a Carte Musées et Monuments, available from the tourist office and participating museums. You only need to visit two sights a day to break even and, better still, it allows you to skip the queues.

It is valid at the following:

Arc de Triomphe
Cité des Sciences et de l'Industrie
(not including La Géode or la Cité des Enfants)
La Conciergerie
Les Egouts
Musée Cognacq-Jay
Musée de l'Armée – tomb of Napoleon
Musée d'Art Moderne de la Ville de Paris
Musée de l'Assistance Publique
Musée Carnavalet
Musée du Louvre
Musée de la Marine
Musée de la Monnaie
Musée de la Musique
Musée National d'Art Moderne –
Centre Georges Pompidou
Musée National des Arts d'Afrique et d'Oceanie
Musée National des Arts Asiatiques
Musée National des Arts et Traditions Populaires
Musée National du Moyen Age –
Thermes de Cluny
Musée Nissim de Camondo
Musée d'Orsay
Musée Picasso
Musée Plan Reliefs
Musée Rodin
Notro Dame bell towers
Panthéon
Sainte Chapelle
Musée Condé – Château de Chantilly
Château de Vincennes
Musée National de Châteaux de Versailles

kids out

Since most Parisian children live in garden-less apartments, the city is obliged to provide them with lots of open spaces and areas to run about in. Each district has at least one playground and most of the larger public parks and gardens boast a variety of dedicated children's attractions – these can range from playgrounds, boating ponds and puppet theatres to adventure playgrounds, children's zoos and even mini-funfairs. In the more formal parks the grass is often out of bounds – look for the signs saying *pelouse interdite* (lawn forbidden). For a large expanse of grass to run around on, you'll have to head out to the two wooded areas on the eastern and western outskirts of the city, the Bois de Vincennes and the Bois de Boulogne. Most parks are open daily from early morning till dusk.

In late December 1999, Paris was hit by the worst storms in living memory. Winds of over 150 miles per hour uprooted an estimated half a million trees. Many of its parks and gardens, including the Bois de Boulogne, the Bois de Vincennes, Parc Monceau and the Jardin des Plantes, will be closed during the early months of 2000 while the debris is cleared. The tourist office believes things should be back to normal by early summer.

Bois de Boulogne

16th

Ⓜ Porte Dauphine, Les Sablons

The Bois de Boulogne began life in the Middle Ages as a royal hunting ground and was only formally landscaped in the mid 19th century on the orders of Napoleon III who wanted to create a Parisian version of London's Hyde Park. It has many similar features including bridal paths and a boating lake although, being a much larger space, it also has room for numerous cycle paths, a couple of racecourses, a flower garden, an open air theatre, an artificial waterfall and numerous acres of woodland.

Jardin d'Acclimatation

✆ 01 40 67 90 82

Ⓜ Porte Dorée, Château de Vincennes

Open: summer daily 10–7; winter daily 10–6

Adm: adult 40F, under 16s 30F, under 4s free

Le Petit Train runs Wed, Sat and Sun and everyday during the school holidays, 11–6 every 15 minutes; single fare 6F

The main reason for visiting the Bois de Boulogne is this 25-acre amusement park for children hidden within its northern confines. To reach it, simply hop aboard the jaunty little mock-steam train at Porte Maillot (known as *le Petit Train*) which will take you straight there. Laid out in a circular pattern, the park contains a small zoo (where kids can pet the long-suffering goats and sheep), a hall of mirrors, a marionette theatre, a mini golf course, dodgems, a couple of junior-size (still rather hairy) rollercoasters, a riverboat ride, a bowling alley, an archery range, a mini motorbike course. There's also lots of fast food, a babysitting service (in summer), and the following two museums:

Musée en Herbe

✆ 01 40 67 97 66

Open: Mon–Fri and Sun 10–6, Sat 2–6

Adm: adult 41F, under 18s 14F, under 4s free

This children's museum tries to bring art history alive through interactive exhibits and painting workshops.

Musée National des Arts et Traditions Populaires

✆ 01 44 17 60 00

Open: Mon and Wed–Sun 9.30–5.30

Adm: adult 22F, under 25s 15F, under 5s free

This museum is dedicated to French folk art and the culture of agricultural life, and contains an eclectic selection of exhibits ranging from puppet theatres and musical instruments to old toys and circus equipment.

Bois de Vincennes

12th

Paris' largest park has cycle paths, a race track, a baseball pitch, acres of woodland, two lakes where you can hire rowing boats and model sailing boats, a flower garden where entertainments are laid on for children throughout the summer (*see* below) and a Buddhist Temple containing the largest statue of Buddha in Europe. There's also an annual funfair, the Foire du Trône.

Zoo de Paris

53 Avenue de St Maurice, 12th

✆ 01 44 75 20 10

Ⓜ Porte Dorée, Château de Vincennes

Open: summer 9–6; winter 9–5.30

Adm: adult 40F, under 16s 30F, under 4s free

This is the park's biggest draw, one of the largest zoos in Europe, where you'll find hippos, rhinos, pandas, lions, tigers, kangaroo, bison and elephants. Its centrepiece is a 65m artificial mountain laid out on several lift-accessible platforms. Originally built in the 1930s, it has recently been renovated and is now home to herds of free-ranging mountain goats. All the animal enclosures have been carefully landscaped in order to conceal their fences and moats thereby giving the complex as natural and wild a look as possible. Once a day, kids are invited to help feed the sea lions. There's a miniature steam train which trundles around the zoo's perimeter.

Parc Floral de Paris
Entrance on Route de la Pyramide
Open: daily 9.30–6.30
Adm: summer: adult 10F, under 18s 5F, under 6s free; winter: adult 5F, under 18s 2.50F, under 6s free
This park has an excellent adventure playground with slides, swings and climbing frames, a walk-through butterfly house and a miniature steam train which wends its way through the trees. The park is also home to a dedicated children's drama company, the Théâtre Astral, and the Maison Paris-Nature where (French-speaking) children can learn about nature through exhibitions and workshops.

Château de Vincennes
Avenue de Paris, 12th
✆ 01 48 08 31 20
Ⓜ Château de Vincennes
Open: summer 10–6; winter 10–5
Adm: adult 32F, under 16s 25F
This palace-cum-fortress was built in the 1300s in the middle of what was then a royal hunting ground. In the early 17th century it was often used as an overflow prison, whenever Louis XIV got into one of his 'moods' – no other French king locked up so many people – but fell out of favour later in the century following the royal family's move to Versailles. In the early 1800s it was turned

into a fortress and was the site of the Napoleonic army's last stand. From the outside, the palace looks rather dour and militaristic although the inside has a fairy-tale-like opulence with beautiful gilt-covered salons.

Parks

Champ de Mars
7th
Ⓜ Bir-Hakeim, Ecole Militaire
RER: Champ de Mars
For more information see p.54.

Jardin des Enfants aux Halles
105 Rue Rambuteau, 1st
✆ 01 45 08 07 18
Ⓜ Les Halles
RER Châtelet-Les Halles
Adm: 2.50F for a one hour session
For more information see p.66.

Jardin du Luxembourg
Entrances on Place Auguste-Comte, Place Edmond Rostand and Rue de Vaugirard, 6th
Ⓜ Odéon
RER: Luxembourg
For more information see p.80.
This is the place to gather on sunny afternoons to show off your primped and pampered offspring in their latest Bonpoint finery. Despite its neat lawns, sculpted terraces and rather genteel atmosphere, this is still one of Paris' best parks for children: you'll find them playing in the sandpit, clambering over the climbing frames in the adventure playground, sailing toy boats on its hexagonal pond or dashing madly around its gravel pathways. That, of course, is when they're not enjoying a pony ride or a puppet show. Older visitors are catered for with several *boules* pitches and tennis courts.

Jardin des Plantes

Entrances on Place Valhubert, Rue Buffon and Rue Cuvier, 5th

☏ 01 40 79 30 00

Ⓜ Gare d'Austerlitz, Jussieu

For more information *see* p.78.

Jardin des Tuileries

Rue de Rivoli, 1st; entrances on Rue de Rivoli, Place de la Concorde and Avenue du Général Lemonnier

Ⓜ Tuileries, Concorde

Open: summer 7–9; winter 7.30am–7.30pm

For more information *see* p.39.

Parc André Citroën

Entrances on Rue Balard, Rue St Charles and Quai Citroën, 15th

Ⓜ Javel, Balard

Balloon rides daily 9am–dusk every 15mins; until 31 December 2000

Tickets: adults 66F, under 18s 33F

This park occupies the site of an old Citroën car factory. It bills itself as a 'Park for the 21st Century' and is the most modern looking of the city's parks, with six colour-coded high-concept flower gardens, angular glass houses filled with tropical plants and a computer-controlled water garden. Pack your swimsuit for the water jet garden: a concrete plateau lined with dozens of single jet fountains which erupt according to a random pattern which children rush around trying to predict (happily getting soaked in the process). Its most recent feature is the Fortis Balloon, the largest hot air balloon in the world, which offers passengers the chance to view Paris from a vantage point some 150m in the air.

Parc des Buttes Chaumont

Entrances on Rue Botzaris, Rue Manin & Rue de Crimée, 19th

Ⓜ Buttes Chaumont

This used to be a quarry. Today, head to the lake where the central rocky island (reachable by two bridges) offers great views of the city. There's also a an artificial cave complete with artificial stalactites and stalagmites (remember, tights come down) out of which an artificial waterfall cascades, a couple of playgrounds and donkey rides in summer.

Parc Monceau

Boulevard de Courcelles, 17th

Ⓜ Monceau

Only the Jardin du Luxembourg attracts greater numbers of well-dressed children on Sunday afternoons. Again the emphasis here is on elegance and formality, with neat lawns, neat children, neat gravel pathways and a tidy little pond. The park's most interesting features are its 18th- and 19th-century follies which include a replica Egyptian pyramid and a Venetian-style bridge.

Parc Montsouris

Boulevard Jourdan, 14th

RER: Cité Universitaire

In the south of the city, the Parc Montsouris (literally 'Mount Mouse') has a special play area for children, a duck pond (which is also home to several turtles), a waterfall, a replica Moorish Palace and dozens of colourful flower beds.

Parc St Cloud

St Cloud

Ⓜ Pont de Sèvres

Finally, a Parisian park where you are actually allowed to walk on the grass (or lie or run, or jump). Unfortunately, it's slightly outside Paris proper (11km west) but well worth a visit if you have time. Of course, being French, it also pretty formal with lots of landscaping, fountains and elegant shaded avenues. The castle which once overlooked the park was Napoleon's favourite Parisian residence. It was destroyed by fire in 1870.

Parc de la Villette
Avenue Corentin Cariou, 19th
Ⓜ Porte de la Villette
For more information *see* pp.96–7.

Place des Vosges
4th
Ⓜ Bastille, Chemin Vert
For more information *see* p.61.

Les Serres d'Auteil
3 Avenue de la Porte d'Auteuil, 16th
✆ 01 40 71 75 23
Ⓜ Porte d'Auteuil
Open: daily 10–5
Adm: adult 5F, under 18s 2.50F, under 6s free
These sweatily hot tropical glass houses hold a wonderful collection of palms, rubber plants and exotic fish-filled pools – perfect for a cool autumn day.

and for something slightly different...

Cimetière du Père-Lachaise
Boulevard de Ménilmontant, 20th
✆ 01 43 70 70 33
Ⓜ Père Lachaise
Open: daily 9–5.30
Anyone coming to Père Lachaise looking for a little ghoulishness and gore will be sorely disappointed, and would be better off visiting the Catacombs. Paris' most famous cemetery is actually a rather romantic place: a beautiful, grassy, tree-lined space. Many of the country's most illustrious citizens are buried here including Abelard and Héloïse, Balzac, Delacroix, Proust, Molière and Edith Piaf, although it's the graves of international celebrities Oscar Wilde and Jim Morrison which attract the most attention. Morrison's grave is covered in grafitti and has to have its own security guard. A map guiding you to all the most famous graves can be picked up at the front gates for 10F.

River trips

Taking a trip on one of the famous *bateaux mouches* sightseeing boats is one of the best and most enjoyable ways of getting to know the city. The boats depart from the Pont de l'Alma, just east of the Eiffel Tower, and head upriver as far as the Ile St Louis. The commentary is recorded and relayed through loudspeakers in four languages – French, English, Spanish and German (in that order). Lunch is available on Saturdays for 300F and on public holidays for 350F; there's a fancy dress cruise in summer which costs 500F.

Bateaux Mouches
Pont de l'Alma, 7th
✆ 01 42 25 96 10
Infoline: ✆ 01 40 76 99 99
www.bateaux-mouches.com
Ⓜ Alma Marceau
RER: Pont de l'Alma
Sailing times: summer daily 10am–11pm every 30mins; winter daily 11am–9pm every hour.
Fares: adults 40F, under 15s 20F, under 5s.
Lunch 300–350F; dinner 500–700F.
Wheelchair access
Suitable for all ages
The tour lasts one hour

There are several other companies offering sightseeing trips up the Seine:

Bateaux Parisiens
from the Port de La Bourdonnais, 7th
Ⓜ Bir-Hakeim/Iéna
Fares: adult 50F, under 12s 25F

Vedettes du Pont Neuf

from Sq du Vert Galant, Ile de la Cité, 1st

Ⓜ Pont Neuf

Fares: adult 50F, under 12s 25F, under 4s free

Vedettes de Paris

from the Port de Suffren, 7th

Ⓜ Bir-Hakeim

Fares: adult 50F, under 12s 25F, under 4s free

Paris Canal

Ⓒ 01 42 40 96 97

from the Musée d'Orsay

Fares: adult 100F, under 25s 75F, under 12s 60F, under 4s free

Live commentary in French (and English if there is sufficient demand)

Trips up the Canal St-Martin to La Villette, passing through old locks and tunnels.

Batobus

Ⓒ 01 44 11 33 99

Fares: adult 60F, child (under 12) 30F; 25% reduction with a Paris Visite pass.

The boat bus also offers a passenger/sightseeing service up and down the Seine (without commentary). There are six stops: Eiffel Tower, Musée d'Orsay, St Germain des Prés, the Louvre, Notre Dame and Hôtel de Ville.

Sightseeing buses

Balobus

Between the Grande Arche de la Défense and Gare de Lyon

Each Sun and public holiday from 1st Sun in April to last Sun of Sept 1.30–8 every 15mins

The full trip takes an hour and uses up three single tickets.

The RATP runs a sightseeing service along a 12km route between the Grande Arche de la Défense and Gare de Lyon, taking in the Place de la Bastille, the Marais, Notre Dame, the Louvre and the Place de la Concorde.

Cityrama

Ⓒ 01 44 55 61 00

Tours: summer daily 9.30–4.30;

winter daily 9.30–1.30

Departs: Place des Pyramides, 1st

Recorded commentary in English

Fares: adult 150F, child (under 12) free

Parisbus

Ⓒ 01 42 88 69 50

Tours daily every 30mins 10–5 on red London double decker buses

Departs: Eiffel Tower

Recorded commentary in English

Tickets are valid for two days, during which time you can get on and off as often as you like.

Fares: adult 125F, child (under 12) 60F

Paris Vision

Ⓒ 01 42 60 30 01

Tours daily 9.30–3.30

Multilingual commentary

Fares: adult 150F, child (under 12) 75F, under 4s free

Walking tours

Older children may appreciate a stroll in the company of a knowledgeable and experienced guide. The following companies offer guided walking tours in English of all the major tourist attractions:

Anne Hervé

Ⓒ 01 47 90 52 16

Tickets: 50F

Paris Contact

Ⓒ 01 42 51 08 40.

Tickets: 60F

Paris Walking Tours

Ⓒ 01 48 09 21 40.

Tickets: 60F, under 10s free

A particular favourite of children as the tour takes you down into Paris' sewers.

entertainment

Don't let your concerns about language put you off. While the pickings may be slimmer for non-French speakers there's still lots to do in Paris, and in any case the sort of entertainment children like usually requires little translation. Marionette shows, circus performances and carousels may all have a distinct gallic flavour, but they also have universal appeal.

Theatre

Paris has a hugely vibrant theatre scene producing a good number of family-orientated shows each year. There's also a handful of theatres whose entire output is devoted to a younger audience. Of course, in order to appreciate these performances, children will need to be able to speak French to quite a high standard. However, non-French speakers needn't despair. In recent years there has been a significant increase in the number of **English language** shows being produced in Paris.

in French

Théâtre Astral
Parc Floral de Paris, Route de la Pyramide
Bois de Vincennes, 12th
✆ 01 42 41 88 33
Ⓜ Château du Vincennes
Tickets: 33F
Stages dramatized fairytales and morality plays.

Théâtre Dunois
108 Rue du Chevaleret, 13th
✆ 01 45 84 72 00
Ⓜ Chevaleret
Tickets: 35–100F
Plays host throughout the year to various dedicated children's theatre companies.

Théâtre des Jeunes Spectateurs
26 Place Jean Jaurès, 93100 Montreuil
✆ 01 48 70 48 91
Ⓜ Mairie de Montreuil
Tickets: 40–65F
Stages plays with a strong moral and/or political message for children.

in English

Théâtre du Nesle
8 Rue de Nesle, 6th
✆ 01 46 34 61 04
Ⓜ St Michel, Odéon
Regularly stages English language productions featuring both classics (Shakespeare, of course) and modern works.

Théâtre de Ménilmontant
15 Rue de Retrait, 20th
✆ 01 40 33 64 02
Ⓜ Gambetta
Plays host to a variety of English language touring companies.

Cinema

Paris can justifiably call itself the cradle of cinema, for it was here on Rue Scribe in 1895 that the Lumière brothers held the first ever public film screening using their newly invented *cinématographe*. The film itself was just a few minutes long and showed workers leaving the Lumière factory for their lunchbreak.

America aside, no other country enjoys such a strong cinematic tradition. The capital is full of picture houses – from huge, modern popcorn-filled multiplexes to small, Left Bank art houses – and more are being built all the time. Most cinemas show a programme made up of roughly one third domestic titles and two thirds international (i.e. American). Most international films are dubbed into French (marked VF, Version Française) although you will find some cinemas showing the original version with French subtitles (VO, Version Originale). Admission prices range from 25 to 50F.

Child-friendly cinemas

MK2 Sur Seine cinema
14 Quai de la Seine, 19th
☎ 08 36 68 48 07
Ⓜ Stalingrad
Special children's programmes are shown on Wednesday and weekend mornings.

Gaumont Grand Ecran Italie
30 Place d'Italie, 13th
☎ 08 36 68 75 13
Ⓜ Place d'Italie
The 24m x 10m screen is the biggest conventional cinema screen in the city.

UGC Ciné Cité Les Halles
Place de la Rotonde
Nouveau Forum des Halles, 1st
☎ 08 36 68 68 58
Ⓜ Châtelet-Les Halles
16 screen multiplex in the Forum des Halles shopping and cultural complex.

IMAX cinemas

Paris has two IMAX cinemas showing all the latest 3-D releases on vast building-sized screens.

Dôme IMAX
La Défense ✉ 92044
☎ 01 46 92 45 50
Ⓜ/RER: La Défense
Tickets: one film 57F, two films 80F, under 4s free
Next to the Grande Arche de la Défense on the western edge of the city.

La Géode
26 Avenue Corentin Cariou, 19th
☎ 01 40 05 12 12
Ⓜ Porte de la Villette
Open: hourly sessions daily 10am–9pm
Tickets: 57F
In La Villette's huge metal sphere outside the Cité des Sciences et de l'Industrie.

Circus

A trip to the circus in Paris is a Christmas tradition. These days, in addition to oldfashioned sawdust and sword-swallower circuses, Paris also plays host to some very modern troupes performing skills like juggling in new and modern ways (with chainsaws!).

Cirque de Paris
115 Boulevard Charles de Gaulle
✉ 92390 Villeneuve-la-Garenne
☎ 01 47 99 40 40
✆ 01 47 99 02 22
Ⓜ Porte de Clignancourt
Open: Oct–June Wed and Sun
Journée au Cirque (a day at the circus) 10–5
Showtime: 3–5
Tickets: Journée au Cirque: 195F–230F; show only: adult 70–155F, child 45–95F
An all encompassing circus experience – during the morning kids can try their hand at circus skills and train with the clowns, conjurors, contortionists, trapeze artists and tightrope walkers. They then have lunch with the performers before watching the professionals at work at an afternoon performance. It's a hugely popular birthday treat.

Cirque Tzigane Romanes
12 Avenue de Clichy, 18th
☎ 01 43 87 16 38
Ⓜ Place de Clichy
Showtime: Sept–May daily 8.30pm,
Sat also 3pm and 5pm
Tickets: adult 100F, under 18s 50F
Wirewalkers, contortionists, gymnasts and musicians put on a beguiling show.

Espace Chapiteaux
Parc de la Villette, 19th
☎ 08 03 07 50 75
Ⓜ Porte de la Villette
Showtimes: Wed–Sat 8.30pm, Sun 4pm

Tickets: adult 110F, under 25s 90F, under 15s 50F, under 4s free

Various visiting troupes throughout the year ranging from the most modern experimental ensembles to traditional companies.

Cirque d'Hiver

110 Rue Amelot, 11th
✆ 01 47 00 12 25
Ⓜ Filles du Calvaire
Showtimes vary; call in advance
Tickets: adult 150F, under 18s 70F
Probably the most famous circus venue in the world, built in 1852 it was originally called the Cirque Napoleon and today plays host to a variety of visiting troupes.

Puppet theatres

Puppetry is a great Parisian tradition. Almost every park has a marionette theatre or Guignol (named after the leading character, a sort of Gallic version of Mr Punch). As ever, violence (though not domestic violence) is the mainstay of the action. Performances are usually on Wednesday afternoons and Saturday mornings.

Guignol du Jardin d'Acclimatation

Jardin d'Acclimatation, Bois de Boulogne, 16th
✆ 01 45 01 53 52
Ⓜ Les Sablons
Le Petit Train from Porte Maillot
Shows: Wed, Sat and Sun 3pm and 4pm

Guignol de Paris

Parc des Buttes Chaumont, 19th
✆ 01 43 64 24 29
Ⓜ Buttes Chaumont
Shows: Wed, Sat and Sun from 3pm

Marionnettes des Champs-Elysées

Jardin des Champs-Elysées

by the Rond Point, 8th
✆ 01 40 35 47 20
Ⓜ Champs-Elysées-Clémenceau
Shows: Wed, Sat and Sun, and daily during the school holidays, 3pm, 4pm and 5pm

Marionnettes du Champs de Mars

Champ de Mars, 7th
✆ 01 48 56 01 44
Ⓜ Ecole Militaire
Shows: Wed, Sat and Sun 3pm and 4pm

Marionettes du Luxembourg

Jardin du Luxembourg, 6th
✆ 01 43 26 46 47
Ⓜ Vavin, Notre Dame des Champs
Shows: Wed, Sat and Sun from 3pm

Marionnettes de Montsouris

Parc Montsouris, 14th
✆ 01 46 63 08 09
Ⓜ Cité Universitaire
Shows: Tues, Sat and Sun from 3pm

Marionnettes du Parc Georges Brassens

Parc Georges Brassens
✆ 01 48 42 51 80
Ⓜ Porte de Vanves
Shows: Wed, Sat and Sun from 3pm

Carousels

The French have a great fondness for vintage carousels or *manèges*. You can take an old-fashioned spin at the foot of the Eiffel Tower, on the other side of the Pont d'Iena In front of the Jardins du Trocadéro, in the Parc Monceau, at the foot of the stairway in front of Sacre Coeur, by the entrance to Ⓜ St Paul, in the Place de Batignolles, in the Parc des Buttes Chaumont, and on the concourse in front of the Grande Arche de la Défense.

sport
and activities

Whether you want to take part or just watch, Paris has an activity for you. At the moment the most popular pastime with the younger generation is roller skating – to get some idea of how popular it is, sit at a pavement café for a few minutes and see how many roller bladers come shooting past. Every Friday thousands of skaters gather at the Place d'Italie for a 30km whizz through the Parisian streets. For something a little more sedate, head to the parks, many of which have public tennis courts and *boules* pitches. The most prestigious spectator sports are tennis (the star studded French Open takes place every May) and rugby (internationals are played at the state-of-the-art Stade de France, just outside the Périphérique), although football has managed to raise its profile following France's success in the 1998 World Cup.

Cycling

The French love cycling, and they host the world's most prestigious cycle race, the Tour de France, which starts and finishes every July on the Champs-Elysées (with a round trip of several thousand miles in between). Almost everywhere you go in the country you'll see hordes of lycra-clad enthusiasts peddling furiously along the roads. The lack of proper cycling facilities in the capital itself is therefore puzzling.

There are several good cycle paths in the Bois de Vincennes and the Bois de Boulogne, but recent attempts to increase the number of cycle lanes in the centre of town have, as yet, had only a limited effect and you should certainly avoid cycling in the centre, particularly during the week. On Sundays the *quais* beside the Seine are closed to traffic, which allows cyclists and pedestrians to meander along the river-banks in peace.

Bikes are not allowed on the métro, but are allowed for free on some RER lines out into the Paris suburbs. You can hire bikes from 1/2 day, one day or one week from:

A.S.C.
88 Boulevard de la Villette, 14th
Ⓜ Colon Fabien
✆ 01 42 01 28 29

La Maison du Vélo
11 Rue Fénelon, 10th
Ⓜ Gare du Nord
✆ 01 42 81 24 72

Paris à Velo C'est Sympa!
37 Boulevard Bourdon, 4th
Ⓜ Bastille
✆ 01 48 87 60 01
Rentals and a variety of city bike tours.

Star Location
8 Rue des Ecouffes, 4th
Ⓜ St Paul
✆ 01 48 87 83 93
For scooters.

Football

Despite hosting and winning the 1998 World Cup, France's attitude towards football is still rather ambivalent. The game doesn't inspire the same levels of fanatical support that it does in the neighbouring countries of England, Germany, Spain and Italy. In fact, until the country actually qualified for the final, the most notable feature of the tournament was how little public interest there was in it. Victory quickly changed all that, of course, bringing the largest crowds since the Liberation out on to the Champs-Elysées to celebrate.

Paris' most popular team is Paris St Germain (PSG), who play their home games at the Parc des Princes stadium. International football (and rugby, *see* below) matches are played at the state-of-the-art Stade de France in the suburb of St-Denis, built at a cost of several billion francs for the 1998 World Cup.

Parc des Princes
24 Rue du Commandant Guilbaud, 16th
✆ 01 42 30 03 60
Ⓜ Port de St Cloud
You can pick up tickets at the Paris St Germain club shop at 27 Avenue des Champs-Elysées.

Stade de France
✆ 01 44 68 44 44
Ⓜ La Plaine Stade de France

Riding

There are miles and miles of bridal paths in the Bois de Boulogne and Bois de Vincennes. Unfortunately, in order to use them you'll have to join a riding club, an impractical choice if you're only in town a few days as the membership period usually runs for at least three months. However, if you are sticking around for a while, and speak good French, you might want to get in touch with one of the following clubs, all of whom offer tuition for complete beginners from the ages of five and over. A three month course will cost something in the region of 1300–1500F.

Your child will be able to go for a short ride on a pony in many of the parks in Paris, including the Jardin d'Acclimatation in the Bois de Boulogne and the Jardin du Luxembourg.

Centre Hippique du Touring
✆ 01 45 01 20 88

Cercle Hippique du Bois de Vincennes
✆ 01 48 73 01 28

Club Bayard Equitation
✆ 01 43 65 46 87

Roller-skating/ice-skating

The roller-skating craze has caught on big time in Paris. You'll see roller skaters and roller bladers pretty much everywhere: on every pavement, on every road and in every park. It's an efficient way to get around and avoid the traffic jams.

There are indoor rinks in the 19th *arrondissement* and, outside the Boulevard Périphérique, at Boulogne-Billancourt and

Asnières-sur-Seine. However, the most picturesque (and central) place to skate is just outside the Hôtel de Ville where an outdoor rink is set up every year between December and March. Use of the rink is free and you can hire skates (30–50F).

La Maison du Patin
21 Rue des Quatres Cheminées
✆ 01 46 08 29 27
You can hire roller skates and protective pads for between 30F and 80F a day.

La Main Jaune
Place de la Porte de Champerret, 17th
✆ 01 47 63 26 47
Ⓜ Porte de Champerret
Roller-skating rink open Wed and Sat 2.30–7; roller-disco Fri and Sat 10pm to dawn, Sun 3–7.30
Skate hire available

Patinoire Edouard Pailleron
30 Rue Edouard Pailleron, 19th
✆ 01 42 08 72 26
Ⓜ Bolivar
Skate rental available
The only ice-skating rink in Paris.

Ice-skating rinks outside the Périphérique
1 Rue Victor Griffuelhes
Boulogne-Billancourt
✆ 01 46 94 99 74

Boulevard Pierre de Coubertin
Asnières-sur-Seine
✆ 01 47 99 96 06

Rugby

Rugby is France's most popular team sport. The annual Six Nations matches played in Paris inspire a level of passion and commitment among French spectators that the football authorities can only watch with envy. The matches, which pit France against England, Ireland, Scotland, Wales and Italy (for the first time in 2000), are played at the futuristic Stade de France where, in 1998, the French football team won the World Cup.

Stade de France
Rue Francis de Pressensé
✉ 93210 St-Denis
✆ 01 55 93 00 00
Tickets: 40–600F.

Swimming

Aquaboulevard
4 Rue Louis Armand, 15th
✆ 01 40 60 10 00
Ⓜ Balard
Open: daily 10am–8pm, Fri & Sat until 12 midnight
Adm: adult 77F, under 11s 56F, under 3s free
Huge swimming complex just beyond the périphérique, with slides, a wave pool and a tropical lagoon.

Piscine Suzanne-Berlioux
Forum des Halles
10 Place de la Rotonde, 1st
✆ 01 42 36 98 44
Ⓜ Les Halles

Piscine Jean-Taris
16 Rue Thouin, 5th
✆ 01 43 25 54 03
Ⓜ Cardinal Lemoine

Piscine Armand-Massard
66 Boulevard du Montparnasse, 15th
✆ 01 45 38 65 19
Ⓜ Montparnasse-Bienvenue

Piscine Emie-Anthoine
9 Rue Jean Rey, 15th
✆ 01 53 69 61 59
Ⓜ Bir-Hakeim

Piscine Hébert
3 Rue des Fillettes, 18th
✆ 01 46 07 60 01
Ⓜ Marx Dormoy

Piscine Georges-Vallerey
148 Avenue Gambetta, 20th
✆ 01 40 31 15 20
Ⓜ Porte des Lilas

Tennis

to watch
Each May, the world's top tennis players congregate in Paris to take part in the French Open, one of the sport's most prestigious events and one of the tournaments which makes up the Grand Slam. The tournament is played at the Roland Garros stadium on distinctive red clay courts which produce a slower, more tactical game than the grass courts of Wimbledon.

Roland Garros
2 Avenue Gordon Bennet, 16th
✆ 01 47 43 48 00
Tickets: 45–280F

to play
Paris has over 170 municipal courts, and your best chance of getting a game is just to turn up at a court and wait. Perhaps the most idyllic courts in the capital are in the Jardin de Luxembourg (where waiting is no great chore).

'Allô Sports'
✆ 01 42 76 54 54
For full list of municipal courts. Rates are usually 37F per hour for an outdoor court, 53F per hour for a floodlit court and 72F per hour for a covered court.

where to shop

Paris is a great place to shop for high fashions and antiques, and it's also a good place to shop with children. No other city is quite so concerned with the appearance of its younger inhabitants, and you'll find hundreds of children's clothes shops ranging from bland bargain centres to ultra-chic emporia frequented by film stars and royalty.

Détaxe Refund Scheme

If you are from a non–EU country and have spent more than 120F in any one shop, you can claim a refund on any VAT paid (VAT currently stands at 20.6%) when you leave the country – so long as you don't stay longer than 90 days. Pick up a Détaxe form at the shop, fill in the appropriate details, get the form stamped by customs and then send it back to the shop who will refund the money direct to your bank account or credit card.

Sales

Look out for the Paris sales which usually take place twice a year in January and July.

Opening hours

Unless stated otherwise, shops are open Monday to Saturday from 10am to 7pm.

Arts, crafts, gifts & hobbies

Graphigro
157 Rue Lecourbe, 15th
℡ 01 42 50 45 49
Ⓜ Vaugirard

If you've been inspired by the views and fancy joining the artistic throng on the Left Bank come to Graphigro, Paris' largest (and cheapest) arts suppliers to pick up a set of watercolours and brushes.

Marie Papier
26 Rue Vavin, 6th
℡ 01 43 26 46 44
Ⓜ Vavin, Notre Dame-des-Champs

Pop granny a line on a sheet of Marie Papier's beautiful hand-made writing paper – every colour available.

La Maison du Cerf-Volant
7 Rue de Prague, 12th

℡ 01 44 68 00 75
Ⓜ Ledru-Rollin
Open: Tues–Sat 10–7

Every type of kite imaginable: stunt kites, box kites and racing kites, as well as novelty kites in the shape of dragons or butterflies.

Nature et Découvertes
Forum des Halles, 1st
℡ 01 40 28 42 16
Ⓜ Châtelet les Halles

Carrousel du Louvre, 1st
℡ 01 47 03 47 43
Ⓜ Palais Royal Musée du Louvre

Palais de la Découverte, 8th
℡ 01 45 63 46 36
Ⓜ Franklin D. Roosevelt

Passage du Havre, 9th
℡ 01 42 82 72 80
Ⓜ St Lazare

61 Rue de Passy, 16th
℡ 01 42 30 53 87
Ⓜ Passy
Open: daily 10–8

An eclectic range of goods themed very loosely on nature: aromatherapy kits, South American turquoise jewellery, iron weather vanes, pots made out of cinnamon, paper made from coffee beans, etc. The first floor is a dedicated kids section where you'll find boxes of painted wooden toys, zoetrope lanterns, rocking horses, dinosaur model kits, mini hammocks, even mini accordions.

Pylones
57 Rue Tardieu, 18th
℡ 01 46 06 37 00
Ⓜ Abbesses

57 Rue St Louis en l'Ile, 4th
℡ 01 46 34 05 02
Ⓜ Pont Marie

52 Galerie Vivienne, 2nd
℡ 01 42 61 51 60
Ⓜ Pyramides
Open: 10.30–7.30
A huge range of fun gadgets and toys for both children and adults: colourful plastic aliens, shark staplers, painted tea pots, designer toasters, wacky toothbrushes, toy cars, etc.

Why!
22 Rue du Pont Neuf, 1st
℡ 01 42 33 40 33
Ⓜ Pont-Neuf

14–16 Rue Jean Jacques Rousseau, 1st
℡ 01 42 33 36 95
Ⓜ Les Halles, Etiene Marcel

41 Rue des Francs-Bourgeois, 4th
℡ 01 44 61 72 75
Ⓜ Chemin Vert

14–16 Rue Bernard-Palissy, 6th
℡ 01 45 48 71 98
Ⓜ St Germain des Prés, Mabillon
Open: Mon–Sat 10.30am–7.30pm
A temple of tackiness: furry lava lamps, hummingbird shaped key rings, glow-in-the-dark bags, etc.

Books

Chantelivre
13 Rue de Sèvres, 6th
℡ 01 45 48 87 90
Ⓜ Sèvres Babylone
Open: Tues–Sat 10–7, Mon 1–7
Dedicated children's bookshop with a large English language section.

Galignani –
Librarie Française et Etrangère
224 Rue de Rivoli, 1st
℡ 01 42 60 76 07

Ⓜ Tuileries
Claims to have been Europe's first English language bookshop. Stocks a wide range of English, American and French titles.

WH Smith – The English Bookshop
248 Rue de Rivoli, 1st
℡ 01 44 77 88 99
whsmith.france@wanadoo.fr
Ⓜ Concorde
Open: Mon–Sat 9–7.30, Sun 1–7.30
Packed with Brits stocking up on the latest magazines. In addition to its huge magazine and newspaper section, it has over 70,000 English language books, and there's a large children's section on the first floor. Kids can practise their French by picking up a French/English version of children's classics such as *Animal Farm* or *James and the Giant Peach*.

Chocolate

Alliance Chocolat
1 Place Victor Hugo, 16th
℡ 01 45 00 89 68
Ⓜ Victor Hugo
Open: Tues–Sat 10.30am–7.30pm
Very well-to-do confectioners; its intricate chocolate and glacé fruit arrangements are somehow more reminiscent of a jewellers than a sweet store.

Jadis et Gourmande
49bis Avenue Franklin D. Roosevelt, 8th
℡ 01 42 25 06 04
Ⓜ Franklin D Roosevelt
Open: Tues–Sat 10.30–7.30pm, Mon 1pm–7pm
Great novelty chocolate shop – you can pick up chocolate animals, Eiffel Towers and Christmas decorations. If you order in advance you could also buy a special treat –

a box with your child's name picked out in white and dark chocolate tiles.

La Maison du Chocolat
225 Rue du Faubourg-St-Honoré, 8th
✆ 01 42 27 39 44
Ⓜ Ternes
Open: Mon–Sat 9.30am–7.30pm
The French always take their chocolate seriously but at La Maison du Chocolat it is treated with a reverence bordering on the sacred – wide-eyed customers/worshippers silently browse the aromatic rows of hand-painted, exquisitely wrapped treats. It's perhaps more for adults than children, but children don't usually object to being surrounded by chocolates (if they can choose what takes their fancy).

A la Petite Fabrique
12 Rue St-Sabin, 11th
✆ 01 48 05 82 02
Ⓜ Bastille
Open: Tues–Sat 10.30am 7.30pm
At la Petite Fabrique, you can see the creative process behind the chocolates – watch how a big vat of steaming sticky syrup is turned into a tray of elegant eclairs.

Clothes

Agnes B (Children's)
10 Rue du Jour, 1st
✆ 01 4508 49 89
Ⓜ Les Halles
Designer baby and kids clothes plus mini versions of adult lines, by one of the most fashionable names in town.

Baby Dior
252 Boulevard St Germain, 7th
✆ 01 42 22 90 90
Ⓜ Solferino, Rue du Bac

The clothes may be smaller, but the prices are just as steep as in the adult version. You can pick up all your toddler essentials – quilted fur-collared jackets and tailored sailor suits with gold buttons – as well as a wide range of children's perfumes.

Baby Tuileries
326 Rue St-Honoré, 1st
✆ 01 42 60 42 59
Ⓜ Tuileries
Stalwarts of the 'children are mini-adults' school of fashion, this is the place to come for fur coats, tartan skirts and trousers, button down collars, corduroy suits, hooded duffel coats and knickerbockers.

Bonpoint
320 Rue St-Honoré, 1st
✆ 01 49 27 94 82
Ⓜ Tuileries

67 Rue de l'Université, 7th
✆ 01 45 55 63 70
Ⓜ Assemblée Nationale, Solférino

229 Boulevard St Germain, 7th
✆ 01 40 62 76 20
Ⓜ Solferino, Rue du Bac

12 Avenue Montaigne, 8th
✆ 01 47 20 42 10
Ⓜ Franklin D. Roosevelt

15 Rue Royale, 8th
✆ 01 47 42 52 63
Ⓜ Concorde, Madeleine

64 Avenue Raymond Poincaré, 16th
✆ 01 47 27 60 81
Ⓜ Victor Hugo, Trocadero
The most exclusive name in town; Bonpoint is the favourite establishment of parents whose children have balls and gala dinners to attend. With clients that include Princess Caroline of Monaco, the Duchess of York

and the Chirac family, Bonpoint can afford to charge pretty much whatever it likes (and it does). The clothes, however, are adorable: lots of velvet and frills for the girls, sharp suits and knickerbockers for the boys.

Boudezan
24 Rue Yvonne-Le-Tac, 18th
✆ 01 42 62 82 86
Ⓜ Abbesses
Reasonably priced children's clothes made from natural fibres in trendy, but tasteful, colours and designs.

La Boutique de Floriane
17 Rue Tronchet, 8th
✆ 01 42 65 25 95
Ⓜ Madeleine
Elegant baby clothes in a variety of pastel hues, many sporting animal motifs.

Catamini
23 Boulevard Madeleine, 1st
✆ 01 49 27 01 78
Ⓜ Madeleine

6 Rue des Francs-Bourgeois, 3rd
✆ 01 42 72 72 66
Ⓜ St Paul

114 Avenue des Champs-Elysées, 8th
✆ 01 53 76 21 51
Ⓜ George V, Charles de Gaulle Etoile

114 Boulevard Montparnasse, 14th
✆ 01 43 22 05 30
Ⓜ Vavin

311 Rue de Vaugirard, 15th
✆ 01 48 28 36 30
Ⓜ Vaugirard, Convention

155 Avenue Victor Hugo, 16th
✆ 01 47 27 93 01
Ⓜ Rue de la Pompe, Victor Hugo
Fast becoming one of the top names in contemporary children's ware, with funky printed romper suits, voile dresses and co-ordinating accessories.

Croissant
5 Rue St Merri, 4th
✆ 01 48 87 32 88
Ⓜ Rambuteau, Hotel de Ville
Small, friendly boutique in the Marais, selling new and second-hand baby clothes.

Dipaki
20 Rue Pont Neuf, 1st
✆ 01 40 26 21 00
Ⓜ Pont Neuf, Châtelet

5 Rue Bréa, 6th
✆ 01 43 26 04 37
Ⓜ Vavin

22 Rue Cler, 7th
✆ 01 47 05 47 62
Ⓜ Ecole Militaire

46 Rue Université, 7th
✆ 01 42 97 49 89
Ⓜ Rue du Bac, Solferino

18 Rue Vignon, 8th
✆ 01 42 66 24 74
Ⓜ Madeleine
Reasonably priced baby clothes and nursery equipment in bright, primary colours.

D. Porthault
370 Rue St Honoré, 1st
✆ 01 47 03 09 43
Ⓜ Tuileries
Posh baby clothes with lots of lace, frills and bows, for parents who want their newborns to look just-so.

Du Pareil au Même
14 Rue St Placide, 6th
✆ 01 45 44 04 40
Ⓜ Sèvres-Babylone

168 Boulevard St Germain, 6th
✆ 01 46 33 87 85

Ⓜ St-Germain des Prés, Mabillon

15 Rue des Mathurins, 8th
✆ 01 42 66 93 80
Ⓜ Havre Caumartin

24 Rue Mogador, 9th
✆ 01 42 82 13 33
Ⓜ Trinité

165 Rue Château des Rentiers, 13th
✆ 01 45 83 03 08
Ⓜ Place d'Italie, Nationale

10 Boulevard Brune, 14th
✆ 01 45 39 65 95
Ⓜ Porte de Vanves

97 Avenue Victor Hugo, 16th
✆ 01 47 27 06 31
Ⓜ Victor Hugo

In a city of high fashion madness, Du Pareil au Même is an oasis of bargain priced common sense. You can get good, sturdy dungarees, thick coats and brightly coloured T-shirts as well as copies of designer labels at reasonable, department store prices.

Gap Kids
102 Rue de Rivoli, 1st
✆ 01 44 88 28 28
Ⓜ Châtelet

14 Rue Lobineau, 6th
✆ 01 44 32 07 30/31
Ⓜ Mabillon

62 Rue de Rennes, 6th
✆ 01 53 63 00 39
Ⓜ Saint-Sulpice

90 Rue St Dominique, 7th
✆ 01 44 18 18 50
Ⓜ Latour Maubourg

Galaries Lafayette Haussmann, 4ème étage
40 Boulevard Haussmann, 9th
✆ 01 42 82 99 71
Ⓜ Chausée d'Antin

Passy Plaza, 53 Rue de Passy, 16th
✆ 01 44 96 30 50 69/69
Ⓜ Passy, La Muette

28 Avenue Victor Hugo, 16th
✆ 01 53 64 11 00
Ⓜ Victor Hugo

The American chain has seen its popularity grow enormously in recent years. Its no-nonsense US styles – sweatshirts, T-shirts, denims, etc – are a welcome alternative to the over-designed lines of many Paris boutiques. Some branches also contain a subsidiary, Baby Gap, which sells a colourful range of sturdy, practical baby clothes.

Gaspard de la Butte
10 bis Rue Yvonne-le-Tac, 18th
✆ 01 42 55 99 40
Ⓜ Abbesses

A wide selection of hand-made clothes for under-6s, including gorgeous dungarees and sweaters in ochres and reds.

Jacadi
4 Avenue Gobelins, 5th
✆ 01 43 31 43 90
Ⓜ Gobelins

76 Rue Assas, 6th
✆ 01 45 44 60 44
Ⓜ Notre-Dame des Champs

256 Boulevard St Germain, 7th
✆ 01 42 84 30 40
Ⓜ Solférino

17 Rue Tronchet, 8th
✆ 01 42 65 84 90
Ⓜ Madeleine

54 Boulevard du Temple, 11th
✆ 01 48 06 13 10
Ⓜ République

Ultra-neat shop displays and the sweet aroma of baby perfumes. Nothing too gaudy or controversial: sharp cut suits and formal smocks with cutesy motifs (usually rabbits).

Kerstin Adolphson

157 Boulevard St Germain, 6th

✆ 01 45 48 00 14

Ⓜ St Germain des Prés

Welcoming shop, chaotically arranged with great piles of clothes and shoes all over the place, a tile floor and wooden beams poking through the ceiling. These are the sorts of clothes kids will choose for themselves: patterned socks, bright jackets and painted wooden clogs.

Miki House

366 Rue St Honoré, 1st

✆ 01 40 20 90 98

Ⓜ Concorde, Madeleine, Tuileries

1 Place des Victoires, 1st

✆ 01 40 26 23 00

Ⓜ Pyramides

1 Rue du Vieux Colombier, 6th

✆ 01 46 33 77 55

Ⓜ St Sulpice

Nice, bright cheerful clothes; lots of red and yellow t-shirts and shirts, corduroy dress all bearing the miki smiling-bear motif.

Natalys

32 Rue St Antoine, 4th

✆ 01 48 87 77 42

Ⓜ Bastille, St Paul

74 Rue de Rivoli, 4th

✆ 01 40 29 46 35

Ⓜ Hôtel de Ville

47 Rue de Sèvres, 6th

✆ 01 45 48 77 12

Ⓜ St Sulpice, Sèvres Babylone

92 Avenue des Champs-Elysées, 8th

✆ 01 43 59 17 65

Ⓜ George V

42 Rue Vignon, 9th

✆ 01 47 42 61 83

Ⓜ Madeleine

117bis Rue Ordener, 18th

✆ 01 42 23 92 91

Ⓜ Jules Joffrin

Well-priced children's clothes, shoes, nursery equipment and toys: fur-collared coats, thick woollen jackets, corduroy trousers and dresses as well as nice wooden cribs and high chairs.

Petit Bateau

81 Rue de Sèvres, 6th

✆ 01 45 49 48 38

Ⓜ Sévres Babylone, Vaneau

161 Rue de Grenelle, 7th

✆ 01 47 05 18 51

Ⓜ La Tour-Maubourg

13 Rue Tronchet, 8th

✆ 01 42 65 26 26

Ⓜ Madeleine

41 Rue Vital, 16th

✆ 01 45 25 55 19

Ⓜ La Muette

Petit Bateau is posh, but not too posh, and if you rummage hard enough you should be able to turn up something affordable. The twirly pajamas, for instance, are very reasonable, and there are lots of nice print T-shirts

.

Petit Faune

33 Rue Jacob, 6th

✆ 01 42 60 80 72

Ⓜ St-Germain des Prés

Coordinated knitwear for babies and toddlers, patterned sweaters and smocks for older children.

Petit Petons

20 Rue St Placide, 6th
© 01 42 84 00 05
Ⓜ St Placide

2 Rue Cler, 7th
© 01 47 53 81 70
Ⓜ Ecole Militaire

135 Rue Faubourg St Antoine, 11th
© 01 40 19 07 19
Ⓜ Ledru Rollin
Reasonably priced children's shoes.

Six Pieds Trois Pouces

223 Boulevard St-Germain, 7th
© 01 45 44 03 72
Ⓜ St Germain des Prés

85 Rue Longchamp, 16th
© 01 45 53 64 21
Ⓜ Rue de la Pompe
Exquisitely crafted children's footwear, all
soft leather, Italian designs and high prices.

Tartine et Chocolat

24 Rue de la Paix, 2nd
© 01 47 42 10 68
Ⓜ Opéra

266 Boulevard St Germain, 7th
© 01 45 56 10 45
Ⓜ Solférino

22 Rue Boissy d'Anglas, 8th
© 01 40 17 09 03
Ⓜ Madeleine, Concorde

105 Rue du Faubourg Saint Honoré, 8th
© 01 45 62 44 04
Ⓜ St-Philippe du Roule

60 Avenue Paul Doumer, 16th
© 01 45 04 08 94
Ⓜ Trocadero, La Muette
A wide range of tasteful, formal baby clothes
and nursery furniture. Pastel shades – lots of
apple greens – and natural fibres.

Tout Compte Fait

62 Rue Chaussée d'Antin, 9th
© 01 48 74 16 54
Ⓜ Trinité, Chausée d'Antin La Fayette

128 Rue du Faubourg St Antoine, 12th
© 01 43 46 94 32
Ⓜ Ledru Rollin, Faidherbe Chaligny

115 Avenue Victor Hugo, 16th
© 01 47 55 63 36
Ⓜ Victor Hugo
Classic conservative wear for 0–4-year-olds
– button-down suits, formal dresses, duffel
coats, etc.

Department stores

BHV

52–64 Rue de Rivoli, 4th
© 01 42 74 90 00
Ⓜ Hotel de Ville
Open: Mon–Sat 9.30–7, Wed until 10pm
This sturdy no nonsense department store
opposite the Hôtel de Ville has a huge DIY
and electrical goods department in the
basement where you can pick up that forgotten transformer or adaptor. There's also a
large children's clothes and toy section on
the first floor.

Le Bon Marché

24 Rue de Sèvres, 7th
© 01 44 39 80 00
Ⓜ Sèvres-Babylone
Open: Mon–Sat 9.30–7
Children's clothes and toys are in the basement of 'The Good Buy', Paris' first ever
department store. Over 400 square metres
of shop floor dedicated to toys.

Marks & Spencer

35 Boulevard Haussmann, 9th

℡ 01 47 42 42 91

Ⓜ Havre-Caumartin

Open: Mon–Sun 9am–8pm, Wed until 9pm

Branch of the British old faithful, for those underwear emergencies or sudden cravings for microwavable chicken tikka massala.

Galeries Lafayette

40 Boulevard Haussmann, 9th

℡ 01 42 82 34 56

Ⓜ Chausée d'Antin

Open: Mon–Sat 9.30am–7pm, Thurs until 9pm

A truly vast shop; every month the equivalent of the entire population of Paris passes through its doors, and there's an absolutely huge children's clothes section.

Au Printemps

64 Boulevard Haussmann, 9th

℡ 01 42 82 50 00

Ⓜ Havre Caumartin

Open: Mon–Sat 9.30am–7pm, Sat until 10pm

Perhaps Paris' poshest department store – it certainly thinks so. A vast array of fashion concessions and a free fashion show every Tuesday morning. There's a free créche for children aged between 2 and 9, Wed and Sat 2pm–7pm (max 2hrs).

Samaritaine

19 Rue de la Monnaie, 75001

℡ 01 40 41 20 20

Ⓜ Pont Neuf, Châtelet

Open: Mon–Sun 9.30am–7pm, Thurs until 10pm

Samaritaine, on the banks of the Seine, boasts the best toy section of any department store in Paris. There's even a carousel on hand for when your kids tire of browsing the vast hordes of teddies, remote controlled cars and video games. Afterwards, have a coke on the roof top café and enjoy some truly spectacular views of the city.

Flea markets

Marché aux Puces de Saint Ouen

Porte de Clignancourt, 18th

℡ 01 40 11 54 14

Ⓜ Porte de Clignancourt

Open: Sat–Mon 10–6

The largest of Paris' flea markets – reputedly the largest in Europe. It's easy to get lost among its thousands of antique and bric-à-brac stalls. A great place to pick up old toys.

Marché aux Puces de Montreuil

20th

Ⓜ Porte de Montreuil

Open: Sat–Mon 10–6

A rather junky market. The traders here are perhaps a little more likely to let a bargain slip through their fingers than their more wised up counterparts at Saint Ouen.

Marché aux Puces de Vanves

14th

Ⓜ Porte de Vanves

Open: Sat–Sun 10–6

The most amateurish of the three, and thus the best hunting-ground for bargains. Lots of old toys and books.

Toys

Baby Rêve

32 Avenue Rapp, 7th

℡ 01 45 51 24 00

Ⓜ Ecole Militaire

Open: Tues–Sat 9.30–7

Pre-school toys and educational games.

La Ciel est à tout la Monde

Carrousel du Louvre, 99 Rue de Rivoli, 1st

℡ 01 49 27 93 03

Ⓜ Palais Royal-Musée du Louvre

7 Avenue Trudaine, 9th

✆ 01 48 78 93 40

Ⓜ Anvers, Barbes Rochechouart

10 Rue Gay-Lussac, 5th

✆ 01 46 33 53 91

Ⓜ Luxembourg

Large selection of traditional toys: marionettes, dolls houses, rocking horses and over a hundred varieties of kite.

Gault

206 Rue de Rivoli, 1st

✆ 01 42 60 51 17

Ⓜ Tuileries

Open: Mon–Sat 10–7, Sun 11–7

Dedicated to miniatures: tiny models of famous cartoon characters like Tin Tin and Snow White, and beautifully crafted dioramas, miniature house interiors and mini paper and porcelain houses.

Territoire

30 Rue Boissy d'Anglas, 8th

✆ 01 42 66 22 13

Ⓜ Madeleine

Near the very plush Place de la Madeleine, this is a very plush traditional toy shop selling dolls houses, carved wooden animals and puppets.

Jouet International du Monde

28 Rue des Trois-Bornes, 11th

✆ 01 43 57 68 44

Ⓜ Parmentier

Open: Mon–Sat 12noon–8pm

I land crafted toys and games from around the world: boomerangs, yo yos, frisbees, kites, etc.

Au Nain Bleu

406–410 Rue St Honoré, 8th

✆ 01 42 60 39 01

Ⓜ Concorde, Madeleine

Open: Mon–Sat 9.45–6.30

Founded in 1836, Au Nain Bleu has vast vaults of toy cars, dolls houses and board games as well as some truly magical window displays.

L'Oiseau de Paradis

211 Boulevard St Germain, 7th

✆ 01 45 48 97 90

Ⓜ Rue du Bac

Friendly toy shop selling plastic animals, drum kits, dolls, wooden forts and sailing boats.

La Grande Récré

Centre Cial Italie, 230 Avenue Italie, 13th

✆ 01 53 62 15 12

Ⓜ Place d'Italie

Open: Mon–Fri 10–8, Sat 10–7

A vast toy supermarket with a very large pre-school section.

Le Train Bleu

55 Rue St-Placide, 6th

Ⓜ St Placide

Specialists in electric toys: train sets, remote controlled cars and aeroplanes, etc.

Toys R Us

Centre Commercial Quatre Temps

La Défense, ✉ 92800

✆ 01 47 76 29 78

Ⓜ La Défense

Open: Mon–Sat 10–10

Vast branch of the international toy supermarket in the shopping centre next to the Grande Arche de la Défense.

where to eat

French cooking is synonymous with culinary sophistication, and Paris certainly has more than its share of swanky restaurants, but unfortunately many of them have a tolerant rather than welcoming attitude towards children. There are, however, lots of family-friendly restaurants serving good, relatively inexpensive fixed-price dinners – which usually consist of an *entrée* (appetiser), a *plat* (main course) and dessert – for between 70 and 120F a head. Most will be more than willing to provide children's portions. Also, look out for Hippopotamus, a French fast-food chain which provides colouring books, balloons and games at every table. For a snack, *crêpes* – as sold at countless street stalls – are popular with Parisian school children, who fold them into quarters and munch them marching along the street; or pop into a *patisserie/boulangerie* for warm *pains au chocolat* (chocolate-filled croissants), fresh from the oven.

Note: if you want the fixed-price meal in a restaurant you need to ask for *le menu*; if you want the menu you need to ask for *la carte*; and remember that burgers, like steaks, come medium-rare unless ordered *bien cuit* (well done).

Chains

Bistro Romain

26 Avenue des Champs-Elysées, 8th
© 01 43 59 93 31
Ⓜ Franklin D. Roosevelt

6 Place Victor Hugo, 16th
© 01 45 00 65 03
Ⓜ Victor Hugo

Open: daily 11.30–1am
Fixed price menu: 59F, 79F, 99F, 149F
Children's menu: 45F

The Romain chain prides itself on its family service with large tables and a menu full of kiddies' favourites – chips, burgers and chocolate mousse – as well as a range of simple pasta dishes. If you're particularly ravenous, you could always take on the challenge of the all-you-can-eat beef.

Hippopotamus

1 Boulevard Beaumarchais, 4th
© 01 44 61 90 40
Ⓜ Bastille

42 Avenue des Champs-Elysées, 8th
© 01 53 83 94 50
Ⓜ Franklin D. Roosevelt

9 Rue Lagrange, 5th
© 01 43 54 13 99
Ⓜ Maubert Mutualité

Open: daily 11.30am–5am
Fixed price menu: 98F, 143F
Children's menu: 47F

The Hippo chain specializes in family meals. The menu is simple – burgers, steaks, ribs, etc. – and you can ask for games and puzzles from the super-friendly staff. A favourite spot for children's parties.

Recommende

Altitude 95

First Level, Eiffel Tower, Champ de Mars, 7th
© 01 45 55 20 04
Ⓜ Bir-Hakeim
RER: Champ de Mars
Open: daily 11.30–3pm
Fixed price menu: 98F, 127F, 150F, 250F
Children's menu: 46F

Surely the best location in Paris: on the first level of the Eiffel Tower where the views are, as you would expect, spectacular – insist on a window table. The interior is deliberately unconventional (all struts and weird pieces of metal), the food is reasonable and they're very welcoming to families. One of the perks of dining here is that you get to use the private lift and can avoid the lengthy queues below.

L'Ancien Trocadéro

2 Place Trocadéro et 11 Novembre, 16th
© 01 47 04 94 71
Ⓜ Trocadero
Open: daily 11.30–1am

Sit at a pavement table for views of the Palais du Chaillot and, if you crane your neck, the Eiffel Tower. It's a bit touristy but the food is simple and reasonably priced.

Androuet

6 Rue Arsène Houssaye, 8th
© 01 42 89 95 00
Ⓜ Charles de Gaulle-Etoile
Open: Mon–Fri 12 noon–3 and 6.30pm–1am,
Sat 6pm–1am
Fixed price menu: lunch 210F, dinner 230F

A veritable temple of cheese, for fondues, raclettes and green salads with hot goat's cheese. Perhaps the best option is a sampler platter laden with a dozen different cheeses accompanied by some freshly baked bread. It's not cheap, but it will appeal to older, more adventurous children. Reserve.

Aux Délices d'Asie

119 Rue St Antoine, 4th

✆ 01 42 72 94 81

Ⓜ St Paul

Open: daily 10am–10.30pm

Cheap good quality noodle house next to Ⓜ St Paul, serving Chinese, Vietnamese or Thai dishes. Either the chicken with black mushrooms or beef with green peppers and onions should prove popular with children – neither are overspiced. The portions are generous and you can eat in or take away.

Bertillon

31 Rue St Louis en l'Ile, 4th

✆ 01 43 54 31 61

Open: Wed–Sun 10–8

By far and away the best and most popular ice cream parlour in town, which unfortunately means in summer you will have to queue for a good ten minutes before being served. It's worth the wait: thick, creamy and with over 70 flavours, this is the ambrosia of desserts.

Blue Elephant

43 Rue de la Roquette, 11th

✆ 01 47 00 42 00

Ⓜ Bastille

Open: Mon–Fri and Sun 12 noon–2.30 and 7–midnight, Sat 7–12 midnight

Fixed price menu: 150F, 275F

International chain of Thai restaurants, particularly welcoming to families at weekends. Kids will love the jungle-like decor.

Bofinger

5–7 Rue de la Bastille, 4th

✆ 01 42 72 87 82

Ⓜ Bastille

Open: Mon–Fri 12 noon–3 and 6.30pm–1am, Sun 12 noon–1am

Fixed price menu: 119F, 178F

Don't be intimidated by its hi-falutin reputation and luxurious Art Deco interior (or even the initial starchiness of the waiters) – as long as your children behave, they'll be made very welcome. Although a touch pricey, your meal shouldn't break the bank even if you decide to leave the safety of the set-price menu. For dessert, try the vanilla and strawberry vacherin. A smaller, cheaper version of the brasserie, 'Le Petit Bofinger' is just across the road.

Brasserie de l'Ile St Louis

55 Quai de Bourbon, 4th

✆ 01 43 54 02 59

Ⓜ Pont Marie

Fixed price menu: 150F

Mid-priced, good quality brasserie with views of Notre Dame and the Ile de la Cité. Check out the stuffed stork in the main dining room.

Brasserie XVième Poincaré

45 Avenue Raymond Poincaré, 16th

✆ 01 47 27 72 19

Ⓜ Trocadéro

Open: daily 12 noon–12 midnight

Simple, cheerful brasserie serving simple tasty fare. Excellent omelettes, and nobody turns up their nose if you ask for ketchup.

La Bûcherie

41 Rue de la Bûcherie, 5th

✆ 01 43 54 78 06

Ⓜ Maubert Mutualité, St Michel

Open: 12 noon–2.30pm and 7.30pm–11pm

Quiet Latin Quarter bistro with good views of Notre Dame, and a fire in winter.

Café Cannibale

93 Rue Jean Pierre Timbaud, 11th
✆ 01 49 29 95 59
Ⓜ Couronnes
Open: daily 9–2

Special children's area with mini tables and chairs; a popular spot with local families on Sunday afternoons.

Café Floré-en-l'Ile

42 Quai d'Orleans, 4th
✆ 01 43 29 88 27
Ⓜ Cité, Sully Morland
Open: Mon–Sat 10am–10.30pm

The perfect place to sample French-style hot chocolate: you are brought two pots – one filled with chocolate, one with hot frothy milk – to be mixed to suit your own taste.

Café in Halle St Pierre

2 Rue Ronsard, 18th
✆ 01 42 58 72 89
Ⓜ Anvers, Abbesses
Open: Mon–Sat 10–6

Just inside the entrance of the Halle St Pierre, Montmartre's dedicated cultural complex for children, this is a family café serving coke and grenadine to hordes of small children throughout the day.

Café in the Musée Rodin

Hôtel Biron, 77 Rue de Varenne, 7th
✆ 01 44 18 61 10
Ⓜ Varenne
Open: summer Tues–Sun 9.30–5.45, winter Tues–Sun 9.30–4.45

A lovely quiet spot for a light snack and a think while your kids run amok in the secluded garden. Mothers with prams get in free.

Cafés et Thés Verlet

256 Rue St Honoré, 1st
✆ 01 42 60 67 39
Ⓜ Palais Royal-Musée du Louvre, Tuileries

Open: daily 9am–7pm

The perfect place for afternoon tea: a family-friendly teashop filled with the aroma of tea and coffee which wafts from the open sacks on the tables. There are baskets of glacé fruits and sweets for the kids.

Le Carré

47 Avenue Raymond Poincaré, 16th
✆ 01 44 05 05 44
Ⓜ Trocadéro
Open: 12 noon–2.30pm and 7.30pm–11.30pm
Fixed price menu:

A small, cosy Italian restaurant serving excellent ravioli and pesto dishes. Slightly cramped but very friendly.

Chartier

7 Rue du Faubourg Montmartre, 9th
✆ 01 47 70 86 29
Ⓜ Grands Boulevards
Open: daily 12 noon–3 and 7–10

Children are welcome but are expected to behave at this bustling 19th-century eaterie. Good, basic fare at good, basic prices.

Chez Alexandre

39 Rue Descartes, 5th
✆ 01 40 46 82 20
Ⓜ Cardinal Lemoine, Place Monge
Open: Mon–Sat 12 noon–2.30
and 6.30–12 midnight
Fixed price menu: 49F, 75F

Bustling eaterie near the Rue Mouffetard market, serving tasty tarragon chicken, grilled steak, and superb desserts.

Chez Léna et Mamille

32 Rue Tournefort, 5th
✆ 01 47 07 72 47
Ⓜ Place Monge
Open: daily 12 noon–2 and 7.30–11
Fixed price menu: 98F, 185F

Located in a narrow street south of the

Panthéon, this restaurant is worth a visit to take on the all-you-can-eat chocolate mousse. The terrace has views of a pretty park where kids can burn off any excess calories.

Chicago Meatpackers
8 Rue Coquillière, 1st
✆ 01 40 28 02 33
Ⓜ Les Halles
Open: daily 11.30am–1am
Fixed price menu: 59F, 74F
Children's menu: 59F

Kids love this full-on American eaterie with line-dancing waiters and a model steam train that chugs its way around a track laid out above your heads, as well as the usual burgers, spareribs, chicken wings, chocolate cake and pecan pie. Children's entertainment is laid on on Wednesdays and at weekends.

Le Chinon
49 Rue des Abbesses, 18th
✆ 01 42 62 07 17
Ⓜ Abbesses
Open: daily 9am–12 midnight

Away from the crowds, this small café is a perfect afternoon pit stop. The omelettes are excellent and the service is friendly.

Crêperie des Arts
27 Rue St André des Arts, 6th
✆ 01 43 26 15 68
Ⓜ St Michel
Open: daily 12 noon–1am
Fixed price menu: 49F (lunchtime only)

Fully deserves its reputation as the best crêperie in town; it serves a huge range of savoury and sweet snacks.

Dame Tartine
59 Rue de Lyon, 12th
✆ 01 44 68 96 95

Ⓜ Bastille
Open: daily 12 noon–11.30

Friendly popular café opposite the Stravinsky fountain – a good place for a quick sandwich or *croque monsieur*.

Le Frog & Rosbif
116 Rue St Denis, 2nd
✆ 01 42 36 34 73
Ⓜ Etienne Marcel
RER: Châtelet-Les Halles
Open: Mon–Fri 12 noon–3 and 7.30–10.30, Sat and Sun 12 noon–4 and 7.30–10.30

Tuck into a range of traditional pub grub: sheperd's pie, toad-in-the-hole and, of course, chicken tikka marsala.

Le Grenier de Notre Dame
18 Rue de la Bûcherie, 5th
✆ 01 43 29 98 29
Ⓜ St Michel, Maubert Mutualité
Open: daily 12 noon–2 and 7.30–11.30
Fixed price menu: 75F, 78F, 105F

Excellent and cheap vegetarian restaurant. There's a children's menu and kids are invited to create their own non-alcoholic cocktails.

Hard Rock Café
14 Boulevard Montmartre, 9th
✆ 01 53 24 60 00
Ⓜ Grands Boulevards
Open: daily 11.30am–2am
Children's menu: 39F

The original burgers and memorabilia franchise, the Hard Rock Café is still packing them in. The children's menu is very good value and there are big screens showing a constant stream of high-energy videos.

L'Ilot Vache
35 Rue St Louis en l'Ile, 4th
✆ 01 46 33 55 16
Ⓜ Pont Marie
Open: Tues–Sun 12 noon–3 and 7–12 midnight, Mon 7–12 midnight

Fixed price menu: 185F, 248F

Excellent, reasonably priced steaks and sea food, decorated to a suitably bovine theme.

Indiana Café

14 Place de la Bastille, 11th

℗ 01 44 75 79 80

Ⓜ Bastille

Open: daily 12 noon–1am

Children's menu: 50F

Huge Tex-Mex diner decorated with American Indian motifs.

Korean Barbecue

22 Rue Delambre, 14th

℗ 01 43 35 44 35

Ⓜ Vavin

Open: daily 11–2 and 7–11

Fixed price menu: 150F, 275F

Interactive food for restless kids – children can cook their own meal at the table-set grill. Try the thin strips of beef soaked in a special sesame seed marinade.

Le Loir dans la Théière

3 Rue des Rosiers, 4th

℗ 01 42 72 68 12

Ⓜ St Paul

Open: Mon–Fri 11–7, Sat and Sun 10–7

Super snazzy tea salon serving mouth-watering goodies: raspberry cheesecake, chocolate fondant and lemon pie.

Le Maquis

69 Rue Caulaincourt, 18th

℗ 01 42 59 76 07

Ⓜ Lamarck Caulaincourt

Open: Mon–Sat 12–2.30 and 7–12 midnight

Fixed price menu: 100F, 159F

Montmartre's top choice, frequented by both culinary aficionados and local families. The 159F fixed price dinner is excellent value and consists of an entrée, main course, dessert, wine and coffee. The steaks are particularly recommended as is the chocolate fondant.

Marais Plus

20 Rue des Francs Bourgeois, 4th

℗ 01 48 87 01 40

Ⓜ Rambuteau, Hôtel de Ville

Open: 10am–7pm

Cheap café serving tasty quiches and pastries above a children's shop.

Le Mosque du Paris

1 Place du Puits de l'Ermite, 5th

℗ 01 45 35 97 33

Ⓜ Censier Daubenton

Open: daily 10am–12 midnight

The perfect pit stop after a morning in the Jardin des Plantes. The café has been designed as an architectural tribute to Spain's Alhambra, and stands next to Paris' largest mosque. Beautiful blue and white tiles and graceful arches provide a wonderfully relaxed setting in which to enjoy a mint tea and a fig-filled pastry.

New Nioullaville

32 Rue de l'Orillon, 11th

℗ 01 40 21 96 18

Ⓜ Belleville

Open: daily 12–3 and 7pm–1am

This vast 500 seat Chinese restaurant is filled with families at the weekend tucking into shrimp balls, dim sum and crispy duck. The menu is one of the largest in Paris.

Patachou

9 Place du Tertre, 18th

℗ 01 42 51 06 06

Ⓜ Anvers

Open: daily 12 noon–12 midnight

This pleasant, somewhat touristy café is a good vantage point from which to survey the artistic bustle on the Place du Tertre and, beyond, the Eiffel Tower.

Planet Hollywood

78 Avenue des Champs-Elysées, 8th
✆ 01 53 83 78 27
Ⓜ Franklin D. Roosevelt
Open: daily 11.30–1am
Fixed price menu: 89F

Surely we didn't come to Paris in order to eat at Planet Hollywood, you'll be telling yourself as you're dragged through the door. Despite the chain's recent financial problems, this branch is still doing well and there's no doubt that its mix of burgers and movie memorabilia really does appeal to children (particularly older ones) who'll demand an overpriced baseball cap.

Polidor

41 Rue Monsieur le Prince, 6th
✆ 01 43 26 95 34
Ⓜ Odéon
Open: Mon–Sat 12–2.30 and 7pm–12.30am,
Sun 12–2.30 and 7–11
Fixed price menu: 100F

A hugely popular traditional bistro near the Jardin du Luxembourg, with great long tables that can accommodate the entire family. The dishes are sturdy French staples such as *boeuf bourgignon*, veal in white wine sauce and snails with garlic. The chocolate tarts are particularly recommended. And as a final treat for your children – Turkish-style squat toilets.

Le President

1st Floor, 120–4 Rue du Faubourg du Temple, 11th
✆ 01 47 00 17 18
Ⓜ Belleville
Open: daily 12–2.30 and 7pm–1am

One of the grandest Chinese restaurants in town; the menu is hugely varied with plenty to attract the fancy of younger visitors. Try the mini dim sum (chinese dumplings).

Quai Ouest

1200 Quai Marcel Dassault, ✉ 92210 St Cloud
✆ 01 46 02 35 54
Ⓜ Porte de St Cloud
Open: daily 12–3 and 8pm–12 midnight

Children's entertainment, in the form of face painting and conjuring, is laid on at weekends in this large converted warehouse overlooking the Seine. The food is mainly American based, laced with a few French basics. It's a popular birthday party venue.

Rendez-vous des Chaffeurs

11 Rue des Portes Blanches, 18th
✆ 01 42 64 04 17
Ⓜ Marcadet Poissonniers
Open: daily 12–2.30 and 7.30–11
Fixed price menu: 65F

A good budget choice. The lunch menu is a sturdy bistro meal worth twice the price. The home-made apple pie with chocolate sauce is a particular speciality.

Le Sancerre

35 Rue des Abbesses, 18th
✆ 01 42 58 08 20
Ⓜ Abbesses
Open: daily 7am–2am

It's kinda groovy, and older kids will like it. The food is decent and the atmosphere merry with live jazz musicians on weekends.

Terrasse de la Samaritaine

Quai du Louvre, 1st
✆ 01 40 41 20 20
Ⓜ Pont Neuf, Châtelet
Open: Mon–Sun 9.30–7, Thurs until 10pm
Fixed price menu: 80F, 105F

Have a sandwich and a coke, settle back and enjoy one of the best views in Paris. This pleasant café is located on the roof of the Samaritaine department store, next to the Louvre on the banks of the Seine. The food is good and reasonably priced.

Thoumieux

79 Rue St Dominique, 7th
℅ 01 47 05 49 75
Ⓜ Invalides, La Tour Maubourg
Open: Mon–Sat 12–3.30 and 6.30–12 midnight,
Sun 12 noon–12 midnight
Fixed price menu: 82F, 160F

Traditional bistro packed with local families
at weekends. Children are very welcome,
although good behaviour and smart dress
are expected. The food is basic bistro classics – thick bean-heavy *cassoulets* and
crème caramel.

Le Totem

Musée de l'Homme
17 Place du Trocadéro et du 11 Novembre, 16th
℅ 01 47 27 28 29
Ⓜ Trocadero
Open: daily 12 noon–2.30am

The Musée de l'Homme's groovy café welcomes families and tourists for snacks and
coffee during the day, although it's a touch
more exclusive at night when it reverts to
full-on restaurant mode. The décor should
interest children, particularly the two giant
totem poles and an exhibition of American
Indian art. When they tire of this they can
always admire the magnificent views of the
Eiffel Tower.

Ty Breiz

52 Boulevard de Vaugirard, 15th
℅ 01 43 20 83 72
Ⓜ Montparnasse Bienvenüe, Pasteur
Open: Mon–Sat 12–3 and 7–11

Bargain-priced Breton restaurant, very popular with local families. Savoury galettes
(potato or buckwheat pancakes) are the
house speciality. Pick your own filling from
tomatoes, ham, cheese, mushrooms, egg,

salmon or artichokes (or anything else if
they've got it in stock).

Le Vieux Bistro

14 Rue du Cloître Notre Dame, 4th
℅ 01 43 54 18 95
Ⓜ Cité
RER: St Michel
Open: daily 12–2 and 7.30–11

Shadowy, traditional bistro, just yards from
Notre Dame. Good, old-style French cooking. Try the *tarte tatin*, a caramelized upside-
down apple pie. You'll have to order it with
the rest of your food as it takes around 45
minutes to cook.

Au Virage Lepic

61 Rue Lepic, 18th
℅ 01 42 52 46 79
Ⓜ Blanche
Open: daily 12–3 and 6pm–2am
Fixed price menu: 98F

A lovely backstreet bistro popular with
locals, with an accordionist on hand to
entertain the diners at weekends.

Virgin Café

Virgin Megastore, 52 Champs-Elysées, 8th
℅ 01 49 53 50 00
Ⓜ Franklin D. Roosevelt, Charles de Gaulle-Etoile
Open: Mon–Sat 10am–12 midnight,
Sun 12 noon–12 midnight

Watch the bustle of the Champs-Elysées
from a window table in the top floor café.
The food is surprisingly good and relatively
child-friendly – salmon on toast, hamburgers, etc. – and reasonably priced,
considering the location.

what to eat

Menus seem to be more and more international these days, and the same things pop up wherever you are in the world, particularly when it comes to fast food. But while you're in Paris, try to taste some French specialities; the following glossary is designed to help out whether you're ordering a meal in a restaurant or buying a snack from the local *boulangerie* (baker) or *épicerie* (grocer).
Also *see* **Language**, pp. 246–7.

Starters and soups

bouillon	broth	*potage*	thick vegetable soup
consommé	clear soup	*velouté*	thick smooth soup
crudités	raw vegetable platter	*vol-au-vent*	puff pastry case with savoury filling

Fish, shellfish

anchois	anchovies	*huîtres*	oysters
cabillaud	fresh cod	*limande*	lemon sole
carrelet	plaice	*lotte*	monkfish
Coquilles St-Jacques	scallops	*loup (de mer)*	sea bass
crabe	crab	*maquereau*	mackerel
crevettes grises	shrimps	*moules*	mussels
crevettes roses	prawns	*saumon*	salmon
cuisses de grenouilles	frogs' legs	*sole (à la meunière)*	sole (with butter, lemon and parsley)
escargots	snails		
friture	deep fried fish	*thon*	tuna
fruits de mer	seafood	*truite*	trout
homard	lobster		

Meat and poultry

agneau	lamb	*dinde, dindon*	turkey
ailerons	chicken wings	*entrecôte*	ribsteak
andouillette	chitterling (tripe) sausage	*foie*	liver
		fricadelle	meatball
biftek	beefsteak	*gigot*	leg of lamb
blanc	breast or white meat	*graisse*	fat
bœuf	beef	*jambon*	ham
boudin blanc	sausage of white meat	*jlapin*	rabbit
		lard (lardons)	bacon (diced bacon)
boudin noir	black pudding	*os*	bone
brochette	meat (or fish) on a skewer	*porc*	pork
		poulet	chicken
canard	duck	*rôti*	roast
cheval	horsemeat	*saucisses*	sausages
côte, côtelette	chop, cutlet	*veau*	veal
cuisse	thigh or leg		

Salad and vegetables

artichaut	artichoke	(rouges, blancs)	(kidney, white)
asperges	asparagus	haricots verts	green (french) beans
aubergine	aubergine (eggplant)	laitue	lettuce
avocat	avocado	maïs (épi de)	sweetcorn (on the cob)
champignons	mushrooms		
chou	cabbage	oignons	onions
chou-fleur	cauliflower	petits pois	peas
concombre	cucumber	poireaux	leeks
courgettes	courgettes (zucchini)	pomme de terre	potato
épinards	spinach	riz	rice
frites	chips (french fries)	salade verte	green salad
haricots	beans	tomate	tomato

Desserts and pastries

biscuit	cake	gâteau	cake
bonbons	sweets, candy	glace	ice cream
brioche	light sweet bread	madeleines	small sponge cakes
compote	stewed fruit	pain au chocolat	chocolate-filled pastry
coupe	ice cream		
crème anglaise	custard	palmier	heart-shaped flaky pastry biscuit
crème chantilly	sweet whipped cream		
		petits fours	tiny cakes & pastries
feuilleté	turnover	sablé	shortbread
(aux pommes)	(apple)	tarte, tartelette	tart, little tart

Fruit and nuts

abricot	apricot	miel	honey
ananas	pineapple	mûres	mulberry, blackberry
banane	banana	noisettes	hazelnuts
cacahouètes	peanuts	noix	walnuts
cassis	blackcurrant	pamplemousse	grapefruit
cerise	cherry	pêche	peach
citron	lemon	poire	pear
fraises	strawberries	pomme	apple
framboises	raspberries	prune	plum
marrons	chestnuts	raisins (sec)	grapes (raisins)

Miscellaneous and snacks

l'addition	the bill	*grillé*	grilled
ail	garlic	*hachis*	minced
au four	baked	*huile (d'olive)*	oil (olive)
baguette	long loaf of bread	*moutarde*	mustard
beurre	butter	*nouilles*	noodles
bien cuit	well done steak	*œufs*	eggs
bleu	very rare steak	*pain*	bread
confiture	jam	*pâte*	pastry, pasta
cornichons	gherkins	*poché*	poached
crème	cream	*poivre*	pepper
crêpes	thin pancakes	*quenelles*	dumplings of fish or poultry
croque-monsieur	toasted ham and cheese sandwich		
cru	raw	*quiche*	savoury tart
cuit	cooked	*raclette*	toasted cheese with potatoes, onions and pickles
frais, fraîche	fresh/cold (drinks)		
frit	fried		
fromage	cheese	*sel*	salt
fromage de chèvre	goat cheese	*sucre*	sugar
fumé	smoked	*sucré*	sweet
garni	with vegetables	*tartine*	bread and butter
(au) gratin	topped with crisp browned cheese and breadcrumbs	*tranche*	slice
		vapeur (à la)	steamed
		vinaigre	vinegar

Drinks

bière (pression)	beer (draught)	*jus d'orange*	orange juice
bouteille (demi)	bottle (half)	*lait*	milk
café	coffee	*limonade*	lemonade
chocolat (chaud)	chocolate (hot)	*orange pressé*	freshly squeezed orange juice
citron pressé	freshly squeezed lemon juice		
eau (minérale)	water (mineral)	*sirop d'orange/ de citron*	orange/ lemon squash
gazeuse	sparkling	*thé*	tea
glaçons	Ice cubes	*verre*	glass
infusion (or *tisane*)	herbal tea	*vin blanc/rouge*	wine white/red

where to sleep

Finding family accommodation in Paris can be difficult, especially for large families (many hotels are not insured to take more than three people in one room), but it is not the impossible task that some guidebooks make out. Many chains pride themselves on their family service, and there are various hotels which offer good deals for families, often including free accommodation for under 12s, babysitting, cots and connecting rooms.

The main tourist office, 127 Avenue des Champs-Elysées, 8th, ⓒ 01 49 52 53 54, has numerous brochures and can book you a hotel room for the night.

The big chains

Hotels which are part of an international chain are nearly always a safe bet. They are usually standardized and may be rather impersonal, but you can guarantee that the rooms will be clean and well equipped, and the staff will be used to dealing with children.

Westin Demeure

Central Reservations: ☎ 33 01 44 58 45 00
The Westin group operates some of the swishest hotels in town including the Castille, the Baltimore, the Astor and Le Parc. Each has a distinct ambience. Unlike many other chains the décor and fittings are not imposed by central office but are left to the discretion of the hotel manager. Nearly all offer a range of facilities for families including duplex suites, cots and a babysitting service.

Holiday Inn

Central Reservations: toll free ☎ 0800 905 999
The family-friendly American favourite operates nine hotels in Paris, only one of which, the Holiday Inn Paris St Germain des Prés, is actually near the centre of town.

Novotel

Central Reservations: toll free ☎ 800 668 6835
Novotel is perhaps the most child-friendly chain, having recently taken the decision to consult its younger guests on how best to improve the facilities. As a result the chain has come up with a number of new features including welcome packs for different age groups, soft drinks in the rooms and cost-cuts for parents. There are 10 properties in Paris, mostly on the outskirts, although there is one in the 1st *arrondissement* overlooking the Jardin des Halles.

Look out for...

Here is a list of things to look out for when hotel-hunting:

❀ Special family packages or discounts
❀ Babysitting service
❀ Separate children's meal times
❀ Children's menus
❀ Availability of books, games and toys for children

Ibis

Central Reservations: ☎ 01 53 02 30 30
Most of Paris' 20 Ibis hotels are located on the edge of town. All cater for families.

Sofitel

There are six Sofitel hotels in Paris including two just off the Champs-Elysées:
Sofitel Paris Arc de Triomphe
☎ 01 53 89 50 50
Sofitel Paris Champs-Elysées
☎ 01 40 74 64 64.

Recommended hotels

Expensive and luxury

****Hotel Baltimore
88bis Avenue Kléber, 16th
☎ 01 44 34 54 54
✉ 01 44 34 54 44
Ⓜ Boissière
RER: Charles de Gaulle-Etoile
Double rooms: 950–2,550F
Easily the pick of Paris' Westin hotels, with friendly service, good family facilities and large, airy rooms, many with balconies over-

looking this smart residential avenue. The Eiffel Tower is just a five minute walk away.

****Castille

33 Rue Cambon
1st
✆ 01 44 58 44 58
🖷 01 44 58 44 00
Castille_hotel@Compuserve.com
Ⓜ Madeleine
Double rooms: 2,160–2,760F
Suites: 3,200–4,000F

A former annexe of the Ritz, just across the road, this is the most centrally located of the Westins. As with its siblings, it can offer duplex suites, interconnecting rooms and cots, and the facilities are generally excellent, although the rooms are a bit bland for the price and the views are nothing to write home about.

****The Crillon

10 Place de la Concorde, 8th
✆ 01 44 71 15 00
🖷 01 44 71 15 02
crillon@crillon-paris.com
www.crillon-paris.com
Ⓜ Concorde
Double rooms: 3,950–4,300F
Suites: 4,950–31,000F

The Crillon and the Ritz currently vie for the title of most exclusive hotel in town. Their room rates are largely similar (i.e. hugely expensive) and both have tastefully opulent interiors although the Ritz is, of course, much the better known establishment – which in the eyes of most Crillon aficionados is no bad thing. The Crillon is certainly the most welcoming to families. If you've got the cash (and you'll need around 5,000F a night) book a suite overlooking the delightful central courtyard.

****Hotel Intercontinental

3 Rue de Castiglione, 1st
✆ 01 44 77 11 11
🖷 01 44 77 14 60
Ⓜ Concorde, Tuileries
Double rooms: 2,200–2,700F

A very grand hotel with ornate furnishings, luxurious interiors and fabulous views – the rooms on the south side of the hotel overlook the Louvre and the Jardin des Tuileries. To emphasize its grand standing, three of its seven 19th-century imperial ballrooms are listed as national monuments. Despite all this, it's very family friendly: there are several large family rooms with cots and small beds, and interconnecting rooms for older children (although note that children under 18 sharing their parents room stay for free). Babysitting is available and the restaurant can provide children's portions.

****Hotel Le Parc

55 Avenue Raymond Poincaré, 16th
✆ 01 44 05 66 66
🖷 01 44 05 66 00
104751.150@compuserve
Ⓜ Trocadéro
Double rooms: 2,100–4,000F
Suites: 4,000F

Very comfortable hotel in the Westin chain, with supposedly English-style fittings (English seems to translate as tweeds, tartans and pictures of dogs on the wall). But it's cosy, the staff are friendly and it's situated in a quiet residential street near the Eiffel Tower. Cots can be provided and there are a couple of duplex suites – mini apartments with the service and facilities of a hotel. The restaurant is run by the celebrated chef Alain Ducasse and can provide (rather expensive) half portions for children.

****Meridien Montparnasse

19 Rue du Commandant René Mouchotte, 14th

✆ 01 44 36 44 36

✆ 01 44 36 49 00

www.lemeridien-paris.com

Ⓜ Montparnasse Bienvenüe

Double rooms: 1,600–2,600F

This modern 35-storey gleaming white behemoth overlooks the Gare Montparnasse. The restaurant lays on children's entertainment with Sunday brunch, and the slightly unfashionable location means that rates are very reasonable for a four star.

****Relais St Germain

9 Carrefour de l'Odéon, 6th

✆ 01 44 27 07 97

✆ 01 46 33 45 30

Ⓜ Odéon

Double rooms: 1,560–1,800F

Large and competitively priced rooms, individually decorated. Four have kitchenettes, making them perfect for families. There's a laundry service.

****Le Terrassee

12 Rue Joseph de Maistre, 18th

✆ 01 46 06 72 85

✆ 01 42 52 29 11

Ⓜ Place de Clichy, Abbesses

Double rooms: 1,070–1,280F

Highly recommended: ask for one of its three junior suites, decorated in delightful, harlequin colours. Under 13s stay for free in their parents' room; older children can stay in an interconnecting room. The restaurant is very family-friendly. There are beautiful views of the city from the seventh floor terrace where in summer there's a restaurant. The prices are much more reasonable than you would pay for something of this quality in the centre of town.

Moderate

***Fleurie

32–34 Rue Grégoire de Tours, 6th

✆ 01 53 73 70 00

✆ 01 53 73 70 20

bonjour@hotel-de-fleurie.tm.fr

www.hotel-de-fleurie.tm.fr

Ⓜ Odéon

Double rooms: 900–1,200F

A friendly family-run hotel furnished with antiques. There are interconnecting rooms, and under 12s stay for free.

***Grands Hommes

17 Place du Panthéon, 5th

✆ 01 46 34 19 60

✆ 01 43 26 67 32

Ⓜ Maubert Mutualité

Double rooms: 780–800F

Good value three star hotel near the Panthéon, with antique furnishings, exposed wood beams and a hifalutin literary reputation – this is where André Breton defined surrealism in the 1920s. Babysitting is available, and there are great views from the 6th floor balconies.

***Hôtel Lenox Montparnasse

15 Rue Delambre, 14th

✆ 01 43 35 34 50

✆ 01 43 20 46 64

Ⓜ Vavin

Double rooms: 560–690F

The Montparnasse area's most elegant hotel, with beautiful furniture and fittings and a family-friendly atmosphere.

***Relais du Louvre

19 Rue des Prêtres St Germain l'Auxerrois, 1st

✆ 01 40 41 96 42

✆ 01 40 41 96 44

au-relais-du-louvre@oleane.com

Ⓜ Louvre Rivoli

Double rooms: 860–990F

Small, 20-room hotel within sight of the great museum. Most of the rooms are quite small although there are a couple of large penthouse apartments with fully equipped kitchens perfect for families.

***Université

22 Rue de l'Université, 7th
℃ 01 42 61 09 39
@ 01 42 60 40 84
www.hoteluniversite.com
Ⓜ St Germain des Prés
Double rooms: 850–1,300F

Delightful refurbished 17th-century town house, although its fashionable St Germain location means that the room rates are slightly above average. Reduced rates for kids sharing a room with their parents.

Inexpensive

**Hôtel des Arts

7 Cité Bergère, 9th
℃ 01 42 46 73 30
@ 01 48 0094 42
Ⓜ Grands Boulevards
Double rooms: 360–400F

A family-run hotel, with 26 cosy rooms just around the corner from the Musée Grévin. The lobby and staircase are decorated with hundreds of theatre and museum posters. Cots are available.

**Grand Hôtel Jean d'Arc

3 Rue de Jarente, 4th
℃ 01 48 87 62 11
@ 01 48 87 37 31
Ⓜ St Paul
Double rooms: 400–490F

In a Marais side street, this hotel is well priced for its location. Some rooms are tiny and a little gloomy while others are spacious and light – make sure you know what you're getting. All twin rooms have two double beds. There's no room service or babysitting, but the staff are friendly and helpful.

**Hôtel St Jacques

35 Rue des Ecoles, 5th
℃ 01 44 07 45 45
@ 01 43 26 82 53
hotelstjacques@wanadoo.fr
www.france-hotel-guide.com/h75005stjacques.htm
Double rooms: 430–590F

35 well-equipped rooms in a refurbished 19th-century town house around the corner from the Sorbonne. Families are welcome and they can provide cots. Several scenes from the 1960s film *Charade* starring Cary Grant and Audrey Hepburn were filmed here.

**Vieux Marais

8 Rue de Pilatre, 4th
℃ 01 42 78 47 22
@ 01 42 78 34 32
Ⓜ Hôtel de Ville
Double rooms: 660–690F

One of the better hotels in the Marais. The rooms have TV, telephones and ensuite bathrooms, and cots can be provided.

Aparthotels

For families looking for a little flexibility, aparthotels – a hybrid of an apartment and a hotel – can often be a good alternative to standard hotels. You get both the freedom and privacy of an apartment – each aparthotel apartment is self contained and comes with a fully equipped kitchenette – plus the services and facilities of a hotel including 24 hour reception, baby equipment rental, laundry, dry cleaning, housekeeping and often babysitting and a gym. Two of the best aparthotel chains are:

Aparthotel Citadines
Central Reservations
✆ 01 41 05 79 05
✉ 01 41 05 78 83
www.citadines.com
Rates: 550–750F per day; discount if you stay longer than seven nights
Eleven locations, including Bastille, Montmartre, Opera, Place Vendôme and the Champs-Elysées.

Orion Aparthotels
Central Reservations
✆ 01 41 05 79 05
✉ 01 41 05 78 83
sales@apartmenthotels.com
www.apartmenthotels.com
Rates: 550–750F per day; discount if you stay longer than seven nights
Five locations: Bastille, Les Halles, the Louvre, Tour Eiffel and Place d'Italie.

Apartments

For a stay of several weeks, or even months, you would be well advised to rent an apartment. Not only does this make sound economic sense (with a bit of hunting you should be able to get something for just a few thousand francs a week, although this will rise considerably if you want to stay right in the centre of town) but it will also give you the chance to become familiar with the local community – meeting the neighbours, buying and cooking food from local shops, etc.

Self-catering allows you to do what you like when you like. You can get up when it suits you, nurse your colicky newborn at 3am, and scramble eggs whenever your toddler gets peckish. Again, there are some important questions that are worth asking:

▪ How far is your accommodation from the nearest shops, supermarket, launderette, restaurants, transport and park?

▪ How many bedrooms does the flat have? The term 'sleeps 6' does not necessarily mean that there will be three bedrooms; often a sofa in the living room converts into a bed, and you may even need to rearrange the room in order to create enough sleeping space.

▪ Are cots supplied and, if so, is there an additional charge for them?

▪ Are the children's rooms fitted with bunk beds and, if so, do these have safety rails?

▪ Is the garden or pool fenced off and are there any nearby ponds, streams or other potential hazards?

▪ Is it safe for children to play unsupervised in the garden?

▪ Can babysitting be arranged locally?

France Appartements
97–99 Avenue des Champs-Elysées, 8th
✆ 01 56 59 31 00
✉ 01 56 89 31 01
Ⓜ George V
www.apartments-of-France.com

Paris Apartments Services
69 Rue d'Argout, 2nd
✆ 01 40 28 01 28
✉ 01 40 28 92 01
www.paris-appartements-services.fr

Rothray
6 Rue Bertin, 1st
✆ 01 48 87 13 37
✉ 01 42 78 17 72

Paris' year

Events and entertainment suitable for families take place throughout the year in Paris. From festivals and parades to firework displays and grand sporting occasions, there's always something going on. Summer is a particularly good time for kids as this is when the great funfairs at the Bois de Vincennes and Jardin des Tuileries are open, with their vast array of rides, games and stalls.

January

La Grande Parade de Paris

1 January
Porte St Martin to the Madeleine by way of
the Grands Boulevards
℗ 01 43 65 10 10
The New Year's Day parade, with a huge
procession of decorated floats with bands,
cheerleaders, vast floating balloon characters, jugglers, clowns and lots of music.

Chinese New Year

Late January or early February
Around Avenue d'Ivry and Avenue de Choisy, 13th
Ⓜ Porte d'Ivry, Porte de Choisy
Chinatown celebrates Chinese New Year
with firecrackers, paper lanterns and papier-
mâché dragons that dance down the street.

April

April Fool's Day

1 April
April Fool's Day in France is celebrated with
a range of hoaxes and practical jokes,
poissons d'avril, the most popular of which
involves sticking a paper fish to someone's
back without them noticing.

Foire du Trône

mid April–early June
Bois de Vincennes, Pelouse de Reuilly, 12th
Everyday from 2pm till late
℗ 01 46 27 52 29
Ⓜ Porte Dorée
Adm: free; rides cost between 20 and 30F each
Traditional funfair with a huge Big Wheel,
rollercoasters, carousels, arcades and candy
floss – *barbe à Papa*.

Marathon de Paris

A Sunday in mid April
Start: 9am
℗ 01 53 17 03 10

20,000 people run (or jog or walk) the 26
mile course between the Place de la
Concorde and the Hippodrome de
Vincennes. Pick a vantage point along the
quais and watch the seething mass pass by.

Les Grandes Eaux Musicales

Every Sunday from mid April–mid October
Parc du Château de Versailles
℗ 01 30 84 74 00
RER: Versailles-Rive Gauche
Adm: 30F, under 10s free
Music and water themed days throughout
the summer: Versailles' fountains are set in
motion accompanied by classical music.

May

May Day

1 May
The streets are full of people selling sprigs of
lily of the valley (*muguet*), the traditional May
Day flower, to bring good luck.

La Course au Ralenti

30 May
In Montmartre between Rue Lepic and
Place du Tertre
℗ 01 46 06 79 56
Vintage car race up Montmartre's steep *butte*.

French Open Tennis Championships

Two weeks in late May
Roland Garros Stadium,
2 Avenue Gordon Bennet, 16th
℗ 01 47 43 48 00
www.rolandgarros.org
Ⓜ Porte d'Auteuil
Tickets: 45–280F
One of the events that makes up tennis'
Grand Slam, played on distinctive red clay
courts which produce a slow tactical game.
The matches are hugely popular; you'll have
to queue if you want to get tickets.

June

Fête de la Musique
21 June
All over town, particularly Palais Royal , Place de la
République and Institut du Monde Arabe
✆ 01 40 03 94 70
On the longest day of the year, the city
comes alive with the sound of music.
Musicians give impromptu performances on
street corners, in parks, outside cafés, to any
audience, however small. More formal performances are given by classical orchestras
at the Palais Royal, the Musée d'Orsay and
the Place de la République. Arab musicians
perform at the Institut du Monde Arabe.

Foire St-Germain
Early June–early July
St Germain des Prés
✆ 01 40 46 75 12
Ⓜ St Sulpice
A well-to-do antique and cultural fair in
Paris' most well-to-do district. Children are
entertained with a small circus and miniature
steam train.

Feux de la St-Jean
Mid June
Quai St Bernard
Ⓜ Gare d'Austerlitz
Adm: free
The feast of St John the Baptist is marked
with a firework display over the Seine.

Course des Garçons et Serveuses de Café
End of June
From the Hôtel de Ville via the Grands Boulevards
and St Germain des Prés, and back again
✆ 01 42 96 60 75
Ⓜ Hôtel de Ville
The race of the waiters. Over 500 waiters
and waitresses in full serving uniform race a
five mile course starting and finishing at the
Hôtel de Ville and, just to make it interesting,
they have to carry a tray all the way. It's
strange but very popular.

Funfair at Jardin des Tuileries
Mid June–end of August
Jardin des Tuileries
Ⓜ Tuileries, Concorde
One of Paris' most popular funfairs sets up
for business every summer in the neat
manicured Tuileries gardens. There are great
views of the city from the huge ferris wheel.

July

Bastille Day
14 July
The storming of the Bastille is celebrated
throughout the city with a variety of events.
At 10am the President inspects a military
parade on the Champs-Elysées. There are
numerous *bals de pompiers* (parties organized by local firestations) and a party at the
Place de la Bastille. The evening finishes
with a firework display at the Trocadéro.

Grands Fêtes de Nuit de Versailles
Certain weekends from July to September
Parc du Château de Versailles
✆ 01 30 83 78 88
RER: Versailles Rive Gauches
Adm: 70–250F
Lavish recreation of a 17th-century royal
party with dancing, fancy dress, music
and fireworks.

Tour de France
Early and late July
Champs-Elysées, 8th
✆ 01 41 33 15 00
Ⓜ Charles de Gaulle-Etoile, George V, Franklin D.
Roosevelt, Champs-Elysées-Clemenceau,
Concorde

The world's pre-eminent cycle race starts and finishes each year on the Champs-Elysées – with a round trip of several thousand miles in between. Huge crowds line the route on the final day.

October

Salon du Chocolat

End of October
Espace Eiffel Branly, 23 Quai Branly, 7th
☎ 01 45 03 21 26
Ⓜ Alma Marceau
Adm: 50F
The festival of chocolate will encourage both adults and children to stuff themselves silly with sticky treats. Look out for the chocolate sculptures.

Hallowe'en

31 October
Hallowe'en has caught on big time in Paris in recent years, although nobody is quite sure why. Largely ignored just a few years ago, it's now one of the restaurant and costuming industry's biggest nights and provides an excuse for everyone to dress up and decorate their houses. Trick or treating, however, is unheard of.

December

Salon Nautique de Paris

Early December
Paris Expo, Porte de Versailles, 15th
☎ 01 43 90 47 10
Ⓜ Porte de Versailles
Adm: 30–60F
International boat show

Salon du Cheval, du Poney et de l'Ane

Early December
Paris-Expo, Porte de Versailles, 15th
☎ 01 49 09 64 27

Ⓜ Porte de Versailles
Adm: 30–60F
Festival of equestrianism where you can watch and pet as many horses and ponies as you could possibly want.

Patinoire de l'Hôtel de Ville

Mid December to early March
Hôtel de Ville
Ⓜ Hôtel de Ville
Adm: free; skate hire from 30F
Grab your mittens, bobble hats, scarves and other such wintertime essentials for a skate on the open air ice rink outside the Hôtel de Ville. Surrounded by fir trees specially brought in for the occasion, this has a wonderfully Christmassy feel. There are a couple of mini-carousels on hand for non-skating children.

Festival Mondial du Cirque du Demain

Late December
Chapiteau Arlette Gross, 12th
☎ 01 44 61 06 00
Ⓜ Porte Dorée
Adm: 70–150F
Circus performers do their thing for the Christmas crowds. Clowns, jugglers, tightrope walkers, etc.

Christmas

In particular, look out for the Christmas lights on the Champs-Elysées, Avenue Montaigne and Boulevard Haussmann. Carousels throughout the city are free to children during the Christmas period.

New Year's Eve

Also known in France as the Fête de la St-Sylvestre. The Champs-Elysées is still the prime spot at midnight.

Paris for free

Be under no illusions, Paris is not a cheap city. However, if you know where to look there are still some savings to be made. Many museums don't charge for under 18s, and the city's beautiful parks and churches are always free. Also, if you come at the right time of year, you may be able to catch a major free event such as the Paris Marathon, the Bastille Day celebrations or the climax of the Tour de France.

Churches

Admission is free to all Paris' churches, although you'll have to pay if you want to see the views from the top of either Notre Dame or Sacre Coeur.

Events and festivals

Various free events are put on throughout the year for the Parisian population – and you can watch too. *See* pp.150–53 for more details of the Paris year.

Annual Events

January
La Grande Parade de Paris
New Year's Day Parade along the Grands Boulevards.

Chinese New Year
(Occasionally takes place early February.)

April
April Fool's Day

Marathon de Paris

May
May Day

La Course au Ralenti
Vintage car race up Montmartre's steep 'Butte'.

June
Fête de la Musique
Festival of music, with free performances given throughout the city.

Feux de la St-Jean
Feast of St John the Baptist, marked with a firework display over the Seine.

Course des Garçons et Serveuses de Café
500 waiters and waitresses race a 5-mile course, starting and finishing at the Hôtel de Ville.

July
Bastille Day
France's National Day, celebrated with organized parties and fireworks.

Tour de France
Watch the climax of the world's most famous cycle race on the Champs-Elysées.

December
Patinoire de l'Hôtel de Ville
Every year an ice rink (*patinoire*) is erected outside the Hôtel de Ville. You can skate for free, but you'll have to pay for skate hire.

Christmas Lights
In particular, check out the Champs-Elysées, Avenue Montaigne and Boulevard Haussmann.

Christmas Carousels
Carousels throughout the city are free to children during the Christmas period.

New Year's Eve
The focus of Paris' New Year celebrations is on the Champs-Elysées.

Museums, galleries and monuments

Free to all

Musée Fragonard
9 Rue Scribe, 9th
✆ 01 47 42 93 40
Ⓜ Opéra
Open: Mon–Sat 9–5.30
See p.106

Musée de la Préfecture
1bis Rue des Carmes, 5th
✆ 01 44 41 52 54
Ⓜ Maubert Mutualité
Open: Mon–Fri 9–5, Sat 10–5
See p.81

Free for under 18s

Musée National du Louvre
Palais du Louvre, Quai du Louvre, 1st
℡ 01 40 20 53 17
Ⓜ Palais Royal-Musée du Louvre
Open: daily 9am–6pm (Wed until 9.45pm);
closed Tues
See pp.36–8

Musée d'Art Moderne de la Ville de Paris
11 Avenue Président Wilson, 16th
℡ 01 53 67 40 00
Ⓜ Iéna, Alma Marceau
Open: Tues–Sun 10–5.40, Sat and Sun until 7
See p.55–6

Musée Carnavalet
23 Rue de Sévigné, 3rd
℡ 01 42 72 21 13
Ⓜ St Paul, Chemin Vert
Open: Tues–Sun 10–5.40. The 19th- and
20th-century rooms are usually only open from
10–11.30, while the Louis XV period rooms don't
open until 1.30.
See p.62

Musée Cognacq-Jay
Hôtel Denon, 8 Rue Elzévir, 3rd
℡ 01 40 27 07 21
Ⓜ St Paul
Open: Tues–Sun 10–5.40
See p.63

Musée de la Monnaie de Paris
11 Quai de Conti, 6th
℡ 01 40 46 55 35
Ⓜ Pont Neuf
Open: Tues–Fri 11–5.30,
Sat and Sun 12–5.30
See p.74

Musée National des Arts d'Afrique et d'Oceanie
293 Avenue Daumesnil, 12th
℡ 01 44 74 84 80

Infoline: ℡ 01 43 46 51 61
Ⓜ Porte Dorée
Open: Mon and Wed–Sun 10–6
See p.106

Musée Nationale des Arts Asiatiques – Guimet
6 Place d'Iéna, 16th
℡ 01 45 05 00 98
Ⓜ Iéna
Open: Mon and Wed–Sun 9.45–5.45
See p.55

Musée National du Moyen Age
6 Place Paul Painlevé, 5th
℡ 01 53 73 78 00
Ⓜ Cluny-La Sorbonne
RER: St Michel
Open: Mon and Wed–Sun 9.15–5.45
See p.81

Musée Nissim de Camondo
63 Rue de Monceau, 8th
℡ 01 53 89 06 40
Ⓜ Monceau, Villiers
Open: Wed–Sun 10–5
See p.106

Musée d'Orsay
1 Rue de Bellechasse, 7th
℡ 01 40 49 48 48
Infoline: ℡ 01 45 49 11 11
Ⓜ Solférino
RER: Musée d'Orsay
Open: Tues–Sat 10–6, Sun 9–6
See p.71–2

Musée Picasso
Hôtel Salé, 5 Rue De Thorigny, 3rd
℡ 01 42 71 25 21
Ⓜ Chemin Vert, St-Sébastien Froissart
Open: summer 9.30–6; winter 9.30–5.30;
closed Tues
See p.62–3

Musée Rodin
Hôtel Biron, 77 Rue de Varenne, 7th

© 01 44 18 61 10
Ⓜ Varenne
Open: summer Tues–Sun 9.30–5.45,
winter Tues–Sun 9.30–4.45
See p.54

Musée Nationale d'Art Moderne
Rue Beaubourg, 4th
© 01 44 78 12 33
Ⓜ Hôtel de Ville, Rambuteau
RER: Châtelet-Les Halles
Open: centre: Mon, Wed–Sun 11am–10pm;
musée: Mon, Wed–Sun 11am–9pm
Adm: centre: free; musée adults 30F,
under 18s free
See p.60

Free for under 12s

Arc de Triomphe
Place Charles de Gaulle, 8th
© 01 55 37 73 77
Ⓜ/RER: Charles de Gaulle-Etoile
Open: summer 9.30am–11pm,
winter 10am–10.30pm
See p.43

La Conciergerie
1 Quai de l'Horloge, 1st
© 01 53 73 78 50
Ⓜ Cité, Châtelet
Open: Tues–Sat 10–6, Sun 9–6
See p.72

Hôtel des Invalides
Esplanade des Invalides, 7th
© 01 44 42 37 72
Ⓜ Invalides
Open: summer 10–5.45; winter 10–4.45; summer
Napoleon's tomb 10–7
See p.51–2

Musée de l'Assistance Publique
Hôtel de Miramion
47 Quai de la Tournelle, 5th
Open: Wed–Sat 10–5, closed Mon, Tues and Aug
See p.81

Parks

Paris' parks, gardens and woods are all free although you'll have to pay for some specific attractions such as the Jardin d'Acclimatation at the Bois de Boulogne, the flower garden at the Bois de Vincennes and the annual funfair at the Jardin des Tuileries.
See **Kids Out**, pp.108–13 for more information.

Views

Paris is a city of a thousand views. Some have to be paid for; the following are free:

Place de la Concorde
From Paris' most famous square you can see down the Champs-Elysées to the Arc de Triomphe; the Jardin des Tuileries and the Louvre; and the Assemblée Nationale.
See p.40

Sacre Coeur
From the steps of Montmartre's basilica you can see the entire city stretched out before you.
See p.88

Samaritaine
19 Rue de la Monnaie, 1st.
There are spectacular views of Paris from the store's top-floor terrace.
See p.45

Trocadéro
From the Jardins du Trocadéro there is one of the best views of the Eiffel Tower and the Champ de Mars.
See p.53

themed days

Paris has so many wonders, so many great places to visit, that it's sometimes difficult to know where to start. Often your best bet is to plan your family's sightseeing route according to a particularly theme or topic. Here are some suggestions for themed itineraries.

Lions, tigers & bears

Morning
Take the métro/RER to Gare d'Austerlitz to visit the Ménagerie in the Jardin des Plantes, a rather small, old fashioned zoo where you can see llamas, monkeys, deer and bears. Then, take a quick tour of the recently reopened Grande Galerie de l'Evolution in the Musée National d'Histoire Naturelle to find out more about the evolution of modern species.

Lunch
Café of Le Mosque du Paris
1 Place du Puits de l'Ermite, 5th
© 01 45 35 97 33
Ⓜ Censier Daubenton

Afternoon
Head to Ⓜ Porte Dorée to visit the Zoo de Paris in the Bois de Vincennes, one of Europe's largest zoos, home to lions, tigers and elephants. Kids can help feed the sea lions.

The Musée National d'Histoire Naturelle
57 Rue Cuvier, 5th
© 01 40 79 30 00
See p.78–80

Zoo de Paris
53 Avenue de St Maurice, 12th
© 01 44 75 20 10
See p.109–10

On the trail of the French Revolution

Morning
Start the day at the Place de la Bastille (Ⓜ Bastille), where the French Revolution began on 14 July 1789, when a mob of 8,000 people stormed and destroyed the Bastille, the notorious royal prison. You can see the outline of the fortress set into the pavement.

From here, take the métro to Ⓜ Cité to visit the Conciergerie where Louis XVI and Marie Antoinette were held prisoner before their execution. You can even visit Marie Antoinette's reconstructed cell.

Lunch
McDonald's
184 Rue de Rivoli
Ⓜ Tuileries

Afternoon
Walk through the Jardin des Tuileries to the Place de la Concorde, 1st, where both Louis XVI and Marie Antoinette were executed on a guillotine set up where the Egyptian obelisk now stands.

Then, take the métro to Ⓜ Grands Boulevards for the Musée Grevin where you can see waxwork reconstructions of various scenes from the revolution including the death of the revolutionary leader Jean Paul Marat – he was stabbed while lying in his bathtub.

Alternatively
Take the métro to Ⓜ St Paul for the Musée Carnavalet to find out more about France's most celebrated event and see items of revolutionary memorabilia including a model guillotine carved in bone by French prisoners of war in England, Louis XVI's shaving kit and Napoleon's toothbrush.

La Conciergerie
1 Quai de l'Horloge, 1st
© 01 53 73 78 50

Ⓜ Cité, Châtelet
See p.72

Jardin des Tuileries
Rue de Rivoli, 1st
Entrances on Rue de Rivoli, Place de la Concorde
and Avenue du Gal. Lemonnier
See p.39

Espace Montmartre
11 Rue Poulbot, 9th
See p.89

Musée Carnavalet
23 Rue de Sévigné, 3rd
✆ 01 42 72 21 13
See p.62

On the toy trail

Morning
Head down to the Carrousel du Louvre,
Ⓜ Palais Royal-Musée du Louvre, where
you will find Nature et Découvertes which
has an excellent toy section on the first
floor, and La Ciel est à tout la Monde
which has a large selection of traditional
toys. Around the corner is the miniature
mecca, Gault, on the Rue de Rivoli.

Lunch

McDonald's
184 Rue de Rivoli
Keep your eyes open for one of their
Disney tie-ins or toy promotions.

Afternoon
Walk to Au Nain Bleu, Paris' largest toy
store, on the Rue St Honoré and spend
the rest of the afternoon trying to get your
kids to leave.

Nature et Découvertes
Carrousel du Louvre, 1st

✆ 01 47 03 47 43
See p.123

La Ciel est à tout la Monde
Carrousel du Louvre, 99 Rue de Rivoli, 1st
✆ 01 49 27 93 03
See p.131

Gault
206 Rue de Rivoli, 1st
✆ 01 42 60 51 17
See p.131

Au Nain Bleu
406–410 Rue St Honoré, 8th
✆ 01 42 60 39 01
Ⓜ Concorde, Madeleine
See p.131

Paris from below

The mole's eye view of Paris: spend the
day almost entirely below ground.

Morning
Take the métro to Ⓜ Denfert Rochereau for
a visit to the Catacombs, or 'Empire of the
Dead' – six million skeletons stacked in
neatly arranged piles.

Lunch
Take the métro to Ⓜ Palais Royal-Musée
du Louvre for a meal at one of the
Carrousel du Louvre's subterranean cafés.

Afternoon
Take the métro to Ⓜ Alma Marceau for the
Paris Sewers, *Les Egouts,* where you can
take a tour of part of the network.

The Catacombs
1 Place Denfert Rochereau, 14th
✆ 01 43 22 47 63
See p.84

Les Egouts – The Paris Sewers
Entrance opposite 93 Quai d'Orsay
by Pont de l'Alma, 7th
✆ 01 53 68 27 81
See p.55

Paris from above

The bird's eye view of Paris: from the numerous elevated viewing points around the city:

In the north

Sacre Coeur
34 Rue de Chevalier de la Barre, 18th
✆ 01 53 41 89 00
Ⓜ Abbesses, Anvers
From the steps in front of the basilica.
See p.88

In the centre

Pompidou Centre
Rue Rambuteau, 4th
Rue Beaubourg, 4th
✆ 01 44 78 12 33
Ⓜ Hôtel de Ville, Rambuteau
RER: Châtelet-Les Halles
From the escalators and particularly from the top floor and the café.
See p.60

Samaritaine
19 Rue de la Monnaie, 1st
✆ 01 40 41 20 20
Ⓜ Pont Neuf, Châtelet
From the top floor terrace and café.
See p.45

Notre Dame
Place du Parvis Notre Dame, 4th
✆ 01 42 34 56 10
Ⓜ Cité
RER: St-Michel-Notre-Dame

From the bell tower.
See p.70

In the south

Tour Montparnasse
33 Avenue du Maine, 15th
✆ 01 45 38 52 56
Ⓜ Montparnasse Bienvenüe
From the top floor.
See p.84

In the west

Arc de Triomphe
Place Charles de Gaulle, 8th
✆ 01 55 37 73 77
Ⓜ/RER: Charles de Gaulle-Etoile
From the top, looking up the Champs-Elysées towards the Place de la Concorde, and down the Avenue de la Grande Armée towards the Grande Arche de la Défense.
See p.43

Eiffel Tower
Champ de Mars, 7th
✆ 01 44 11 23 45
Infoline: ✆ 01 44 11 23 23
Ⓜ Bir-Hakeim, Trocadéro
RER: Champ-de-Mars
Paris' must-see viewing point.
See p.50–1

Fortis Balloon
Parc André Citroën
Ⓜ Javel, Balard
Paris' newest viewing point; open until the end of 2000.
See p.111

In the far west

Grande Arche de la Défense
✆ 01 49 07 27 57
Ⓜ/RER: La Défense
See p.44

bored kids

Even though Paris is one of the most exciting cities on earth, it is still possible, if not probable, that your children will, at some point utter the two words guaranteed to send the anxiety levels of the calmest parent soaring – 'I'm bored!' What to do? They've seen the sights, watched the film, eaten the ice cream and they're still kicking their heels. You may have your own tried and trusted techniques for entertaining the, kids but if these fail at any point then the following suggestions may be of some help.

Games

The following games are probably the sort of tactics your parents used on you. They have proved successful and, what is more, there is no need for pricey technical equipment. Use these to jog your memory.

20 questions

Think of a person or object. Everyone must take it in turns to guess what or who this is by asking no more than 20 questions, which can only be answered with a simple 'yes' or 'no'. A variation on this game is Who am I? in which players take it in turns to be a famous person. Everybody else has to guess who you are by asking simple 'yes' or 'no' questions.

Can you see it?

Do a squiggly doodle on a piece of paper and see if someone else can turn it into a picture in 20 seconds.

Charades

Good for the evening. One person selects a book, film, TV programme or character to act out. The other players take turns to guess what this is. The player miming can prompt ideas by acting out associated themes. The player who guesses correctly gets the next turn.

Consequences

Each person writes their name at the top of a piece of paper, folds the top over to conceal the writing, then passes it on. Give a linking phrase ('met', 'went to', 'he said') and ask everyone to write a two- or three-word phrase to complete the line, folding over the paper each time, then passing it on, so nobody knows what anyone else has written. Carry on for six or seven lines.

Finally, unfold the papers and read the short stories aloud. A sample might be

(Edie)
went to… (the moon)
and she met… (a happy face)
they said… (We like sweets)
and decided to go to…(Auntie's house)
but on the way they… (fell asleep)
so they decided to… (rob banks).

You can play the same game by drawing the head of a creature at the top of the paper, folding the paper and passing it on. The next person draws a chest, the next a tummy, the next the legs and so on, folding the paper over each time to conceal the emerging remarkable monster.

I spy

I spy with my little eye something beginning with… Take it in turns to see what you can spot in Paris or Disneyland. Everyone else has to guess. A trifle dull, but reliable.

Three popular French rhymes

Frère Jacques, Frère Jacques
Dormez-vous? Dormez-vous?
Sonnez les matines, Sonnez les matines
Dig, ding, dong! Dig, ding, dong!

Sur le pont d'Avignon
On y danse, on y danse
Sur le pont d'Avignon
On y danse, tout en rond.

Au clair de la lune
Mon ami Pierrot
Prête-moi ta plume
Pour écrire un mot
Ma chandelle est morte
Je n'ai plus de feu
Ouvre-moi ta porte
Pour l'amour de Dieu.

Toys

Anything that can keep children amused is worth taking. It can rain a lot in Paris and even though there is plenty to do indoors, it is still a good idea to bring a few well-chosen games from home to pass the time.

Toys to take

✿ Any large, snap-together plastic construction bricks, such as stickle bricks, Duplo or Mega Bloks. Losing one or two won't be a great tragedy.

✿ Hand puppets for their outstanding versatility. They are always a mood lifter.

✿ Non-stain, washable colouring pens. Enough said.

✿ A disposable, automatic camera for a kid's eye view of the trip. (Boots make a Photo Bug throw-away. Fisher Price make a kid's first 35mm.)

✿ The classic travel toys, Etch a Sketch and Magna Doodle. Pocket versions are now available too.

Toys to leave behind

▲ Irreplaceable favourites which might get mislaid.

▲ Toys with a seriously heavy battery consumption.

▲ Wax crayons. They can melt and are messy.

▲ Play dough which smears, squelches, stains, then tends to dry up and crack.

▲ Talking toys with a mind-numbingly repetitive tone and limited vocabulary.

▲ Toys with lots of crucial parts which can easily get lost, dropped or jammed in tight spots.

Hand-held video games

There is no denying it. Over the age of three, a hand-held video game has to be top of the diversion list. Market leader is the Nintendo GameBoy which has seen off its competitors for the 10th year running. Over 70 million have now been sold worldwide.

A recent addition, the compact GameBoy Pocket, is ideal for travel, as it is 50 per cent lighter and 30 per cent smaller than its chunky big brother. A large part of the GameBoy's appeal is its versatility. Regardless of your children's ages, you will find over 1000 multi-level games to suit every conceivable taste and skill level. A few accessories will transform it into a digital camera with its own printer. Even more valued is the revamped GameBoy Color with its vivid, high resolution colour graphics on a new reflective screen.

Electronic learning toys

Interactive learning games are big right now. Alongside companies such as IQ Builders and Leap Frog, award winners Vtech probably make the best range. You can contact Vtech on ✆ UK (01235) 555545 and US (212) 206 0890. The following are some of their best sellers:

Moosical Beads ages 6–30 months

Nursery Rhymes Book ages 3–24 months

Alphabet Desk ages 2–5

Pocket Quiz age 7 upwards

IT Laptop age 11 upwards

Boxed toys

Parker Toys, MB Games and Waddingtons each produce compact travel versions of classic board games such as Cluedo, Monopoly, Scrabble, Connect 4 and Battleships, some with magnetized boards and pieces. Living and Learning, ✆ UK (01945) 463441, make an especially good range of colourful, easily manageable box packs. Alternatively, a simple deck of cards and peg-board versions of games such as chess can prove real winners too. Pin Toy, ✆ UK (01664) 64258, have portable versions of perennial peg favourites Solitaire, Tic-Tac-Toe and Chinese Checkers.

For the baby

Plenty of toys especially designed to captivate your baby will allow you to concentrate on the task at hand. You can buy all sorts of mobile, fold-away diversions that are ideal for keeping your baby amused and helping develop their motor skills at the same time.

One early favourite consists of eye-catching cards which you slot into transparent pockets and attach by velcro to the back of your travel seat. On one side are bold black and white geometric patterns to encourage your baby's focusing ability. On the reverse are basic patterns of sharply contrasting colours intended to engage slightly older babies. This theme is now being used on all sorts of soft toys.

Wrist and sock rattles are are an ideal distraction for babies still finding their hands and feet. Colourful, multi-sensory play mats and activity centres, too, combine all sorts of noises and textures to enhance your baby's sensory awareness.

Peek-a-boo doors, fun sound effects, squeezy figures, mirrors, rattles, shape sorters and teething rings team up together to keep little ones occupied. The most useful portable versions have a clamp which can attach easily to your baby carrier, pushchair, cot, bouncer-seat, or table – in fact just about anywhere.

Most baby retailers and kid's mail order catalogues should have a range of innovative designs. Tomy, Playskool, Mattel, Chicco and Fisher Price are some of the more dependable names to keep an eye out for. Baby Basics, ✆ UK (01793) 697300, MOM, ✆ UK (01225) 332223, and Letter Box, ✆ UK (01872) 580885, are mail-order companies featuring a great selection of toys for newborns upwards.

Four good toy shops

Au Nain Bleu
406–410 Rue St Honoré, 8th
✆ 01 42 60 39 01
Ⓜ Concorde, Madeleine

Baby Rêve
32 Avenue Rapp, 7th
✆ 01 45 51 24 00
Ⓜ Ecole Militaire

La Ciel est à tout la Monde
Carrousel du Louvre, 99 Rue de Rivoli, 1st
✆ 01 49 27 93 03
Ⓜ Palais Royal-Musée du Louvre

10 Rue Gay Lussac, 5th
✆ 01 46 33 53 91
Ⓜ Luxembourg

L'Oiseau de Paradis
211 Boulevard St Germain, 7th
✆ 01 45 48 97 90
Ⓜ Rue du Bac

best of
kids' Paris

Here it is, the pick of Paris for younger visitors: our choice of all the best things to see, eat, visit, shop, ride in and play with in France's capital city.

Best animal attraction
Zoo de Paris at the Bois
de Vincennes, *see* p.109–10.

Best annual jamboree
New Year's Day Parade along the
Grand Boulevards, *see* p.151.

Best café
Le Mosque de Paris, *see* p.85.

Best Christmas experience
Skating on the outdoor ice rink by
the Hôtel de Ville, *see* p.120.

Best church
Sainte Chapelle, *see* p.72–3.

Best cinema
The Géode, *see* p.95.

Best firework display
Bastille Day, *see* p.152.

Best funfair
Summer in the Jardin des Tuileries,
see p.39.

Best for gruesomeness
Conciergerie, *see* p.72, or Les
Egouts (The Sewers), *see* p.55.

Best interactive fun
Cité des Sciences et de l'Industrie,
see p.94–5.

Best market
Marché aux Puces, *see* p.90.

Best museum
Musée National d'Histoire Naturelle,
see p.78–80, or Musée de la
Curiosité et de la Magie, *see* p.62.

Best park
Jardin d'Acclimatation in the
Bois de Boulogne, *see* p.109.

Best restaurant
Altitude 95 on the first floor of
the Eiffel Tower, *see* p.133.

Best shop
Au Nain Bleu, *see* p.131, or
Nature et Découvertes, *see* p.123.

Best sightseeing tour
Bateaux Mouches, *see* p.112.

Best sporting event
Tour de France, *see* p.152–3,
or Course des Garçons et
Serveuses de Café (The Race
of the Waiters), *see* p.152.

Best statue
The 'Stravinsky', *see* p.60.

Best view
Third floor of the Eiffel Tower,
see p.50.

Disneyland® PARIS

Introduction

I think what I want Disneyland to be most of all is a happy place, a place where adults and children can experience together some of the wonders of life, of adventure and feel better because of it.

Walt Disney

Step through the gates of Disneyland® Paris, and you enter one man's fantasy: a cloistered place, isolated from the risks, conflicts and cares of life; litter-free, pretty with perfect flower beds and pastel-coloured buildings; where cartoon characters loom larger than life and classic tales are enacted, fizzed up by thrilling rides and showbiz razzmatazz.

Surrender! Whether you are 2 or 62 years old, sick with excitement or resigned and already exhausted, to get the most out of this truly extraordinary place you must allow yourself to explore it with, or through, the eyes of a child. Just witnessing a child's reaction to all she encounters will be an experience in itself.

This guide takes a less than jaded look at the fabulous phenomenon of Disneyland Paris, Europe's most popular tourist attraction. Follow the advice we provide, and you and your children will have the most fantastic (and economical) time possible.

Survive and enjoy!

The man behind the mouse

Walter Elias Disney was born in Chicago, Illinois, in 1901. As a boy his family moved to Marceline, Missouri, in America's midwest, and bought a small farm. This idyllic setting remained with Walt like a sweet scent, and its turn-of-the-century charm fostered a yearning for romance and simple values which coloured his creative vision for the rest of his life. Main Street, USA is said to be a carefully crafted homage to Marceline.

Getting started

Walt began to draw in high school, and studied cartoon creation in his spare time. Towards the end of the First World War he was working for an advertising agency in Kansas, where he met a talented young artist called Ub Iwerks. In 1922 the two young men started making short animated cartoons together under the studio name Laugh-o-Gram. It was the beginning of an historic creative partnership.

A year later, Walt moved to Los Angeles and re-established the studio with his elder brother, Roy, and Iwerks. They vaulted to fame in 1928 with *Steamboat Willie*, the first cartoon to use synchronized sound, which featured a certain spindly legged mouse called Mickey, whose squeaks were provided by Walt himself. Other animated hits followed. In 1937 Walt again made history, with *Snow White and the Seven Dwarfs*, the first feature-length, colour, animated movie – an enormous commercial and critical success.

A star is born

It was on a train journey that the idea of a cartoon mouse was first discussed. To pass the time, Walt and his wife, Lillian, put together a whimsical character based on the field mice which used to come into their old studio in Kansas. It was Walt's wife who came up with the name Mickey.

Walt's other big idea

Walt's vision was, perhaps, most famously put to use the day he sat on a park bench watching his daughter riding a merry-go-round. Growing increasingly bored, he wondered why there shouldn't be a place specially designed for the whole family to enjoy themselves, and not just the kids? The concept of the theme park, was born. The first park was opened in Anaheim, California, in 1955, and proved an instant success. Work swiftly began on a second site, in Florida. Sadly, Walt did not live to see its completion. A lifelong smoker, he died of cancer in 1966.

Disneyland® Paris

Disney began looking for a European site in 1985, and finally settled on a site near Paris. Work on the mammoth new complex started in August 1988 and involved over 2,000 suppliers, designers and architects (known as 'imagineers'), and some 8,000 construction workers.

A Disneyland Paris glossary

Audio-Animatronics®
A technological breakthrough pioneered by Walt Disney himself, Audio-Animatronics brings the art of animation to 3-D figures, synchronizing mechanical movement and sound effects to give life to many of the figures in the Theme Park.

Cast members
All Disney employees are referred to as cast members. They are trained performers, familiar with the rigorous standards drilled into them at The Disney University Training Center. Lesson no.1 – smile!

Guests
More than mere visitors or customers, you are made to feel a little more special by being addressed as Disney's guests.

Imagineers
The Imagineers turn dreams into reality. Armed with an ideology summed up in three words – imagine, design, build – they have produced such wonders as gold nuggets that really gleam and a tumble-down cowboy town right in the heart of Europe.

Passports
Your entrance tickets into the Theme Park; a reminder that you are entering a strange and exciting new country.

Pre-entertainment Area
Disney-speak for a queue!

Disneyland Paris' dominant landmark, Sleeping Beauty Castle, was unveiled to the public on 12 October 1991. The rest of the Theme Park was opened on 12 April 1992.

The Theme Park is located 20 miles (32km) to the east of Paris, covering an area one-fifth the size of the city. There are ambitious plans for expansion, and a second park is projected for Spring 2002.

> Disneyland will never be finished as long as there is a little imagination left in the world.
>
> Walt Disney

The Disney Years

1923 After his first animated film business fails, Walt and brother Roy start a tiny film studio in Hollywood where Walt directs the first Mickey Mouse cartoon, *Plane Crazy*.

1928 *Steamboat Willie* is the first cartoon with a soundtrack.

1930 Pluto's debut in *The Chain Gang*.

1932 *Flowers and Trees* wins Disney his first Academy Award.

1933 *Three Little Pigs* wins another Academy Award.

1934 *The Wise Little Hen* introduces a brand new character – Donald Duck.

1935 *Music Land*.

1937 *Snow White and the Seven Dwarfs*, the first full-length animated, colour film is a resounding success.

1940 *Fantasia* and *Pinocchio*.

1941 Acclaim grows as *Dumbo* wins an Academy Award for Best Original Score.

1942 *Bambi*.

1943 Donald Duck appears in *Der Führer's Face*, a humourous dig at Nazi Germany.

1948 *Seal Island* is the first of a string of successful nature films.

1950 *Treasure Island* is the first Disney film to use live actors.

1951 *Alice in Wonderland*.

1953 *Peter Pan*.

1954 *20,000 Leagues Under the Sea*.

1955 Launch of the *The Mickey Mouse Club* TV show which continues to draw in audiences for the next four years. Its success coincides with the opening of Disneyland in California. *Davy Crockett – King of the Wild Frontier* and *Lady and the Tramp*.

1959 *Sleeping Beauty*.

1960 *Swiss Family Robinson*.

1961 *One Hundred and One Dalmations*.

1963 *The Sword in the Stone*.

1964 Academy Awards for *Mary Poppins*.

1967 *The Jungle Book*.

1969 *The Love Bug*.

1970 *The Aristocats*.

1971 Disney World opens in Florida.

1973 *Robin Hood*.

1977 *The Many Adventures of Winnie the Pooh*.

1982 Epcot Center (Experimental Prototype Community of Tomorrow) opens in Florida.

1984 Disney President, Walt's son-in-law Ron Miller, starts up Touchstone Pictures to rekindle failing audiences, and produces *Splash*. The film's success coincides with the opening of Tokyo Disneyland.

1988 Mickey's 60th birthday is a double celebration, as *Who Framed Roger Rabbit* wins four Academy Awards.

1989 Disney-MGM Studios Theme Park opens in Florida.

1990 Disney establishes Hollywood Records, a mainstream record label. The same year, *The Little Mermaid* wins two Academy Awards.

1991 *Beauty and the Beast*.

1992 Disneyland® Paris opens amid (subsequently unfounded) French concern over the Park's potential bad effect on the nation's culture.

1993 *Aladdin*.

1994 Disney releases box-office sensation, *The Lion King*, which wins an Academy Award for Elton John's score.

1995 *Pocahontas* and *Toy Story* are released. *Pocahontas* brings in over $140 million and is the third largest grossing film of the year.

1999 *A Bug's Life* and *Tarzan*™.

Contents

The Top 10

1. Space Mountain
2. Big Thunder Mountain
3. Pirates of the Caribbean
4. Star Tours
5. Phantom Manor
6. Honey, I Shrunk the Audience
7. Indiana Jones™ and the Temple of Peril: Backwards!
8. Peter Pan's Flight
9. Blanche-Neige et les Sept Nains
10. Les Voyages de Pinocchio

Booking

The price difference between the major operators is negligible and you won't save much by going it alone. If immersion in the Disney experience is your aim, you should book direct with Disneyland® Paris or one of the dedicated operators who offer added frills. But if you only want to visit the Theme Park for part of your holiday, then plan your own trip or choose an operator offering combined holidays.

Booking through Disneyland® Paris

✆ UK (08705) 030303,
✆ USA (407) 934 7639
✆ 01 60 30 60 53
(lines are open until late, 7 days a week)
www.disney.co.uk

Covers all the hotels on site, plus a selection of 3- and 4-star hotels off site (including several in Paris). Packages on offer include transport via Eurostar, ferry or scheduled flights. Each package also incorporates breakfast and unlimited access to the Theme Park.

Specialist tour operators

A handful of operators are recognized by Disneyland® Paris, as healthy competition. The main advantage of booking with a specialist company is that many of its staff will have visited the resort, and will be able to answer your questions and offer advice.

Bridge Travel Service

✆ UK (01992) 456651
selfdrive@bridge-travel.co.uk

Multi-centre holidays, combining Disneyland® Paris with some of the best family-friendly destinations in Europe.

Cresta Holidays

✆ UK (0161) 926 9999

A wide choice of hotels, plus scheduled flights from 18 UK airports, Eurostar, and self-drive or coach transport to the resort. Special offers and free kids' places.

Eurocamp

✆ UK (01606) 787878
www.eurocamp.co.uk
enquiries@eurocamp.co.uk

Family accommodation at the Davy Crockett Ranch® or at a range of other campsites within easy reach of the resort.

Going Places

✆ UK (0161) 908 7950

Transport to the resort by Eurostar, or by air from the UK's main airports. Both options include transfers to Disneyland® Paris hotels. If you want to take your car, there is a choice of cross-channel ferry routes, or Le Shuttle.

Leger Coach Tours

✆ UK (01709) 839839
www.leger.co.uk

Transport by coach from over 300 locations across England and Wales. In addition to the Disneyland® Paris hotels, Leger feature Ibis, Holiday Inn, Campanile and Mercure hotels, with transport to and from the Theme Park at the beginning and end of each day.

Osprey Holidays

✆ UK (0990) 605 605

Scheduled flights from Edinburgh and Glasgow year round, and on certain flights from Newcastle. The package includes coach transfers on both outward and return journeys, unlimited entry to the Theme Park and accommodation at any of the Disneyland® Paris hotels.

Paris Travel Service

✆ UK (01992) 456100

disney@bridge-travel.co.uk

Holidays combining central Paris and Disneyland® Paris can be arranged.

Thomson

✆ UK (020) 8210 4575

Transport options include Eurostar, self-drive with Le Shuttle and P&O Stena Line, or flights from many regional UK airports.

Travelscene

✆ UK (020) 8427 4445

Budget programme with travel by Eurostar and accommodation at an off-site hotel within easy reach of the Theme Park.

Two-centre holidays

For those who do not wish to spend their entire time at Disneyland Paris, several major operators offer two-centre holidays, combining a stay in central Paris with a day or more in the Theme Park.

British Airways

✆ UK 0870 242 4243

Eurostar Holidays Direct

✆ UK 0870 167 6767

Keycamp

✆ UK (020) 8395 4000.

Kirker

✆ UK (020) 7231 3333

Magic Cities

✆ UK (020) 8563 8959

Other booking options

Both the Internet and, in the UK, Teletext are a good bet for finding last-minute and discounted package fares. The majority of companies you come across are established and respectable – a few are not.

What will it cost?

Park entry
high season adult *c*. £23, child *c*. £18, low season adult *c*. £17, child *c*. £14

By Eurostar (return)
Apex adult fare from £89, Apex child fare (4–11 years) £55

By ferry (return)
c. £135 for a car and up to 9 people

By air (return)
c. £70 for cheapest adult fare (*c*. £40 for child aged 3–11 years).

Always check for the IATA and ATOL symbols, which will guarantee that your money is safe in the unlikely event that the company folds. Three UK companies worth considering are:

Frenchlife
✆ UK (0113) 259 0777

Magical Breaks
✆ UK (020) 8324 4033

MAT Travel
✆ UK 0870 700 8543

Theme Park entry

Buying tickets at the Park gates is not recommended as it takes you much longer to get in. Tickets, or 'passports', are available in advance from:

▪ Any Disney Store in the UK.

▪ Thomas Cook Bureaux de Change at the UK Eurotunnel Passenger Terminal, and Dover and Portsmouth ferry terminals.

▪ On board P&O Stena Line Ferries sailing between Dover and Calais.

▪ The Disney Store and Virgin Megastore, Champs-Elysées, Paris.

▪ Paris Tourist Offices at Orly and Roissy-Charles de Gaulle airports, and on the Champs-Elysées, Paris.

Disneyland connections

By road

From central Paris

The Theme Park is about 20 miles (32km) east of Paris. Head southeast (take the Porte de Bercy exit from the Périphérique) and pick up the A4 motorway (Autoroute de l'Est) east toward Metz-Nancy. Follow signs for Marne-la-Vallée until you see the exit signs for 'Parc Disneyland' with a picture of Mickey (junction 14 from the A4).

From the airport

From Roissy-Charles de Gaulle Airport, follow signs for Marne-la-Vallée on the A104 (La Francilienne). After some 17 miles (27km), exit from the A104 to the A4 in the direction of Metz-Nancy. From Orly Airport head towards Paris, following signs for Créteil on the A86. Exit on to the A4 towards Metz-Nancy. Exit 13, for the Theme Park, is 17 miles (27km) along this road.

Self-drive

Disneyland® Paris is easily accessible by car thanks to the excellent French motorway system. The following gives an idea of how much time to allow once you disembark.

Top tips

▲ The Davy Crockett Ranch® is a short way from the main complex, on the other side of the A4, so watch out for the separate signs (junction 13 Provins-Serris).

▲ Major roads in France now have both a local Autoroute (A) number and a newer Euroroute (E) designation.

Boulogne	3 hours
Caen	2.5 hours
Calais	3 hours
Cherbourg	4.5 hours
Dieppe	3 hours
Le Havre	2.5 hours

Airport bus transfers

Paris has two airports: Roissy-Charles de Gaulle (CDG) and Orly. Buses run seven days a week at 45-minute intervals starting at 8.30am and continuing until 7.45pm. The Friday and Sunday service from CDG runs every 30 minutes until 10.30pm. All the bus pick-up points are signposted 'Navettes (Shuttle) VEA Disneyland Paris'.

CDG Terminal 1
Go to Departure Level Gate 30

CDG Terminals 2A and 2C
Use Gate A-11 or C-1

CDG Terminals 2B and 2D
Use Gate D-12

CDG Terminals 2F
Use Gate E

Orly South (International)
Coach Station, Platform 2

Orly West (Domestic)
Use Gate C, Level 0

Tickets cost 85F per adult or 65F per child (aged 3–11) each way. Taxis are also available; the fare will be around 300F.

VEA
✆ 01 64 30 66 56

Automatic information service
✆ 01 49 64 47 08

By rail

Direct by Eurostar from the UK

A dedicated daily service runs from London Waterloo, Mondays to Saturdays at 9.27am, and on Sundays at 9.14am. Return journeys from Disneyland leave daily at 7.35pm. The service operates between April and September, as well as during the February half-term and Christmas school holidays. A weekend service operates year round, leaving Waterloo on Friday and returning on Sunday. The trip takes three hours. Passport control, and even check-in at your resort hotel, can be done either at Waterloo or once you are on the train. Under the same system, you can have your luggage sent to the station ahead of you on your departure. Kids receive a free Disney pack. On arrival, you are greeted by Disney characters on the station platform, which is only minutes from the Theme Park.

Non-direct Eurostar services

When there are no direct services available, you can take the Eurostar as far as Lille (two hours) and change platforms to a TGV (high-speed train), which will deliver you to the Theme Park within 90 minutes. Eurostar to Paris (three hours) is less convenient, as it involves either a hike at Gare du Nord to the Châtelet-Les Halles RER (overground train), or a more complex switch via the métro. You can telephone the Eurostar booking line on ✆ UK 0990 186 186.

To get to the Theme Park via Lille contact Rail Europe ✆ UK 0990 848 848, who will be able to book both the Eurostar and TGV connection for you in advance.

Don't miss the train!

Eurostar's service adheres to strict security codes. Much the same as when taking a scheduled flight, you are expected to check in (at least 20 minutes before the train is due to depart). Otherwise the gates are closed and your ticket is rendered useless.

TGV rail connections

The TGV railway station at Disneyland® Paris allows for rail connections from Lyon (1 hour 45mins) and Lille (90mins), offering full flexibility for access to the Theme Park.

UK passengers arriving via the Channel Tunnel should change at Lille (not Paris) to join the TGV route for Roissy-Charles de Gaulle airport and on to Disneyland Paris.

RER express train from Paris

The quickest way to get straight to Disneyland Paris from the capital is to take the RER 'A' express train. It takes 40 minutes and drops you at the Theme Park gates. Trains run until 12 midnight.

You can pick up the RER 'A' line from any station on the eastbound Torcy A4 route. Suitable stations within the central Paris métro area are Ⓜ La Défense (business district), Ⓜ Charles de Gaulle-Etoile (Arc de Triomphe), Ⓜ Auber (Opéra) Ⓜ Châtelet-Les Halles (central Paris), Ⓜ Gare de Lyon (major TGV train station) and Ⓜ Nation.

Make sure you purchase an RER ticket before you board as Paris métro tickets are not valid. Also note that this is a branch route so check that your train is heading in the direction of Marne-la-Vallée–Chessy, and that it actually stops there.

For current details, there is an English-language RER information line on ✆ 83 66 84 114 (calls are charged at the Premium Rate of 2F per minute).

On arrival

The closer they get to Disneyland® Paris, the more excited children become. Getting them to sit tight and *be-have!* is impossible as soon as they realise Mickey and friends are just minutes away. And when they finally reach the Theme Park, and join the throng of other children passing through the main gates, the thrill of their shared anticipation is almost palpable.

At the station

The Marne-la-Vallée–Chessy station is located between Disney® Village and the Theme Park entrance, just a couple of minutes' walk from the main gates.

When you step off the direct Eurostar service you are ushered up the escalators to the first floor. There, you are greeted by Disney characters who guide you towards a shuttle bus which takes you to your hotel.

If you arrive under your own steam and already have a Disneyland® Paris hotel booked, head upstairs to the Disney Express Counter on the first floor, where you can drop off your luggage to be transported to your hotel ahead of you. This leaves you free to head straight to the Theme Park and leave the tiresome jobs of checking-in and unpacking until later. The service costs 25F per item, unless you have booked a package which specifically includes hotel and luggage transfer.

There are lockers at the station, but you will probably find it more convenient to use the lockers located just within the Main Gate of the Theme Park itself. There are also currency exchange booths on the first floor of the station, but there are more scattered throughout the resort, so do not feel you have to exchange all your money in one go.

Turn right after leaving the station building to get to the Theme Park, or left for Disney® Village and the hotel complex. If you would rather freshen up first and explore later, then head left and follow the station building around to the bus station from which the free shuttle service to the hotel complex leaves every few minutes.

Top tips

- 🌀 For drivers, a 24-hour Esso Service station is located by Hotel Sante Fe®.
- 🌀 You can leave and re-enter the Park as often as you like each day provided you have your hand stamped with a pass-out permit, available at the right-hand set of exit gates.
- 🌀 There are lockers at the station, but it is more convenient to use the ones just inside the main gates.
- 🌀 An excellent information office is located in the main forecourt of Marne-la-Vallée station which can give details of any travel arrangements you may want to make out of the Park.

At your hotel

Check-in can be a drawn-out process. The main snag is that you cannot book in until 3pm. Cast members are well trained in apologizing and enthusiastically suggesting that you leave your luggage with them and head straight for the Theme Park. If you have arrived by coach or car, this may be the last thing you feel like doing. If this is the case, head instead for a snack at one of the hotel bars or restaurants, take a stroll around Lake Disney® or make for the shops and eateries at Disney® Village, less than five minutes away.

All the hotels are within walking distance of the entrance gates to the Theme Park, although, to make life even easier, a fleet of yellow shuttle buses whirl around the resort at frequent intervals, delivering guests close to the turnstiles. There are free car parks at each of the Disneyland® Paris hotels. A valet parking service is available at the Disneyland® Hotel and Hotel New York®.

At the car park

The visitors' car park has room for 12,000 cars. Each row of parking spaces is named after a Disney character – Alice, Bambi, Donald, Fleur, Jiminy, Minnie, Pinocchio, Winnie and Tigger (who is reserved for coaches). Take care to make a note of the name of the row in which you have parked, along with the number and letter of your individual parking space.

Parking is free for all hotel guests and Annual Plus passport holders.

A moving walkway links the main car park to the centre of the resort, next to the railway station. There is a picnic area at the end of the walkway, and an Animal Care Centre for boarding pets during your stay.

A special car park reserved for disabled visitors is located nearer to the entrance to the Theme Park.

Guest parking

Motorbikes and side-cars
25F per day (20F after 5pm)

Cars
40F per day (20F after 5pm)

Campers and caravans
60F per day

At the main gates

The car park walkway and the railway station both lead into Disney Square. From there head for the magnificent floral gardens sculpted into the shape of Mickey. To reach the main entrance turnstiles you will need to pass under the Disneyland® Hotel.

If you have not been issued with an entry ticket (known as a Disneyland® Paris Passport), queue at the ticket booths. A child passport is available for children aged between three and eleven years. Children under the age of three are admitted free.

A one-day Passport gives unlimited access to nearly all the Theme Park attractions. (There are a few exceptions, such as the video games, for which you have to pay a nominal pay-to-play fee.) You can also buy a two- or three-day Passport, both of which are valid for the duration of the season (high or low) and need not be used on consecutive days.

It is worth remembering that credit cards and traveller's cheques are both accepted in the shops; you only need cash for arcade games and snack carts. Don't worry if you've forgotten to bring French francs, as there are several *bureaux de change* within the Theme Park.

Getting around

Disneyland® Paris

By shuttle bus

Free shuttle buses run every 12 minutes throughout the day (6.30am–11.30pm), connecting the station at Marne-la-Vallée–Chessy, Disney® Village, the Theme Park gates and the Disneyland® Paris hotels (except the Disneyland® Hotel and Davy Crockett Ranch®). They start an hour before the Theme Park opens and stop at least an hour after it closes.

By railroad

A 20-minute round trip is a good way to acquaint yourself with the Theme Park layout. Steam trains chug around the perimeter, starting at Main Street Station and stopping at Frontierland Depot, Fantasyland and Discoveryland on the way. One arrives every 10 minutes or so. Railways were one of Walt Disney's passions, so it is no surprise that these four gleaming locomotives are a highlight of the Theme Park. Every detail is in place from whistles and smoke-stacks to cow-catchers and brass fittings. The carriages are open on one side, with excellent views of the Theme Park as you puff past.

On foot

Disneyland® Paris is quite manageable for adults but, bearing in mind the sheer scale of the place, you will see plenty of quite sizeable kids in strollers. Being a wheelchair-friendly site, these can be used here with ease. Wide shop doors and aisles, generous sidewalks and stroller bays at the entrance to many of the rides keep them from knocking too many ankles in the crowd. If you find you overestimate your children's stamina, you can hire a pushchair for the day within Town Square Terrace (adjacent to the station). The fee is 30F.

By streetcar

In playful contrast to France's high-tech public transport system, the only other modes of transport date from the same era as the railroad. Horse-drawn streetcars offer a trip in reproduction trams of the last century, drawn by magnificent Percheron or Shire horses. They stop at the bandstand in the centre of Town Square. There are elegant vintage vehicles too. Among these are a limousine, a police paddy-wagon and a red fire truck. Simply queue up at the bus-stop outside Ribbons & Bows Hat Shop in Town Square to take a short ride up Main Street, USA and on to Central Plaza.

Guided tours

Guides are on hand to take you on a walking tour. They can provide information about the Theme Park as well as its creator, Walt Disney. Tours last two hours. You can book in advance on ✆ 01 60 45 67 76, or enquire at the main entrance or City Hall on Town Square. The cost is 50F for adults and 35F for children.

The surrounding area

By public transport

On the whole, the Paris public transport system is safer, cleaner and more reliable than anywhere else in Europe. *See* pp.15–17 for more details. In brief, a métro ticket costs 8F while a carnet of 10 tickets will save you money at 55F.

To explore in more depth, get a Paris-Visite tourist ticket, which comes in one-, two-, three- or five-day versions (e.g. a three-day, 5-zone pass costs 245F for adults, 120F for children). This allows unlimited travel on public transport: métro, bus and RER, and on SNCF trains both in Paris and the Ille-de-France Zones 1–5 (Disneyland Paris is in Zone 5). You will need your passport (your real one, not the Disneyland® Paris version) in order to purchase a ticket.

An all-inclusive three-day Parissimo ticket allows you unlimited travel by métro, bus, tram and RER and also includes entrance to the Louvre, plus free access to the Paris L'Open Tour tourist bus and Batobus tour boat which stops off at popular points along the Seine.

The first train for Paris leaves the resort station of Marne-la-Vallée–Chessy at about 5.15am. Thereafter, trains run every 10 to 30 minutes depending on the time of day. The journey lasts 40 minutes. Do make sure, before you board, that you are on the right side of the tracks. Here trains are categorized not according to the direction in which they are travelling, but by their destination station. This can be confusing if they run a different system at home. Lines are indicated by colour and a ringed number; a letter plus a number in the case of the RER lines. For more detailed information, call ✆ France (0836) 68 41 14.

By car

To tour the surrounding area for a few days, it is best to hire a car rather than bring your own. Hertz is the resort's official car-hire company, with a rental office at the Disneyland Paris agency in the Marne-la-Vallée–Chessy station. You can also book rental cars by pressing a Hertz button on your hotel room telephone or alternatively through the information desk at your hotel. Guests staying at the resort receive concessionary rates.

To be eligible for rental, you will need to produce a valid driving licence (held for at least one year) plus your passport (again your real one). An International Driving Permit is recommended for translation purposes but may only be used in conjunction with a National Driver's Licence. The minimum age for renting a car is 21; there is an additional charge for young drivers aged 21–25. Unless you have a major credit card, you will be asked to pay a sizeable refundable deposit.

By taxi

There is a taxi rank outside Marne-la-Vallée–Chessy station. You can also call or reserve taxis at any hotel reception.

Guided tours

Ask at the regional tourist office (Espace du Tourisme, Ile de France, Seine-et-Marne) in Disney® Village, or at the theme hotel receptions, for details of excursions to various places of interest. Most depart for Paris from the Hotel New York® at 10am and return at around 5.30pm. Prices vary, but a Paris day trip costs around 350F for adults and 175F for children. You can contact the tourist office direct on ✆ 01 60 43 33 33.

How things work

The Theme Park is rather better run than most military campaigns, which means that guests do not have much to do but stroll around, gawp, eat, ride, shop and have fun. Cast members are always on hand to help, so there is little you need to know before you arrive. Still, the following should be of use for the first-time visitor.

Babies

You will find a Baby Care Centre (*Relais Bébé*) at the top of Main Street, USA, next to the Plaza Gardens Restaurant. It provides a baby-changing area, a range of baby foods, drinks and nappies for sale, a microwave oven to heat food and milk, plus an area to feed your baby. Most of the toilets are equipped with a pull-down changing table.

Babysitting

A babysitter (*garde d'enfant*) can be booked through any of the hotels. At least two hours notice is required. Disneyland® Paris use an outside company, and the minimum qualification they demand is the same as that required by French summer camps. Up to two children can be cared for per babysitter. The cost structure allows a minimum charge for the first three hours and a set rate per half hour after that. There is an additional fee for all babysitting ending after 11pm.

Buggy hire

The convenience a buggy affords is worth the small outlay. You can rent a sizeable vehicle (to take two kids up to a total weight of 50kg) immediately to the right of the main entrance. There is a standing platform at the back for older kids and a tall pole for you to string all your bags around. Attach something easily identifiable to this and your children will be able to spot the buggy even if they briefly lose sight of you in the crowd. Hire buggies cannot be used outside the Theme Park. Buggies are offered on a first come, first served basis and the queues grow quickly. The cost is 30F per day.

Car parks

Both the hotel car parks and the Theme Park's car parks are free for hotel guests. Show your Disneyland® Paris ID card at the entrance. A separate car park for disabled visitors is next to the Disneyland® Hotel.

Cash

Cash dispensers are located within the Theme Park both in Liberty Arcade and Discovery Arcade (set behind the shops on either side of Main Street, USA). There is a cash machine in Discoveryland (next to the Constellations) and in Adventureland (between Hakuna Matata Restaurant and Colonel Haithi's Pizza Outpost). In Disney® Village, both the Post Office and Gaumont Cineplex have automatic cash dispensers.

You will find foreign exchange booths at the main entrance to the Theme Park and just inside the gates next to City Hall, as well as in Fantasyland and Adventureland. In Disney® Village, exchange facilities are at the post office and at the American Express agency. You can also change money at the hotels and at Marne-la-Vallée station. During your stay, you can pay with travellers cheques in francs or eurocheques just about anywhere.

Credit cards

All the major cards are accepted (American Express, Visa, Eurocard, Mastercard, Diners Club). As the official Disneyland® Paris credit card, American Express also gives cardholders certain privileges, including savings on a host of resort attractions. *See* **Saving Money**, p.245.

Dress code

Though you are pretty much free to wear whatever you want within the Theme Park, you are requested not to go barefoot or bare-chested. Swimwear is frowned upon. The importance of sensible walking shoes cannot be over stressed as there is a tremendous amount of ground to cover. As for rainwear, a lightweight pack-a-mac is a safe bet whatever time of year you visit.

Electricity

The local voltage is 220V.

First aid

First Aid is available next to the Plaza Gardens Restaurant at the far end of Main Street, USA, on Central Plaza. The Center is staffed by fully trained nurses and a doctor. Their services are free.

Guest information

City Hall, on the lefthand side of the entrance to Main Street, USA, is the Theme Park's central information point. There is also a seasonal information point at the far end of Main Street, USA, in Central Plaza. If you still have any unanswered questions or concerns head for the guest relations window situated to the righthand side of the main entrance as you approach the Theme Park, under the railway arch.

Language

Both French and English are official languages here. Though visual clues are used wherever possible, you will find written signs may be spelled out in just one language (but sometimes in both). Most of the attractions work without words. The few which depend upon narration are multi-lingual (English, French and German). If this is not the case, guests are supplied with headphones.

Laundry

Each of the hotels, including the Davy Crockett Ranch®, have coin-operated laundry facilities.

Lockers

Small coin-operated lockers can be found beneath the viaduct at Main Street Station (10F). For large or valuable items, there is a guest storage counter to the right of the main entrance turnstiles, under the railway arch next to guest relations (12F).

Lost & Found

Lost children are ushered towards the Relais Baby Centre, on Central Plaza at the far end of Main Street, USA. Missing items should be reported at City Hall on Main Street, USA. City Hall is also a good place to leave a message if you become separated from your companions. For guest relations at City Hall call ✆ 01 64 74 30 00. If you have already left the Theme Park for the day, there is a Lost & Found counter outside the entrance.

Opening hours

The Theme Park is open all year. In peak season it opens from 9am–11pm. In low season (Nov–April, excepting Christmas, the New Year and public holidays) it is open from 10am–6pm. For the remainder of the year, the Park is open (with some variations) between 9am and 8pm. Much depends on the weather conditions and demand. During peak season the gates may open up half an hour before the official time.

Pets

Besides guide dogs, pets are not allowed inside the Theme Park or anywhere else in the resort. An Animal Care Centre is located at the exit to the main car park. Fees are 50F per day (75F for an overnight stay). You are likely to be asked to produce certificates of health, proof of vaccination and a tattoo identification mark.

Post

Mail is collected daily from post boxes throughout the Theme Park. Stamps are available at several shops, including The Storybook Store on Main Street, USA, and in the hotels. The post office in Disney® Village is open from 11am–7pm (often later during high season) seven days a week, excluding public holidays. If you are staying at one of the hotels, you will find a post box in the lobby.

Photography and video

You are not permitted to take your own flash photographs or use video cameras within any of the attractions. Camera film, batteries and disposable cameras are available at several of the shops and at any of the hotel shops. At Town Square Photography on Main Street, USA you can get your films developed in an hour, and rent cameras and videos. Alternatively, you can take your films to Thunder Mesa Mercantile Building, Sir Mickey's or Star Traders.

Get the picture?

Keep an eye out for the Point Photo Kodak signs which direct you to the best vantage points for snaps. On Space Mountain and Big Thunder Mountain, photos are taken during the ride. These are available for you to buy (45F).

Smoking

Smoking is not permitted within the attractions, nor in the queuing areas. Most restaurants are divided into smoking and non-smoking areas.

Telephones

There are public telephones throughout the resort. Most are card operated. France Télécom phone cards may be purchased at the RER station, at the post office in Disney® Village and at various shops. All Disneyland® Paris hotel rooms feature direct-dial telephone. See p.31 for international dialling codes.

Toilets

Main Street, USA
- either side of Main Street Station
- next to the Barber Shop

Adventureland
- in the Adventureland Bazaar
- next to Colonel Hathi's Pizza Outpost

Frontierland
- next to Phantom Manor
- opposite Big Thunder Mountain
- next to the Legends of the Wild West

Fantasyland
- near the Toad Hall Restaurant
- next to Au Chalet de la Marionette
- near Pizzeria Bella Notte

Discoveryland
- in Videopolis
- between Orbitron and Autopia.

Disney® Village
- mainly in the restaurants

For safety reasons, several attractions are subject to age, height and health restrictions. Health limitations apply to pregnant women, and those who suffer from motion sickness or have heart, back, neck or similar problems.

Frontierland

Phantom Manor
This is dark and spooky and may frighten younger children.

Big Thunder Mountain
Minimum age: 3 years.
Minimum height: 1.02 metres.
Health limitations apply.

Adventureland

Pirates of the Carribbean
Cannon fire and battle scenes may frighten younger children. Health limitations apply.

Indiana Jones™ and the Temple of Peril: Backwards!
Minimum age: 8 years.
Minimum height of driver: 1.40 metres.
Health limitations apply.

Fantasyland

Dumbo the Flying Elephant
Minimum age: 12 months.

La Tanière du Dragon
Very dark and a bit smelly with a huge dragon, so may unnerve younger children.

Blanche-Neige et les Sept Nains
A bit dark at times, so may frighten young or nervous children.

Peter Pan's Flight
The unsteady flight and some startling scenes may frighten younger children.

Parent swap!

This scheme, available on ... , enables adults to take turns holding the baby and taking a ride. One adult queues as far as the loading area. Once there, he or she can enjoy the ride while the other keeps hold of any youngsters who are too small for the attraction. As the ride collects its fresh cargo, the adults are allowed to swap places without having to rejoin the queue.

Mad Hatter's Tea Cups.
Health limitations apply.

Discoveryland

Autopia
Minimum age: 12 months.
Minimum height of driver: 1.32 metres.
Health limitations apply.

Honey, I Shrunk the Audience
This is a pretty racy spectacle and may frighten younger children.

Orbitron
Minimum age: 12 months.
Health limitations apply.

Star Tours
Minimum age: 3 years.
Minimum height for post-ride computer game, Arcade de Jeux Vidéo: 1.02 metres.
Health limitations apply.

Space Mountain
Minimum age: 10 years.
Minimum height: 1.40 metres.
Health limitations apply.

Le Visionarium
Health limitations apply.

Whatever your preconceptions, Disneyland® Paris is likely to come as a surprise. It's a triumph of commercialism, yes, but it's also the product of one man's vision. And whilst you may be a hardened cynic, as soon as you pass through the magic gates you are likely to find a world that's bigger, brighter, busier, brasher, bolder, more beautiful and better fun than you imagined. It's unreal, of course, but it's not hollow or fake – which may be the biggest surprise of all.

A number of Internet sites contain information on Disneyland® Paris; often they offer revealing insights and anecdotes. Disneyland® Paris' official site, *www.disneylandparis.com*, has details of current and forthcoming special events, sound files and music clips and even video sequences. It's available in six languages (English, French, German, Spanish, Italian and Dutch).

The Ultimate Disney Links Page is an unofficial source of Disney theme park information, and contains a list of links to other Disneyland® Paris sites. Check it out at *www.magicnet.net/~tudlp/dlparis.html*.

Commercialism

The Theme Park manages to provide a saccharine cocktail of escapism and consumerism, mixed to such a perfect blend that spending money is all part of the experience.

✿ **Do bring cash, credit cards and traveller's cheques – otherwise, bring blinkers.**

⚠ **Don't charge everything to your hotel ID card without keeping a note of what you are spending.**

Doing it the Disney way

Once you enter the resort, you realize you are not really in France at all. You are in America; or at least an imitation of America, and almost immediately you also realize that everything in this little state comes under the watchful eye of the benevolent Disney machine.

From the moment you arrive to the moment you turn out the light at night, your actions are discreetly but firmly directed by a combination of recorded voices, robots and employees. Even an action as innocent as taking off your shoes will bring instant intervention. In the Theme Park itself, Disney use a combination of technology (security cameras hidden around the park), and physical barriers such as pools, fountains and flower gardens, to ensure, sweetly but undeniably, that you follow an itinerary conceived at the highest level.

In fact, this is not as menacing as it might at first appear. The Disneyland® Paris ethos, set by Walt at the outset, is to offer a complete escape, a total Disney 'experience'; which is something that clearly cannot be achieved without the exertion of a significant level of control. Buy into the dream, if only for a day, and you won't go far wrong.

✿ **Do comply.**

⚠ **Don't take it all too personally, especially if you are directed to do something. It is probably for a good reason.**

Cast members

All cast members have to be trained in and adhere to a system emphasizing safety, courtesy, efficiency and show. Everything they do is governed by the order of these points. Safety comes first and everything else takes a second place – including courtesy – if you or any other guest is in danger.

🌼 **Do** bear in mind that without a police force to take charge, the cast member's continual vigilance is paramount to the safe and efficient running of the Theme Park.

⚠ **Don't** under any circumstances attempt to cross a rope barrier, especially during a parade. That is just about equivalent to poisoning your granny here.

The rides

The Theme Park is essentially a fairground. The fact that kids are convinced Disney do it better is largely down to its five intricate 'film-set' lands, each with a legendary roller coaster at its heart and surrounded by must-do themed rides featuring classic cartoon characters. What kid would not want to boast they had been?

Disney has decreed that big thrills are what every kid needs, so there are plenty of credo-building, high-tech attractions drawing the biggest crowds. Accordingly, you can quite easily spend half your time in the **Theme** Park queuing for rides which rarely last more than three minutes each.

🌼 **Do** combine better known rides with the less overrun attractions.

⚠ **Don't** even bother queuing until you have read the Restrictions section (*see* p.185).

The parades

The attention span of the average child is generally little greater than that of a fish. However, stick one in front of a Disney parade and he or she will happily stand for half and hour or so, enthusiastically waving at Mickey and the rest of his affable pals. You should ensure you see at least the daytime extravaganza during your stay. It may seem like a waste of good riding time but your kids will never forgive you if you don't make it to at least one parade. They take place almost every afternoon at 3pm, and often again at 9pm.

The only difficulty is keeping an eye out for the veteran visitors with their own particular parade agenda. These seasoned Disney fans insist on muscling their way through to the front of the crowd. If they can't find a way through they will shove their kids through, then follow them. Unfortunately, wedging yourself in a position that blocks these pushy types out is impossible; they simply shove through in front of the rope barrier – incredibly dangerous at night when the float drivers can't see what they're doing. Then, safe in the knowledge that a cast member will warn them to step back, they will do so, right in front of you.

🌼 **Do** stake out your spot and be prepared to defend it with ferocious tenacity.

⚠ **Don't** give in to pushy kids; remember, they only become pushy adults!

For younger children

It's tempting to take even the youngest children to Disneyland® Paris: they waive the entrance fee for kids under the age of three, and the hotels don't charge for those under two if they share your room. Yet babies can get little from the experience; and subjecting fidgety infants and toddlers to a route march around the Theme Park, and to long queues for short rides, is sure to lead to tears and tantrums.

For kids under the age of four dark interiors, shaky carriages and eerie scenes on some of the rides may be unsettling. Though they are not signposted as unsuitable, Pirates of the Caribbean, Honey, I Shrunk the Audience, Blanche-Neige et les Sept Nains and Phantom Manor are among those that could create problems. If your child is nervy, ask a cast member for advice before you start queuing.
See **Restrictions**, p.185.

Limit yourself

Most younger children need no more than two low-key, classic rides, such as the Mad

Top tips

- Head for easy-flow attractions and those with plenty of space for your kids to wander without restriction.
- If you are in a Disneyland® Paris hotel, take a nap after lunch, especially in summer when the Theme Park is open until midnight.

Hatter's Tea Cups or Orbitron, during any one day. Around every corner they will be surprised by bright colours, ingenious Audio-Animatronics®, film-set constructions and costumed characters – all of which adds up to quite enough stimulation for the little ones, who have no need for relentless, high-tech, G-force excitement.

For the under 4s

The Disney characters are central to the Theme Park's appeal and you can find out the best time to meet and greet them by picking up a programme at the main entrance or City Hall. Characters tend to hang out by the Ribbons & Bows Hat Shop on the corner of Town Square each morning until lunchtime.

Outside the shop you can take a horse-drawn streetcar or vintage vehicle up Main Street, USA, to Central Plaza. Here a board details just how long queues are on some of the Theme Park's most popular rides.

Close by are the Fantasy Festival Stage and Le Théâtre du Château, which have character appearances and shows at set times throughout the day; some are subject to seasonal closure. You can also often have a souvenir photograph taken at Le Théâtre du Château.

If you do not intend to keep your youngsters up past bedtime for the Main Street Electrical Parade, you should try to catch the daytime parade, which wends it way down Main Street, USA from around 3pm onwards. Grab a kerbside spot at the Central Plaza end of Main Street, USA and watch your children's faces light up.

Fantasyland

The drawbridge leading to Sleeping Beauty Castle takes you into Fantasyland, which is probably the most suitable of the lands for young children. Here Le Carrousel de Lancelot, Mad Hatter's Tea Cups, 'it's a small world', Le Pays des Contes de Fées and Casey Jr. are gentle rides that little ones will probably enjoy. Nearby, Alice's Curious Labyrinth is a topiary maze dominated by the Queen of Hearts' castle and filled with the quirky characters from Lewis Carroll's story. It's an ideal spot to take photos.

Blanche-Neige et les Sept Nains, Les Voyages de Pinocchio, Dumbo the Flying Elephant and Peter Pan's Flight are not restricted for kids over a year old, but are probably best reserved for kids over two.

Frontierland

At Fantasyland Station you can take the railroad to Frontierland. From here the steam train passes through the Grand Canyon Diorama, a subtly lit tunnel containing a huge mural depicting sunrise to sunset in the Grand Canyon, enlivened by music, animated wildlife and sound effects.

Critter Coral has its own petting farm. Lambs, goats, rabbits, chickens and piglets are always a safe bet with toddlers. Your kids can wash their hands at the water-trough outside.

Close by is Pocahontas Indian Village, a scaled-down adventure playground with plenty of seats for worn out adults. It's a safe place to turn your children loose and allow them to let off steam.

Before you leave, enjoy a leisurely paddle-wheel riverboat ride on the *Molly Brown* or *Mark Twain* which board at nearby Thunder Mesa Riverboat Landing.

Adventureland

A short walk will take you to Adventureland, where many of the attractions are more activity based than elsewhere in the **Theme Park**. The central feature is Adventure Isle, a moated twin-isle connected by two suspended rope bridges. A network of wooden staircases leads you up winding stairs and down mysterious passages, into underground caves, past waterfalls, to Captain Hook's Galley and up to La Cabine des Robinson. It is a spectacular spot for kids who like clambering and exploring, though the under 4s may find there are too many steps to contend with and are sure to need a supporting hand over the more precarious parts. Some of the attractions are a bit dark as well, and may frighten younger children. Le Passage Enchanté d'Aladdin attracts few queues and is satisfying in much the same way as window shopping.

Discoveryland

It is worth leaving Discoveryland until last if you are with younger children. There isn't an awful lot for the under 4s to do here – the rides are too thrilling. The exceptions are Autopia and Orbitron, which are tame enough for the over 2s.

However, spectacular shows are staged each day at Videopolis. These are seldom scary, and production values are high enough to keep young kids spellbound for the duration of the show. Videopolis is also a good place to rest tired legs and have a bite to eat; it's huge, so there's always somewhere to sit down.

Meeting the characters

Many children come to the Theme Park with a single idea – they're about to come face to face with their favourite Disney characters. During the parades they strain to catch a glimpse then hop up and down, clapping wildly, as Baloo lumbers round the corner. Elsewhere, crowds of grinning kids threaten to topple Mickey or Donald in the crush for autographs. These are not just actors dressed up as Mickey or Baloo the Bear. This *is* Mickey. This *is* Baloo. This is real.

Good guys and bad guys

All the Disney characters are briefed to act out their specific roles to their utmost and, consequently, there is the odd occasion when they completely misjudge your child's reaction. Watch out especially for the baddies such as Hades (Hercules), Captain Hook (Peter Pan), Prince John (Jungle Book) and Stromboli and Gideon (Pinocchio). Stromboli makes a habit of snatching children's toys. Captain Hook lunges at you with his hook, and others sneer or growl menacingly. It's all done with good humour, of course, and though some children may find it confusing at first, most learn to play the game pretty quickly.

What children seem to enjoy most about the characters, however, apart from the excitement of being close to larger-than-life-size versions of their favourites, is the possibility that they might, just might, be singled out. It's absolutely thrilling for any child to dance with Cinderella, to be given a ticking off by Mary Poppins, to be noticed by the giant Hercules, or receive a hug from Mickey Mouse.

Where to find them

Hotels

Mickey and his pals put in an appearance at the hotels each day; times are listed under 'Just for the kids' in **Where To Stay** (from p.233). Both guests and day visitors are free to visit the characters at any of the hotels.

Character meals

You can dine with the characters throughout the day, and it is worth trying to incorporate one of these treats into your itinerary, especially if you have younger children. Baloo, Chip 'n' Dale, Minnie or Goofy joining you at your table is likely to be an experience that will linger with young children for years.

Top tips

⚙ You can watch the parades from anywhere behind a rope barrier so don't be put off if there's no one else around. Traditionally, Town Square is the last place to fill up and you can usually get a good spot here about 15 minutes before the parade kicks off.

⚠ Some characters suffer restricted vision, because of their costumes. It is dangerous to let young children walk behind them where they cannot be seen.

At both the Disneyland® Hotel's Inventions restaurant and at the Hotel New York®'s Manhattan restaurant, guests can book a special buffet breakfast with the classic characters. At the Davy Crockett Ranch®, Crockett's Tavern hosts a similar event. For other guests there is a character breakfast in the Los Angeles Bar & Grill in Disney® Village between 7am and 10.30am.

An all-you-can-eat brunch is available every Sunday from 12noon to 3pm at the Steakhouse Restaurant in Disney® Village. Tea with characters from *The Lion King* and *The Jungle Book* starts every day at 4.30pm at the Hakuna Matata restaurant in Adventureland.

Theme Park appearances

You can get an eyeful of the gang at the Park entrance on Main Street, USA each morning as you come in. Many more characters wander at leisure around the Theme Park, with set 'Meet and Greet' times throughout the day.

Shows

Special choreographed shows at Videopolis, Fantasy Festival Stage, Le Théâtre du Château and the Chaparral Theatre operate seasonally.

The parades

The best opportunity to see many of the characters together is during the daily parades which wind through the Theme Park, from Fantasyland down to Main Street, USA, culminating in the Town Square. During the daytime parade, children are regularly hand-plucked from the audience and invited to join in the action. Kitted out in miniature costumes they can find themselves fighting Captain Hook, being slipped into a sea shell to become a Little Mermaid or clowning around at the circus with Dumbo.

Disney's ImagiNations Parade

This is made up of seven giant floats, each at least 11m high. On board his airship, Mickey reigns supreme as ambassador of the parade overseeing the floats, each representing a different continent. Minnie Mouse presides over Asia, Chip 'n' Dale represent Africa, Daisy Duck is Australasia, followed by Donald Duck as South America and Goofy bringing up the rear as Europe.

Main Street Electrical Parade

During the summer, as darkness falls, the parade begins its journey through the Theme Park, lighting the way with glittering floats filled with Disney favourites. Over a million light bulbs illuminate the way for what is, by anyone's standards, a spectacular show of lights and sound.

For the very grand finale, and that all important 'ooh!' and 'ah!' factor, a fireworks display next to Sleeping Beauty Castle is topped by the appearance of an acrobatic Tinker Bell who flits and darts, leaving angel dust in her fiery trail.

Hidden Mickeys

Ever since the Theme Park opened, a sub-culture of committed fans has steadily reported sightings of 'hidden Mickeys' dotted around the attractions. Some of the hidden Mickey claims are outrageous, others are more cryptic, but Disney do confirm these subtle touches have been built into the Theme Park – so be sure to keep an eye out. Just a few of the reported sightings are listed here, to get you started.

Main Street, USA

City Hall

❀ There is a hidden Mickey on the clock. The back of the minute hand and hour hand of the clock are two black circles. When they are about 15 minutes apart, they make a perfect Mickey. The hands are the ears, the centre of the clock is the head.

Main Street Station

❀ While queuing for the train you come face to face with a glass mural. On the left is a castle decorated with circular patterns. One of these circles has two Mickey ears.

Liberty Arcade and Discovery Arcade

❀ In both arcades, there are gas lamps. If you invert the three rings, you can see a Mickey.

Frontierland

Riverboat Landing

❀ Look between the two smoke stacks on the paddle steamers and you will see an ironwork lattice with a gold star in the middle. To either side is a perfect hidden Mickey, turned sideways.

Big Thunder Mountain

❀ In the upstairs section of the queuing area is a balcony where you can look down on the queue. Directly below are three barrels. Together they form a hidden Mickey.

❀ Take a look at the out-of-order clock on the wall, facing the queue line, just to the right of the control tower. Mickey is on the hands of the clock.

Phantom Manor

❀ As you walk into the first chamber in Phantom Manor, look up at the ceiling. Above the chandelier in the middle of the room there is a design that forms a double hidden Mickey.

❀ The table setting in the ballroom scene reveals several hidden Mickeys.

Adventureland

Indiana Jones™ and the Temple of Peril: Backwards!

❀ Look at the front of any train. If you look hard, you will see an Inca-style Mickey.

Pirates of the Caribbean

❀ In the battle scene, the hole blown out of the castle wall is in the shape of a Mickey.

❀ Just before the burning town there is a crane suspending three barrels. When the barrels turn so that you view them end-on they form a hidden Mickey.

❀ In the treasure scene, right before the exit, are three tablets displayed on a heap of gold which make up a perfect Mickey.

Fantasyland

Sleeping Beauty Castle

❀ The lanterns on the back entrance of the castle each contain three bulbs – a big one and two smaller ones, which together form a hidden Mickey.

✿ Several of the roof tiles are a different colour and form a typical Mickey head.

Auberge de Cendrillon

✿ In the third room of the restaurant there is a raised area with a wrought-iron railing. The main repeated design in the ironwork is that of a full-figure Mickey.

'it's a small world'

✿ To the lefthand side of the clock on the front facia of 'it's a small world' you will see a panel going from top to bottom entirely made up of hidden Mickeys.

✿ Halfway through the ride you approach an Arabian scene (where the boat makes a sharp turn to the left). If you look towards the left of the scene as you float past you will see Mickey on the wall, rotated 90° counter-clockwise.

Toad Hall Restaurant

✿ In front there are two lamp posts containing the restaurant's menu. The lamps are made of black iron, with hidden Mickeys punched out all around them.

Blanche-Neige et les Sept Nains

✿ In the queue area is a mural with all the characters from the film in the background. In front of Happy's right foot are three flowers that form a hidden Mickey.

✿ Inside the attraction there are three fountains. Inside each one there are three lights which make up a hidden Mickey.

Les Voyages de Pinocchio

✿ Within the attraction there is a pool table. Look closely and you will see that the 8-ball has a hidden Mickey on it.

Peter Pan's Flight

✿ Just after the nursery, you see a painted roof. On the wall, there is a hidden Mickey.

Believe it or not

When the Theme Park is finally complete its outline will make up the biggest hidden Mickey of all. But you'll need a helicopter to spot it.

Alice's Curious Labyrinth

✿ On the taller beige observation stand of the castle overlooking the labyrinth – above the round opening – three stones form a perfect hidden Mickey on its side.

Discoveryland

Le Visionarium

✿ In the scene where Nine-Eye and Jules Verne are in Russia, there is a hidden Mickey on a balloon.

Orbitron

✿ The ride is topped by rotating spheres. For a brief second during the ride, three come together to form a hidden Mickey.

Les Mystères du Nautilus

✿ After the show, there are two paths to the exit. Take the left hand one. You will see a bottle filled with fish. On one of them there is a hidden Mickey.

Around the hotel complex

Disneyland® Hotel

✿ If you are lucky enough to stay at the Disneyland® Hotel on the 'Castle Club' floor you should find six golden coins (chocolate) on your bed each evening. They form obvious Mickey heads.

Hotel Cheyenne®

✿ At the Hotel Cheyenne® reception, in one of the windows, is a red hidden Mickey.

✿ Look closely at the coffee cups and the carpets at the Cheyenne Hotel®.

Lake Disney®

✿ Around the lake are street lamps. Every lamp has a hidden Mickey.

Main Street, USA

From the quaint clapperboard shop fronts and clanking, hooting automobiles to the gas lamps and spotless curbs, nothing is left to chance in this lovingly recreated Disney version of turn-of-the-century, small-town America. It's extraordinarily well done. And, despite the fact that it's almost entirely composed of shops, restaurants and cafés, Main Street, USA, both excites and reassures. You feel you have known this place all your life.

© Disney

Best for quality shops and snacks.
Worst for budgeting.

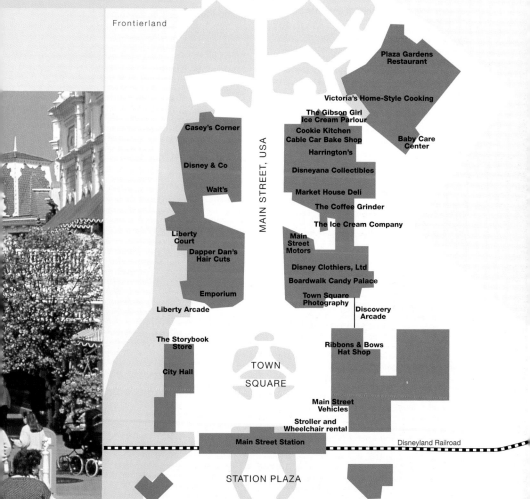

Fantasyland

60 metres
60 yards

N

CENTRAL PLAZA

Discoveryland

Frontierland

Plaza Gardens
Restaurant

Victoria's Home-Style Cooking

The Gibson Girl
Ice Cream Parlour

Casey's Corner

Cookie Kitchen
Cable Car Bake Shop

Baby Care
Center

Harrington's

Disney & Co

Disneyana Collectibles

MAIN STREET, USA

Walt's

Market House Deli

The Coffee Grinder

The Ice Cream Company

Liberty
Court

Main
Street
Motors

Dapper Dan's
Hair Cuts

Disney Clothiers, Ltd

Boardwalk Candy Palace

Emporium

Town Square
Photography

Liberty Arcade

Discovery
Arcade

The Storybook
Store

Ribbons & Bows
Hat Shop

City Hall

TOWN

SQUARE

Main Street
Vehicles

Stroller and
Wheelchair rental

Main Street Station

Disneyland Railroad

STATION PLAZA

Plaza West
Boutique

Plaza East
Boutique

Disneyland Hotel

Main attractions

Disney parades

The parades which pass triumphantly down Main Street, USA are a real focal point of any visit. The characters are on a god-given mission (and for god read Walt) to get children involved at every opportunity. The kids lap it up, and the sound system ensures that even the most cynical of grown-ups can't help but tap a reluctant foot to the beat.

The floats are great hulking constructions of fibreglass and wood, ornately decorated in bright colours, which quiver under their own weight as they pass by. Every now and again there is a jam and Mickey and Goofy *et al* are left dancing on the spot before they can continue. No one seems to mind and it affords an opportunity for friendly banter between audience and cast, as well as that all-important photo opportunity.

Toilets

✿ Close to the Disneyland Railroad Main Street Station, opposite City Hall.

✿ Close to each of the four corners of Town Square.

✿ Within Liberty Arcade.

Seasonal parades operate throughout the year, among them the Disney ImagiNations Parade, Main Street Electrical Parade, Christmas Parade, Halloween Happening, Celtic Parade and some mini-parades.

Disneyland Railroad

Four steam-powered locomotives trundle round the Theme Park, stopping off at Frontierland, Fantasyland and Discoveryland on the way. Inspired by the trains that crossed the American West at the end of the 19th century, they skirt the entire Theme Park, passing through the Grand Canyon Diorama and cutting through the back of the Pirates of the Caribbean ride. The trip, which lasts about 20 minutes,

© Disney

Question 16

What are the names of the four steam-powered locomotives on the Disneyland Railroad?

answer on p.249

is a good way to get a first look at the Theme Park, although your kids are likely to want to jump off as soon as they get a first glimpse and hear the screams from Big Thunder Mountain.

Liberty Arcade
and Discovery Arcade

These form the back entrances to the shops and restaurants on either side of Main Street, USA. Their turn-of-the-century interiors have gas lamps, wrought-iron railings and lavish window displays featuring inventions and curios of American and French origin.

On one side the Statue of Liberty tableau details the French origin of the symbol of New York City, which has stood at the mouth of its harbour since 1886.

On the other side of Main Street, USA, following the covered passageway which leads to Discoveryland, you can stop and re-live the age of invention in Discovery Arcade. Here, cabinets display model flying-machines and other such 19th-century rarities. You will usually find the Silhouette Artist here too. He will cut out and frame paper silhouettes of you to take home.

Main Street Vehicles

Vintage vehicles such as an old-fashioned police paddy wagon, a limousine and a fire truck cruise up Main Street, USA to Central Plaza. It is more of a giggle than anything

Over half a million flowers are planted in the Theme Park each year.

© Disney

On Main Street, USA alone there are over 225,000 light bulbs and 7,653 theme lights.

else as you could walk it in two minutes. - Nevertheless, a short ride on a horse-drawn tram can be quite a treat for youngsters.

Central Plaza

Central Plaza is the hub of the Theme Park, a circular gateway to all five lands. It is an ideal spot to meet up and take souvenir snaps in front of Sleeping Beauty Castle. Look out for the information point here that keeps you updated on waiting times for the Theme Park's most popular rides.

Shopping

One of the best things about Main Street, USA is the shops. You can mooch about here searching for souvenirs while waiting for a parade to begin, get warm, get out of the rain or just do a bit of window shopping.

Plaza West and Plaza East Boutique

Your first (or last) stop for Disneyland® Paris souvenirs, T-shirts and film, set just outside Main Street Station. The kiosks are at the Park gates and normally stay open late.

Emporium

The largest store in the Theme Park, this is the place to find all kinds of toys and games, clothing and souvenirs. The window displays are an attraction in themselves. Inside, the old-fashioned overhead cash exchange system never fails to attract attention.

The Storybook Store

This cosy hometown library is made for browsing. All kinds of books, stationery, videos, posters, CDs and cassettes are available. Tigger is there to add a personalized stamp to your child's new book.

Ribbons & Bows Hat Shop

Hats, clasps, bows and the inevitable Mickey ears. You can have your name custom-monogramed free of charge on an old-fashioned sewing machine.

Lilly's Boutique

This is the place for home-lovers. Plates, glasses, cutlery, oven gloves with a picture of Minnie on them – you name it, they sell it.

Harrington's Fine China & Porcelains

Blown glass giftware is created on site, with personalization available. You will also find Chinese porcelain, crystal, and cut glass.

Dapper Dan's Hair Cuts

Real haircuts, shaves and souvenirs plus a bit of barbershop harmony and gossip from the quartet singers. Not a bad place to get away from the bustle as it is rarely busy.

Disney Clothiers, Ltd.

Plenty of fashion gear plus a sweet section of baby clothes set in a 19th-century house complete with velvet drapes and fireplace.

Disney & Co.

Situated in the block beyond Liberty Court. Plenty of toys, T-shirts, decorative gifts and bath accessories displayed around a large hot-air balloon.

Disneyana Collectibles

A treasure trove for serious Disney collectors – original Disney animation cels, limited-edition lithographs, rare and unusual books and unique ceramic figurines.

Town Square Photography

A replica of a photographer's studio from the last century. Purchase film, disposable cameras and accessories, or rent video and

35mm cameras. This is also the spot where you can pick up your professionally staged photo-encounters with the Disney characters. (7x9 inch print costs 65F).

Boardwalk Candy Palace

Plenty of tooth decay potential with giant lollipops, chocolates and sweets at this sugar-coated paradise. Make sure you try the balls of saltwater taffy, a traditional East Coast treat. The shop is next door to Town Square Photography.

Main Street Motors

A shop originally themed on vintage cars but now entirely devoted to the current Disney darling – Winnie The Pooh.

Where to eat

Main Street, USA is a top spot to eat, but, in keeping with its period style, you won't find anyone serving french fries.

A = table and buffet service, full menu.
B = counter service, full menu.
C = counter service, light snacks.

Walt's – An American Restaurant (A)

A first-class eatery that celebrates the life and times of Walt Disney. The place is decorated with family souvenirs – it is the ideal spot for serious Disney fans, although kids could find the atmosphere a little too formal. The menu includes traditional meat and fish dishes and meal-size salads. Walt's is subject to seasonal closure. *Over 100F.*

Plaza Gardens Restaurant (A)

You can dine in 19th-century splendour at this stylish restaurant near the centre of the Theme Park. The sparkling interior is filled with statues, mirrors and a glass roof which allows the daylight to flood through, even on a cold, wet day. *Between 50F and 100F.*

Market House Deli (B)

Relaxed, New York-style deli serving freshly made, jumbo-size sandwiches and salads, including pastrami, hot turkey and tuna. *Under 50F.*

Casey's Corner (B)

Hot dogs, soft drinks and old-fashioned ragtime music plus the chance to learn about baseball's history – authentic gear, photographs of teams and players such as the Brooklyn Dodgers, Chicago White Stockings and Babe Ruth pay homage to America's beloved national sport. *Under 50F.*

Victoria's Home-Style Restaurant (B)

Lasagne, quiches, mini-pizzas, baked potatoes and desserts in a cosy 1890s family boarding house. *Under 50F.*

The Coffee Grinder (C)

Set mid-way down Main Street, USA, the smell alone will draw you to this vintage coffee house. This is the best spot for fresh coffee and a croissant. *Under 50F.*

The Ice Cream Company (C)

Set in Discovery Arcade, the name says it all: a selection of your favourite flavours in a cone. *Under 50F.*

Cable Car Bake Shop (C)

The shop has booth seating and is decorated to evoke a nostalgic sense of San Francisco. On the way out, the Cookie Kitchen counter may tempt you back for bags of cookies and muffins to take away. *Under 50F.*

The Gibson Girl Ice Cream Parlour (C)

All manner of colourful ice creams and sorbets, as well as frothy milkshakes served up in an old-fashioned milk bar. *Under 50F.*

Frontierland

This is cowboy country – a land of wagon wheels, paddle steamers, old-timers, gloomy houses, disused mine shafts, ranches, corrals and steaks as big as hats. Snake-eyed gun-fighters pace the boards beside the Lucky Nugget Saloon, ready to beat you to the draw should you step into their path, while atop Big Thunder Mountain a lone coyote cackles and howls, bending its back towards a non-existent moon.

© Disney

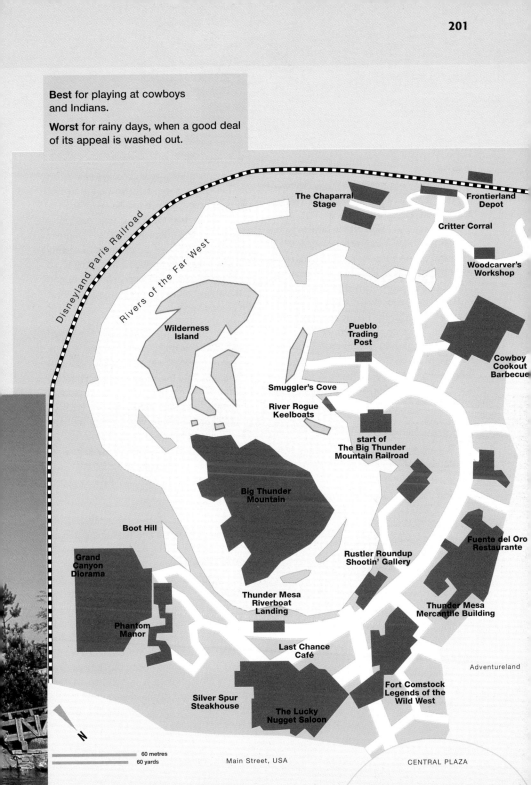

Best for playing at cowboys and Indians.

Worst for rainy days, when a good deal of its appeal is washed out.

Disneyland Paris Railroad

Rivers of the Far West

Wilderness Island

The Chaparral Stage

Frontierland Depot

Critter Corral

Woodcarver's Workshop

Pueblo Trading Post

Cowboy Cookout Barbecue

Smuggler's Cove

River Rogue Keelboats

start of The Big Thunder Mountain Railroad

Big Thunder Mountain

Boot Hill

Grand Canyon Diorama

Rustler Roundup Shootin' Gallery

Fuente del Oro Restaurante

Thunder Mesa Riverboat Landing

Phantom Manor

Thunder Mesa Mercantile Building

Last Chance Café

Adventureland

Fort Comstock Legends of the Wild West

Silver Spur Steakhouse

The Lucky Nugget Saloon

N

60 metres
60 yards

Main Street, USA

CENTRAL PLAZA

Main attractions

Phantom Manor

Just to prove it's not entirely doom and gloom, designers used a hundred different shades of paint to decorate Phantom Manor, not all of them black. This once-stately house, sits high on the hillside with a shutter half off its hinges, flapping lamely in the wind. It is your mission to discover the legend surrounding its past. Led into a dark chamber, the doors slam shut, the lights go out and the walls move in to crush you. Ushered into 'doom buggy' carriages you head off on a spooky journey, filled with cackling ghouls and phantoms. You emerge in daylight up on Boot Hill, the family graveyard. Here the racy epitaphs bring some light relief: *Here lies Shotgun Gus, Holier now than all of us.*

Top tips

▲ Because of the weather, for most of January and February Frontierland does not open until 1pm.

▲ You will need a handful of 10F coins to play on the Rustler Roundup Shootin' Gallery.

▲ Ask about Fast Pass tickets to reduce your queuing time at Big Thunder Mountain.

Toilets

☆ Opposite the entrance to Thunder Mountain in a Mexican-style pueblo.

☆ Left of the entrance to Phantom Manor, next to the undertakers, J Nutterville.

☆ Next to the Legends of the Wild West.

Question 17

How do the paddle boats travel around the Rivers of the Far West?

answer on p.249

Thunder Mesa Riverboat Landing

Mississippi-style paddle boats, *Mark Twain* or *Molly Brown*, can take you on a nostalgic boat cruise around the Rivers of the Far West. From the top deck you get great views of the 33m-high Big Thunder Mountain. It may not be all thrills and spills but it is a leisurely enough way to spend 15 minutes and is especially relaxing during the summer although they are a little short on places to sit.

Rustler Roundup Shootin' Gallery

There is a small charge for this cartoon-style shooting gallery. Even so, it's fairly popular and is a bit of a hoot. Complete with sound effects such as ricochets and exploding dynamite, you can take aim at cacti, a windmill and even (for a big bang) a shack filled with explosives. As many as 20 children can shoot off in all directions at once, so it's pretty difficult to tell just who has hit what.

Big Thunder Mountain

This is the centrepiece of Frontierland. All day, distant rumbles and screams emanate from its depths as the roller coaster weaves and plummets along the tracks at breakneck speed. It is extremely popular and people often jump out of the rickety looking carriages at the end and join the queue again for another go. Even queuing here is fun, as you thread your way through the Thunder Mountain mining company's HQ, growing increasingly nervous, before you reach a point where it is too late to turn back. If you want to play it safe, get into the front cart – the back few are for serious roller-coaster riders, those who are brave or

The oldest visitor so far to Disneyland Paris was 106 years old.

simply just mad. Plunging through tunnels and hurtling around corners, even the most seasoned rider is hard put not to scream with terror/delight when a flooding river washes away part of the track. A camera is there to record your expression. Watch out for the mine explosion, bat-filled cave, famished goat, and stranded coyote. You can view your live-action mug-shot at Big Thunder Photography as you gratefully disembark. *Restrictions apply*.

Disneyland Railroad - Frontierland Depot

Situated on the edge of Frontierland, the diorama is in fact only visible from the Disneyland Railroad (*see* pp.196–97). Trains pass through a 80m-long tunnel, taking you on a journey from dawn to dusk through a recreation of the Grand Canyon in Arizona, one of the natural wonders of the world.

The weather changes too, on your journey, with a dramatic thunderstorm closely followed by a beautiful rainbow. Look out for wild animals: grazing deer, a fox on the hunt, a rattlesnake, squirrels and raccoons.

River Rogue Keelboats

Boat trips on the diesel-powered *Raccoon* or *Coyote* are a shade more exciting than on the stately paddle steamers: the boats weave swiftly in and out, sometimes coming dangerously close to the rocks.

© Disney

Critter Corral

This small farm is entirely enclosed, allowing both barnyard animals and children to mingle freely. Lambs, ducklings, baby goats and rabbits are always a safe bet with kids who will enjoy petting and stroking the cute and cuddly animals.

There's a water trough just outside so the children can wash their hands once they have finished.

The Chaparral Theatre

Superb live stage shows are hosted at this huge outdoor wooden theatre throughout the year. Check your entertainment programme (available at City Hall) for scheduled performances.

Pocahontas Indian Village

There are strategically placed benches for adults seeking a well-earned rest at this outdoor playground inspired by the animated film of the same name.

Legends of the Wild West

As you enter Frontierland, you pass under the timbered stockade of Fort Comstock. If you have 10 minutes to spare, climb the wooden staircase to see a panoramic view of Frontierland and a self-guided history tour that reveals some of the Old West's most popular legends.

You can see famous characters such as Buffalo Bill and Davy Crockett, and even an Indian chief, and there's also a chance to learn about the traditions and customs of Native Americans and to see genuine Cheyenne crafts.

Shopping

Thunder Mesa Mercantile Building

Three rustic stores under one roof, guarded over by the giant figures of Buffalo Bill and Kit Carson.

Tobias Norton & Sons – Frontier Traders
Leather hats, boots, belts and wallets. This is a one-stop shop for western gear. Boys will love the pistols and holsters. If you are not keen on them having toy guns, make a sneaky detour.

Bonanza Outfitters
If you cannot be a cowboy for real, here you can at least dress like one. On sale are brand name boots, Stetsons, shirts, waistcoats, jackets, plus plenty of candy and dress-up wear for the kids.

Eureka Mining Supplies & Assay Office
In this abandoned mining shack, there is staunchly traditionally fare, such as 'Wild Western Salsa', root beer and home-made frontier toys.

Pueblo Trading Post
Here you can buy hand-crafted Indian pottery and woven rugs plus more Disney merchandise.

Woodcarver's Workshop
Watch a skilled woodworker whittle, carve and engrave your very own personalized woodcarving.

Where to eat

A = table and buffet service, full menu.
B = counter service, full menu.
C = counter service, light snacks.

Silver Spur Steakhouse (A)

Rather formal, old-fashioned steak house set opposite the Thunder Mesa Riverboat Landing. You can treat yourself to a top-notch meal of charcoal-grilled meat by the fireside. There is a wine menu and a choice of beers. *Over 100F.*

The Lucky Nugget Saloon (A)

Old-West entertainment in the form of a 30-minute revue, showing here at set times throughout the day. For a fee, you can watch the rollicking can-can girls while you sit back and sample the substantial American fare. For lunch there are sandwiches, salads and chicken wings; pork ribs and prime rib are served at dinner. *Between 50F and 100F.*

Last Chance Cafe (B)

Overlooking Big Thunder Mountain, this is the final outpost on the way to Phantom Manor and a notorious hideout for bandits and rustlers. Enjoy the turkey drumsticks, french fries and barbecue sandwiches, but keep an eye out for the baddies posted around the walls on WANTED posters. *Under 50F.*

Fuente del Oro Restaurante (B)

Traditional Tex-Mex dishes, including tacos, fajitas and chilli con carne. The outside terrace has a Mayan fountain which provides some relief for overheated kids during the summer. *Under 50F.*

Cowboy Cookout Barbecue (C)

This huge wooden hay loft is hard to miss. You can enjoy hearty cowboy grub (spare ribs, chicken and hamburgers) and toe-tapping bluegrass performances from the band. However, when it is not so crowded, the vast interior can seem a little impersonal and the atmosphere becomes more school refectory than cowboy revelry. *Under 50F.*

Adventureland

Adventureland is at once more exotic and at the same time gentler than the other lands. The mix of African, Moorish and Aztec elements, the covered market complex in the Bazar and the wealth of natural vegetation, including a bamboo garden, make it a fascinating place through which to wander, and also one of the most relaxing areas in Disneyland® Paris. In addition, many of the attractions are less sophisticated, offering the chance for kids to clamber about and explore on their own. Yet at its heart there is, of course, another roller coaster, the ever-popular Indiana Jones™ and the Temple of Peril: Backwards!, a fast and furious race through the jungle, culminating in a stomach-churning loop the loop.

© Disney

Best for unsupervised play time, especially as the evening draws to a close.

Worst for weary legs: there's a lot of climbing.

Indiana Jones™ and the Temple of Peril: Backwards!

Blue Lagoon Restaurant

Pirates of the Caribbean

The Shipwreck

Ben Gunn's Cave

Spyglass Hill

Colonel Hathi's Pizza Outpost

Skull Rock

Adventure Isle

La Cabane des Robinsons

Captain Hook's Galley

Trader Sam's Jungle Boutique

Aux Epices Enchantées

Café de la Brousse

Fantasyland

Le Chants des Tam-Tams

L'Echoppe d'Aladdin

Les Trésors de Schéhérazade

La Girafe Curieuse

Le Reine des Serpents

Frontierland

Le Passage Enchanté d'Aladdin

Adventureland Bazar

N

60 metres
60 yards

CENTRAL PLAZA

Main attractions

Pirates of the Caribbean

Housed within the confines of a greystone fortress, the queuing area leads you towards a rocky grotto where skeletons and the remains of shipwrecks offer some odious clues to what lies ahead. You are ushered into boats by friendly pirates (who often stroll around Adventureland trying to drum up trade) and head off on an underground voyage, past scenes of pirate mayhem, roaring cannons and swashbuckling sabres. Menacing eyes peer at you from every dark corner as your boat lurches to dodge stray cannon balls. For younger children, though, the macabre atmosphere, sudden plunges, skeleton scenes, spooky fog and flames that threaten to engulf you may provoke a few nightmares. And don't forget to take your snorkel; you are likely to get splashed a little.
Restrictions apply.

Top tips

▲ Because of the weather, for most of January and February Adventureland does not open until 1pm.

▲ Indiana Jones™ and the Temple of Peril: Backwards! tends to have long queues. Try early in the day or during a parade.

▲ Keep a careful eye on any under 5s at Adventure Isle as there are some precarious spots.

Toilets

☁ Next to Colonel Hathi's Pizza Outpost.

☁ Within the Bazar, close to Le Passage Enchanté d'Aladdin.

Indiana Jones™ and the Temple of Peril: Backwards!

An all too brief, yet frantic roller-coaster ride which climaxes in a breathtaking 360° loop. The queuing area features the abandoned archaeological site, in the depths of the jungle, with tents, 1940s Jeeps and upturned billy cans. To solve this mystery, you enter the ruined Maya temple, watched over by huge stone cobras. Once inside you climb into a rickety old mine cart to race through the long-buried ruins of the Temple of Peril – and all at a stomach-churning speed. For those with strong stomachs, make for the first carriage if you can, to appreciate fully the almost vertical drop at the ride's outset. In the flickering torchlight after dark, the attraction takes on an added dimension that's certain to spur dedicated thrill-seekers. *Restrictions apply*.

Le Passage Enchanté d'Aladdin (Aladdin's Enchanted World)

This is a jewel-encrusted walk-through of miniature scenes from the story of Aladdin. Clever three-dimensional displays, songs and special effects provide light entertainment for young fans.

Adventure Isle

Skull Rock stares with a dead and menacing expression out over the lagoon, daring kids to explore the secret caves, tunnels, waterfalls and rope bridges which cross *La Mer des Bretteurs* to reach a tropical treasure trove. There are two islets, one inspired by the Johann Wyss classic, *Swiss Family Robinson*, the other by Robert Louis Stevenson's *Treasure Island*. To the north, Captain Hook's pirate ship has cast anchor

Over 1,000 artists work at Disneyland – including actors, dancers, musicians, designers, decorators and seamstresses.

in Canonball Cove. A play area on the top deck draws would-be swashbucklers, while at Teetering Rock daredevils can really let off steam. Ben Gunn's Cave provides a series of ominous, underground tunnels which lead to a hidden chamber. It's very dark and easy to get lost as you explore, clinging to the walls until your eyes become accustomed to the gloom. With bats and skeletons, and no fewer than six entrances in and out, it is spine-chilling stuff that kids will revel in for an hour or more. A good place to come and burn off some pent-up energy.

Pirates' Beach

This new outside adventure playground is aimed at younger children, with shipwrecks, climbing frames, walkways, games and toys – a real-life training ground for young pirates.

La Cabane des Robinson (The Swiss Family Robinson Treehouse)

At the Swiss Family Robinson's Treehouse there are some 17,000 individual leaves on the skyscraping tree itself, each positioned by hand. This is something of a literary treat as you discover how this shipwrecked Swiss family make the best of time after surviving a shipwreck. The four levels of this 27m, spreading banyon (fig) tree are reached via makeshift stairs which spiral into the upper branches. Below stairs, a tangled mass of roots reveals a cellar (le Ventre de la Terre), where supplies from the wreck are stored. The wreck itself, lying lop-sided in the water, is to be found under the suspended rope bridge.

© Disney

Shopping

Indiana Jones™ Adventure Outpost

Everything your kids will ever need for a pioneering adventure. Clothing, bush hats, accessories, jewellery and souvenirs based on the classic Indiana Jones™ movies.

Les Trésors de Schéhérazade

Mementoes of far distant lands, left behind by Sinbad the Sailor. You will find magic lanterns, brass bells, oriental dolls and exotic clothing.

Le Coffre du Capitaine (The Captain's Coffer)

At the exit of Pirates of the Caribbean, choose from a treasure-trove of nautical novelties. The skull and crossbones gear is sure to go down well.

La Girafe Curieuse (The Curious Giraffe)

Safari clothing (some non-Disney and eco-friendly) and other gifts, all sold under the watchful gaze of a giraffe, happy nibbling away at leaves.

© Disney

Where to eat

A = table and buffet service, full menu.
B = counter service, full menu.
C = counter service, light snacks.

Blue Lagoon Restaurant (A)

Guests can relax under a perpetual moonlit sky amid the underground tranquility of palm trees and sandy beaches. Fish and spicy Creole specialities are served on a tropical terrace as the boats from the Pirates of the Caribbean drift by. Good for kids and couples alike. *Over 100F.*

Agrabah Café (B)

Set in the Bazar, this atmospheric buffet-style restaurant offers colourful and fragrant Mediterranean and African dishes including couscous, tabouleh and Middle Eastern pastries. *Under 50F.*

Colonel Hathi's Pizza Outpost (B)

Tucked away in a bamboo forest, talking parrots invite you in to dine on the Colonel's private veranda, and enjoy a safari snack of pizza, lasagne and salad. It is worth a visit just to see the authentic colonial gear. *Under 50F.*

Restaurant Hakuna Matata (B)

The mud hut's décor is an array of masks and safari trophies, and the food is just as exotic with kebabs, couscous and other African delicacies. *Under 50F.*

Café de la Brousse (C)

Get some shade in a native grass-thatched hut overlooking Adventure Isle, and refresh yourself with a light snack. *Under 50F.*

Captain Hook's Galley (C)

You can descend into the depths of Captain Hook's galleon for drinks, cookies, sandwiches, hot dogs and apple dough-nuts. The kids can play above deck, while you take a breather below. *Under 50F.*

Fantasyland

© Disney

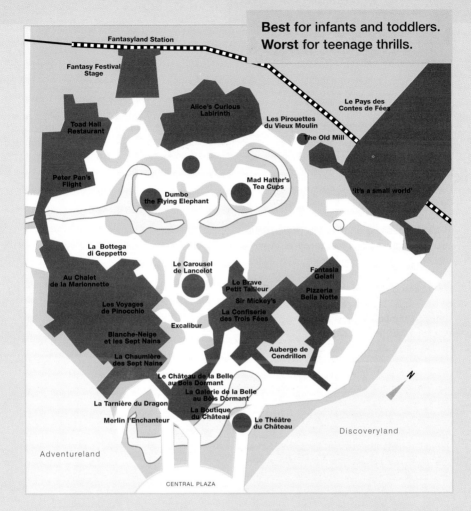

Best for infants and toddlers.
Worst for teenage thrills.

Fantasyland Station

Fantasy Festival Stage

Alice's Curious Labirinth

Le Pays des Contes de Fées

Les Pirouettes du Vieux Moulin

The Old Mill

Toad Hall Restaurant

Peter Pan's Flight

Mad Hatter's Tea Cups

'it's a small world'

Dumbo the Flying Elephant

La Bottega di Geppetto

Le Carousel de Lancelot

Fantasia Gelati

Au Chalet de la Marionnette

Le Brave Petit Tailleur

Pizzeria Bella Notte

Sir Mickey's

Les Voyages de Pinocchio

La Confiserie des Trois Fées

Excalibur

Blanche-Neige et les Sept Nains

Auberge de Cendrillon

La Chaumière des Sept Nains

Le Château de la Belle au Bois Dormant

La Galerie de la Belle au Bois Dormant

La Tarnière du Dragon

La Boutique du Château

Merlin l'Enchanteur

Le Théâtre du Château

Discoveryland

N

Adventureland

CENTRAL PLAZA

Fantasyland is pink. The rides are pink, the ground is pink, the food is pink, even when it's not pink, in spirit it's pink. Younger children will enjoy the gentler rides, such as Dumbo the Flying Elephant and the Mad Hatter's Tea Cups, and race around Alice's Curious Labyrinth squealing with delight as water squirts from stone turrets. There is nothing too scary here, except for the dragon, a two-ton beastie with bad breath and bloodshot eyes, which slumbers beneath the castle and wakes every so often to let out a deafening roar.

Main attractions

Sleeping Beauty Castle

The landmark castle towers 45m above the Theme Park, centrepiece not only of Fantasyland but of the entire complex. Its soaring design is taken from the Disney animated classic, with cubic trees, gothic spires and pink turrets faithfully reproduced to stunning effect.

Most ingenious of all is the cinematique technique of 'forced perspective', which makes the tallest tower seem even higher than it actually is. The walls themselves have been built upwards using increasingly smaller sized bricks, deceiving the eye into believing the battlements at the top are that much further away. Look out, too, for the central oval stained-glass 'polage' window which constantly changes scene.

La Galerie de la Belle au Bois Dormant (Sleeping Beauty Gallery)

A spiral staircase leads to an upstairs gallery where hand-painted storybooks, stained-glass windows and finely woven tapestries recall the romantic tale of Sleeping Beauty. In the corner of the gallery, two guards are supposed to be standing watch. Both are fast asleep and their gruff snoars never fail to raise a titter from children who tiptoe by.

La Tanière du Dragon (The Dragon's Dungeon)

The castle's fire-breathing dragon is Disney's largest Audio-Animatronic® figure, measuring an impressive 27m in length. Weighing in at two tons, the dragon sleeps restlessly beneath the castle in a secret lair. He grumbles and snorts in his misty pool of fetid green water, before awakening with a fearsome growl.

© Disney

Top tips

▲ La Tanière du Dragon is probably a little too terrifying for most toddlers.

▲ The queues for Peter Pan's Flight are among some of the longest. Try during a parade.

Toilets

✿ Next to Au Chalet de la Marionette restaurant.

✿ Close to Pizzeria Bella Notte.

✿ Close to the Toad Hall Restaurant.

Question 19

How many Audio-Animatronic® figures are there in the Park?

a) 500 or less
b) 500–2,000
c) 2,000–4,500

answer on p.249

Le Théâtre du Château

Set to the right of the castle drawbridge, this little theatre stages seasonal open-air shows (currently *Winnie the Pooh and Friends Too*). Check your entertainment programme (available from City Hall) for scheduled performances.

Fantasy Festival Stage

Colourful costumes, music and dancing bring this show to life, as some of the best loved Disney characters step out on stage. You will find the theatre tucked under the arches of Fantasyland Station. Check your entertainment programme (available from City Hall) for scheduled performances and make sure you turn up at least 10 minutes before the show is set to begin or you may be disappointed.

Blanche-Neige et les Sept Nains (Snow White and the Seven Dwarfs)

Heigh-ho, heigh-ho, it's off on the Dwarfs' mine-train you go. From their happy cottage home, you hurtle through unforgettable scenes from the movie (alternately cute then scary) and onwards to the bleak haunted forest where the wicked queen awaits you at every turn. A happy ending is in sight, of course, as Prince Charming arrives to save the day – still this is one ride likely to startle impressionable youngsters.

Les Voyages de Pinocchio (Pinocchio's Travels)

Next door to the Snow White attraction, this is essentially a ghost-train ride which highlights the darker side of Carlo Collodi's classic Italian fairytale. Seated in lurching hand-crafted carriages, you follow Pinocchio on his eventful journey as a wooden puppet in Geppetto's workshop, through temptation and on to his magical reincarnation as a real boy. As you might expect, rousing scenes such as Pleasure Island, Stromboli's birdcage and a ravenous Monstro the whale will fascinate fans over five familiar with the movie version, but may still unnerve younger children.

Le Carrousel de Lancelot (Lancelot's Merry-Go-Round)

The manes and tails of the horses on the carousel are hand-painted in 23 carat gold leaf. Worthy of the Knights of the Round Table, these 86 graceful, galloping horses really add to the fairy-tale atmosphere. There are ornate carriages large enough for whole families to ride together.

Peter Pan's Flight

A covered wooden bridge takes you from Pinocchio's village to the opening setting for J. M. Barrie's spectacular story. Here you board a suspended pirate ship and soar over London. Starting off in the children's nursery you are whisked out of the window and past a series of tableaux from the animated movie, culminating in Never Land with Captain Hook and the Crocodile. Tinker Bell commandeers your escape with a little help from her pixie dust, and you land safe and sound in Mermaid Lagoon.

Alice's Curious Labyrinth

In keeping with Lewis Carroll's classic children's story, *Alice in Wonderland*, this whimsical hedge-maze sets out to baffle and bemuse. You are confronted by signs pointing in every direction, dead ends,

It took 9.5 million kilos of cement, 500,000 litres of paint and 68,000 cubic metres of rock work to complete the Park.

miniature doors and bizarre characters. At the heart of the maze there is a quirky castle filled with distorting optical illusions.

Dumbo the Flying Elephant

Choose just how high or how low you want to fly as Dumbo takes you on this delightful aerial merry-go-round. Another fairground classic, and a perfect photo opportunity. *Restrictions apply*.

Mad Hatter's Tea Cups

Seated in one of 18 giant tea cups you whirl out of control on the Mad Hatter's table. Your cup spins one way, while the saucer turns in the opposite direction. You decide the speed using a steering wheel inside your cup. *Restrictions apply*.

Le Pays des Contes de Fées (Storybook Land)

A gentle boat cruise around miniature landscapes recreated from familiar folk stories and Disney classics. The settings are a little faded, but kids enjoy pointing out Hansel and Gretel, Aladdin, Snow White, *et al*.

Casey Jr. le Petit Train du Cirque (the Little Circus Train)

Straight out of *Dumbo*, this endearing mini roller-coaster train circuits the elaborate villages of Storybook Land and is a guaranteed thumbs-up for younger kids.

Les Pirouettes du Vieux Moulin (Twirling Old Mill)

You get a birds-eye view of Fantasyland from the top of this little wheel. Seated in oversized wooden buckets, it is a novel enough ride, but it takes such a long time to load it may hardly seem worth the wait.

'it's a small world'

A musical tribute to the cultures of the world, your canal boat drifts around the globe passing hundreds of authentically dressed, singing dolls. Despite its rather saccharine theme, the tune is catchy, the scenes captivating and the effects undeniably impressive. At the exit an innovative display from the ride's sponsor (France-Télécom) features tiny buildings with intricate synthetic video scenes playing inside. This is one you won't want to miss.

© Disney

Shopping

La Boutique du Château
Deep inside Sleeping Beauty Castle, it's Christmas all year round. Shop here for Christmas cards and holiday decorations.

La Chaumière des Sept Nains
Children's clothing and costumes, character toys, and film souvenirs.

La Confiserie des Trois Fées
The sweet smell alone will draw you in. Here you'll find delectable sweets and candy in specially packaged gift boxes and tins.

Merlin L'Enchanteur
You can watch crystal being etched and buy ornate medieval figures, jewellery and glass-ware. Set inside the castle, there's a stair-way leading down to the Dragon's Dungeon.

Sir Mickey's
Four stores under just one roof, fronted by a giant beanstalk.

Le Brave Petit Tailleur
Children's clothing and hats, cuddly toys, games and souvenirs.

La Bottega di Geppetto
The woodcarver's shop sells a few wooden puppets, cuckoo clocks and music boxes and hand-carved toys. It also has a good selection of babywear and souvenirs.

La Ménagerie du Royaume
Plush soft toys alongside glassware, ceramic Disney characters, jewellery, videos and other gifts.

La Petite Maison des Jouets
Under the colourful shingled roof of this olde worlde cottage you will find plush toys and other Disneyland® Paris gifts.

Where to eat

A = table and buffet service, full menu.
B = counter service, full menu.
C = counter service, light snacks.

Auberge de Cendrillon (A)
One of the few places in the whole of the Theme Park to eat French food. Cinderella's coach sits in the covered courtyard. Inside, beautiful tapestries depict scenes from the movie. The clink of grown-up cutlery and wine glasses reflects the rather formal atmosphere, but the staff are very friendly and the kid's menu is first rate. The Express Menu is good value for money. *Over 100F.*

Pizzeria Bella Notte (B)
Pizza and pasta are served here in a setting inspired by the spaghetti scene from *Lady and the Tramp*. *Under 50F.*

Au Chalet de la Marionette (B)
Basically a fast-food chicken joint, with Bavarian décor, Pinocchio theme and cosy fireplace. Choose from roast chicken, hamburgers and hot dogs. *Under 50F.*

Toad Hall Restaurant (B)
Timbered country inn, serving British fare: fish 'n' chips, pork pies, steak sandwich-es and hearty puddings. *Under 50F.*

March Hare Refreshments (C)
Sickly sweet doughnuts, cookies, pop-corn and apple turnovers. *Under 50F.*

The Old Mill (C)
Creamy frozen yoghurt, fruit tarts, doughnuts, french stick sandwiches (i.e. Subs) and beverages. *Under 50F.*

Fantasia Gelati (C)
Delicious Italian ice cream in a cone. *Under 50F.*

Discoveryland

© Disney

Discoveryland is really rather beautiful and, of the five lands, architecturally the most interesting because, being a land of tomorrow, it makes its own rules. The glistening, golden balls of Orbitron and the forbidding launch pad of Space Mountain are as much a draw for kids and adults as the rides themselves. Dotted around are other 'exhibits' such as a life-size X-wing fighter from *Star Wars* and a space car by Renault. Budding boffins will love it.

Best for adrenaline rush.
Worst for peak-season queues.

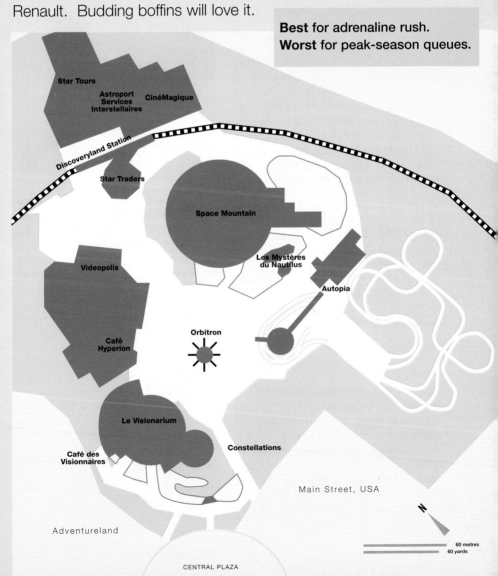

Star Tours

Astroport Services Interstellaires

CinéMagique

Discoveryland Station

Star Traders

Space Mountain

Les Mystères du Nautilus

Videopolis

Autopia

Café Hyperion

Orbitron

Le Visionarium

Constellations

Café des Visionnaires

Main Street, USA

N

Adventureland

60 metres
60 yards

CENTRAL PLAZA

Main attractions

Star Tours

Anyone who climbs aboard the Starspeeder 3000 is in for an out-of-this world space adventure. This *Star Wars*-inspired flight simulator takes you on an astonishingly realistic journey to Endor at turbulent speed, accompanied by amateurish pilot, RX24. There's no real danger of course. The windscreen in front of you is in fact a screen projecting a 70mm showreel. Accompany this with the effects of G-force, propulsion and abrupt deceleration and you will feel as though you are really out there. George Lucas fans will be thrilled to find R2D2 and C3PO among the droids in the intergalactic loading area. They certainly help take the tedium out of queuing. *Restrictions apply.*

L'Astroport Services Instellaires (Star Tours Post-Show)

At the exit to Star Tours is a state-of-the-art video arcade. As well as interactive games and simulator rides, there is a picture-morphing area which allows you to distort your own photographic image. This, as well as the 12-player Star Course game, are especially popular.

Space Mountain – De la Terre à la Lune (From the Earth to the Moon)

Nowhere is Disney's subtle use of dim and near non-existent lighting put to better effect than here. Space Mountain, probably the best ride in the whole park, takes place in near darkness. Inspired by Jules Verne's *From the Earth to the Moon*, this breathtaking indoor roller coaster catapults you from a giant cannon into a series of pitch-black, cosmic loops and spins at a giddying

70km per hour around a full kilometre of track. Thanks to a magnificent feat of engineering, a moonward-bound rocket ship carrying 24 fellow passengers is launched every 36 seconds throughout the day. A near deafening explosion prompts your equally audible screams as the rocket embarks on a supersonic journey through the hostile wastelands of the cosmos. You are never quite sure when the next errant meteorite will appear as you dodge and weave your way into space on this white-knuckle ride.

For the less daring, special gangways allow you to climb the immense copper and bronze mountain and take a closer look at this high-tech, corkscrewing ride. Entrance to the viewing area is around the back, opposite Honey, I Shrunk the Audience. *Restrictions apply.*

Space Mountain cost 600 million francs and can accommodate 2,600 guests an hour.

Arcade des Visionnaires

An interactive video games arcade that tempts you to part with even more of your hard-earned dough.

Honey, I Shrunk the Audience

This is a recent addition to the Theme Park which features the latest in film and digital technology. The misadventure begins as Professor Szalinski presents the invention of the year: an amazing shrinking machine. Unfortunately, it is pointed at the audience, and, what do you know? we all shrink! The combination of tactile, visual and sound effects creates a world of topsy-turvy dimensions. Special 3-D glasses bring you up close to a giant python, roaring lion and sneezing dog. Building on an age-old gag, escaping laboratory mice cause predictable panic. While this is billed as a family attraction, under 4s may be startled.

Le Visionarium (The Visionarium)

Enter into a 360⁰ panoramic time-travel adventure hosted by the eccentric Timekeeper. This circular-vision cinema employs nine interlocking screens which completely surround you. A combination of robotics, computerized special effects and high-impact film footage takes you on a giddy voyage around Europe, as you switch between past, present and future paying tribute to the world's greatest inventions. *Restrictions apply.*

There are 700 speakers strategically placed around the Theme Park, though trying to spot just one of them is a task in itself.

Top tips

▲ The main dialogue on Star Tours is entirely in French, the only drawback to an otherwise superb ride.

▲ At Honey, I Shrunk the Audience, though a large crowd is loaded quickly, expect to spend up to 10 minutes before getting into the auditorium while you are herded together for a Kodak commercial.

▲ The Visionarium is highly recommended but the under 4s may get a bit distracted, as it runs for a full 20 minutes.

▲ Cinémagique is easy to miss. You reach the cinema via a canopied entrance under the railroad.

Toilets

🚽 Within Videopolis.

🚽 Close to Autopia.

Three visionaries

Leonardo da Vinci (1452–1519)

Leonardo da Vinci was a painter, sculptor, architect, musician, engineer and scientist. Far from being a jack-of-all-trades, he was a master at whatever he put his mind to. As early as the 15th century, he invented the basis for a prototype helicopter, aeroplane, tank, machine-gun, power hammer, swivel bridge and parachute. He also painted the *Mona Lisa*, which hangs in the Louvre (*see* p.36).

Jules Verne (1828–1905)

Jules Verne was a French author with a fertile imagination which led him to write *Around The World in Eighty Days*, *A Journey to the Centre of the Earth*, *20,000 Leagues Under The Sea* and *From the Earth to the Moon*. Many of his stories feature incredible machines (such as the submarine) which seemed fantastical to his contemporaries, but which were to become reality over a century later.

H. G. Wells (1866–1946)

H. G. Wells was a British author who, although he wrote all kinds of novels and political works, made his name writing science fiction. Among his most famous books are *The Time Machine*, *The Invisible Man* and *The War of The Worlds*.

Orbitron

Inspired by Leonardo da Vinci's sketches of flying machines, this is your chance to pilot your own spaceship as you soar through a galaxy high above Discoveryland. Though it is essentially a fairground ride, it is beautifully designed and an unmistakable classic. *Restrictions apply.*

Autopia

The Autopia cars cover a distance of 730,000km each year. Junior L-drivers love the highways and byways of this retro, space-age circuit which makes its way around the futuristic city of 'Solaria'. With their cars kept steadily on track by a metal rail, all the kids have to do is press the gas pedal and steer. *Restrictions apply.*

Videopolis

Spectacular live stage shows are put on at regular intervals throughout the day in this huge, high-tech auditorium. The sheer size of the auditorium makes it a touch impersonal but there is no denying the mounting excitement as the time for the scheduled show draws closer. These are no mere fillers but quality productions on a lavish scale. Try to see one if you can.

Les Mystères du Nautilus (The Mystery of the Nautilus)

Explore the darkest depths of the ocean in Captain Nemo's legendary submarine, straight out of Disney's screen version of *20,000 Leagues Under the Sea*. The tour holds a few spine-tingling surprises including an attack by a giant squid. Les Mystères du Nautilus may be a little disappointing unless you know something of the story.

Shopping

Constellations
This planetarium-inspired boutique offers a wide range of Disney merchandise and clothing for aspiring space cadets. Mickey fans will appreciate the whacky, flying-machine centrepiece.

Light Speed Photography
You can prove to everyone that you survived the interstellar speeds of Space Mountain with your own photograph taken at the split second of blast-off.

Star Traders
Mainly sportswear, plus *Star Wars* souvenirs, all sorts of gadgets, gizmos, and a wide assortment of futuristic toys at this solar-panelled, intergalactic trading post.

Where to eat

B = counter service, full menu.
C = counter service, light snacks.

Café Hyperion (B)
Pass under the immense floating Hyperion airship (straight out of a Jules Verne novel) and you enter the futuristic Videopolis amphitheatre. Queue for a burger, sausage, sandwich or salad, then take it easy as multiple-screen cartoons and a live musical stage show keep the kids engrossed. *Under 50F.*

Buzz Lightyear's Pizza Planet (C)
True to its *Toy Story* movie namesake, Pizza Planet looks like something out of a science-fiction comic. The fun décor features a giant rocket-ship filled with three-eyed, mini aliens. Diners can choose from Mickey-shaped pizzas or the house speciality: a hamburger topped with a mini pizza. A unique feature is the supervised theme play area with closed circuit television, enabling you to keep a leisurely eye on the kids. *Under 50F.*

Beating the queues

Queuing can be a dull affair, especially when you spend an hour in the line for a three-minute ride. But it's all showbusiness here, and the trick of whipping up the audience by making them wait and wait is one Disney know well.

Top tips

- Visit in low season. Relatively quiet times are from mid-January to mid-February, late September, November and the first few weeks in December. The Theme Park is also quieter during the week; weekends and national holidays are usually more crowded.

- Watch the shows and parades on your first day and use this valuable time on subsequent visits to ride the big-thrill attractions. Many of the rides are near deserted during the Main Street Electrical Parade, and watching the fireworks from Dumbo the Flying Elephant or Orbitron is a real thrill.

- Watch the main parade from its starting point near 'it's a small world' in Fantasyland. Once the final float has passed by, head for a normally busy ride nearby (such as Star Tours or Peter Pan's Flight).

Top tips

The Fastpass ticket system allows you to book ahead during busy periods for a time that suits you. At the designated time, you are then offered priority in the queue. It is currently valid for Space Mountain, Indian Jones™ and the Temple of Peril: Backwards! and Peter Pan's Flight. Big Thunder Mountain will also be included in the scheme during 2000.

- The lines get increasingly shorter as the day draws to a close. If you can, take a break mid-afternoon and return to the Theme Park after 5pm.

- If you are visiting during the shorter off-peak days, enjoy the rides during the day and leave all your shopping until you visit Disney® Village, which will allow you to buy souvenirs once the gates close.

- On certain days during the summer season, from April to September, Disneyland® Paris hotel guests can enter the Theme Park half an hour before it officially opens. Ask at your hotel about early entry.

Where to head first

The attractions with the slowest moving queues are clearly worth riding first thing. They include Big Thunder Mountain, Indiana Jones™ and the Temple of Peril: Backwards!, Dumbo the Flying Elephant, Star Tours, Peter Pan's Flight, Orbitron and Autopia. Other attractions may appear to have long queues, but load a large group of people quickly so you can leave them until later. These include Pirates of the Caribbean, Les Voyages de Pinocchio, 'it's a small world', Le Carrousel de Lancelot and Le Visionarium.

The early bird catches the worm

To avoid the worst of the queues, you will need to arrive early – even before the gates are open. Wait at the turnstiles until you see Mickey appear. Once you hear the train hooter give two blasts you will know it is time to get on your starting blocks. The red arrow on the front of the turnstile changes to green, giving you the all clear to enter with your passport.

Rainy days

Even Disneyland® Paris loses some of its lustre on cold, bleak days, after all this is northern Europe not Florida. However, 80 per cent of the rides are under cover, so you can still enjoy most of the rides without getting your feet wet.

The Disney Imagineers have considered the weather, of course, and included central heating in all the visitor areas, as well as some roaring log fires and covered queuing areas. You can get from the main gate to Frontierland and then on to Adventureland and Fantasyland without ever confronting the elements.

Even if the rain is falling, there is no need to abandon your plans. If you are caught out unexpectedly, Le Passage Enchanté d'Aladdin (Adventureland), Les Mystères du Nautilus (Discoveryland) and Legends of the Wild West (Frontierland) are an escape from the sudden bad weather outside. Your kids will also have fun exploring Sleeping Beauty Castle (Fantasyland). Don't forget to visit the cellar down below for an encounter with the red-eyed, smoke-snorting dragon.

If the bad weather persists, head for the two covered arcades on either side of Main Street,USA leading up from Town Square. These offer rear access to several welcoming shops and restaurants. On one side Liberty Arcade leads north of Dapper Dan's to Liberty Court where you will find the Statue of Liberty Tableau. On the opposite side of Town Square, Discovery Arcade has a showcase presenting some of the world's greatest inventions.

More ideas

Kids will happily spend a good hour or two at Videopolis, enjoying fast food, a live musical show and cartoons. Buzz Lightyear's Pizza Planet Restaurant, too, has a supervised indoor play area and video screens so that you can keep an eye on their antics from your table. You can get a fair way towards either restaurant under cover if you use Discovery Arcade.

From Liberty Arcade you can reach Frontierland without a drop of rain touching you. From here, head for Adventureland Bazar which is a fun spot to browse in. The exotic covered courtyard has boutiques, murals, fountains and a collection of impressive movie props.

If the rain looks set to last, your kids are likely to feel cheated if you do not brave it and set out to make the most of your time in the Theme Park. Pirates of the Caribbean, Phantom Manor, Star Tours, Le Visionarium and Honey, I Shrunk the Audience last long enough for you to enjoy their sheltered interiors, and for the most part their queuing areas are under cover. Space Mountain is one of the fastest moving rides and doesn't last long but the star-studded corridor to the loading area offers a welcome breather from the rain. For the less brave, gentle rides such as the Mad Hatter's Tea Cups and Peter Pan's Flight are also almost entirely under cover.

Top tips

For the most up-to-date weather reports covering the Paris area, access the net at *www.intellicast.com/weather/par*.

Disney® Village

Best for nightlife.

Its appeal is largely adult.

Set between the Theme Park and the hotels, this vast entertainment complex is marked by enormous silver and red vertical columns, which seem to support nothing more than a bunch of wires. Take a closer look and you'll see that the wires hold hundreds of lights, which beckon the crowds once darkness falls and the Theme Park closes.

Disney® Village, open from 7.30am to 4am daily, attempts to recreate the downtown atmosphere of a small American city. It consists of nightclubs, bars, restaurants, shops, kiosks, a cinema and live shows. There is a good-humoured (if unsophisticated) party spirit here and it is a safe place to wander with your family after dark.

A car park located between Disney® Village and the Newport Bay Hotel® is designated for all those free-flowing visitors who have no intention of using the Theme Park itself.

The main attractions

Most of the attractions focus specifically on evening performances and have limited opening hours. For details of Crescend'O, Buffalo Bill's Wild West Show and Hurricanes see **Entertainment**, p.244.

Gaumont Cinema

An 15-screen cinema complex (including one giant screen) equipped with the latest film technology. You will find it to the right of the entrance to Disney® Village.

Marina Del Ray

You can rent various water vehicles from the dock area for use on Lake Disney®. Limited opening hours during the winter months.

Disney® Village Video Arcade

All the usual video games for hi-tech children with itchy trigger fingers.

Where to eat

Check opening times on arrival as they are subject to change without prior notice.

Annette's Diner
Open all day.
Burger and shakes, chilli, hot-dogs or ice-cream sundaes. If you don't fancy a sit-down meal, order from the takeaway window outside. *Between 50F and 100F.*

Billy Bob's Country & Western Saloon
Open dinner only.
Tex-Mex buffet on the third floor of this atmospheric, mock-up saloon. A five-piece cowboy band helps give it a laid-back appeal. *Over 100F.*

Los Angeles Bar & Grill
Open lunch and dinner.
Breakfast with the Disney characters is also served here between 7.30 and 10.30am. *Between 50F and 100F.*

McDonald's®

Open all day.

An inventive indoor children's play area keeps kids busy while you queue. *Under 50F.*

Planet Hollywood

Open lunch and dinner.

Standard American cuisine in a glam, movie-memorabilia setting. Check out the gift shop and celebrity handprints on your way out. *Over 100F.*

Rainforest Café

Open lunch and dinner.

Features an enormous aquarium, impressive menu and a shop with merchandise that rivals much of Disney's. Look out for the shop's eco-friendly talking tree. *Over 100F.*

Rock 'n' Roll America

Open dinner only.

Pizza, salads and snacks in a 1950s-style, musical setting. *Between 50F and 100F.*

Sandwiches New York Style

Open all day.

Specialities include bagels, pastrami, sand-wiches and cheesecake, served at 1950s-revival formica tables. *Under 50F.*

The Steakhouse

Open lunch and dinner.

You can order succulent prime rib or a thick T-bone steak. There is also an American brunch with the Disney characters here every Sunday. *Over 100F.*

Shopping and services

Buffalo Trading Company

Denims, boots, shirts, hats, belts, bandannas, and turquoise and silver trinkets, at this Wild West general store.

The Disney Store

All the clothes, books, toys, videos, watch-es, jewellery and souvenirs you could want.

Disney® Village Post Office

Open Mon–Sun 11am-7pm
(often later during high season)

Do not be fooled by the futuristic sand-blasted metal décor, this is, in fact, a fully functioning post office. It also sells collector's picture stamps, exchanges foreign currency and has an automatic cash machine that accepts all the major credit cards.

Hollywood Pictures

American film merchandise, books, souvenirs and postcards. Under the spotlights, young would-be film stars will find all their favourite dress-up costumes.

Disney Gallery

A good place to stock up on those Disney collectables.

Team Mickey

This is the place for ice-hockey shirts, USA college logo sweatshirts, basketball and baseball gear. Disneyland Paris golf clubs, balls and polo shirts are also available.

World of Toys

Barbie is the star of the show here, surrounded by all her friends and scores of accessories. Little (and big) boys will head straight for the huge range of model cars.

Where to shop

Shopping is all part of the fun at Disneyland® Paris, providing it doesn't get out of hand. There are outlets aplenty though most sell pretty much the same range of goods – soft toys, hats, T-shirts and scarves, watches, huge lollies, and souvenirs of all kinds. Some shops, however, are more specialized and they are worth tracking down if you know what you are looking for. In all of them, prices are reasonable and the quality is good. You won't find a bargain but neither will anything fall apart once you get it home.

Disney was the first company to combine successfully the notion of entertainment with shopping. In 1930 Walt's brother, Roy, signed the company's first international licensing contract with Borgfeldt & Co. for production and sale of Mickey Mouse merchandise. The first Mickey Mouse watch was sold by the Ingersoll Watch Company in June 1933. By 1954, 700 companies were making more than 3,000 Disney items from pyjamas and underwear to toys, games and school supplies. With Disney characters gazing out from every T-shirt and lunch box, it is no surprise that one in 10 guests leave the resort with a Disneyland® Paris baseball cap.

Shopping made easy

You do not have to weigh yourself down with purchases. As well as storing bulkier items in the lockers beneath Main Street Station, you can use the free shopping service which allows you to shop wherever you want, then collect your purchases at Town Square Terrace as you leave the Theme Park anytime after 5pm. If you are staying on site, deliveries can be made to your hotel, allowing you to collect your shopping after 7pm. Shops will normally exchange faulty merchandise within 10 days of purchase, so long as you can produce your receipt. You are likely to be offered a credit note rather than a refund.

Tax-free shopping

If you are normally resident outside the EU, you can obtain a tax refund on your purchases (this does not apply to cigarettes, alcohol, groceries and beverages). Simply present your receipts at your hotel shop and you will be handed the appropriate form for customs. Minimum purchase is 1,200F.

Unique buys

Serious collectors should head for the shops which sell items from the Walt Disney Classics Collection as well as original 'cellos' (the plates used to create Disney animated movies). Find them at Harrington's Fine China and Porcelains (Main Street, USA), Galerie Mickey (Disneyland® Hotel), Hollywood Pictures and Disney Gallery (Disney® Village) and the New York Boutique (Hotel New York®). For a lasting memory of your visit, you can pay 495F to have your name engraved in a paving stone on Promenade Disney.

As well as selling clothing and gifts, the on-site hotel shops stock items you may need during your stay: sunglasses, film, toothbrushes, toothpaste, razors and a range of childcare products are available. In addition, they each feature a few one-offs in keeping with their individual theme. Hotel Cheyenne®'s General Store, for example, has Western-style souvenirs and clothing.

The Planet Hollywood® restaurant and Rainforest Café, both in Disney® Village, also have their own ranges of merchandise.

Best for babies

La Bottega di Gepetto (Fantasyland)
Disney & Co. (Main Street, USA)
Disney Clothiers Ltd. (Main Street, USA)

Barbie

World of Toys (Disney® Village)

Christmas goodies

La Boutique du Château (Fantasyland)

Confectionery and candy

Boardwalk Candy Palace (Main Street, USA)
La Confiserie des Trois Fées (Fantasyland)

Cowboy Gear

Buffalo Trading Company (Disney® Village)
Thunder Mesa Mercantile (Frontierland)

Dressing-up and costume

La Chaumière des Sept Nains (Fantasyland)
Le Coffre du Capitaine (Adventureland)
Hollywood Pictures (Disney® Village)

Sportswear

Star Traders (Discoveryland)
Team Mickey (Disney® Village)

What you can expect to pay

Disney's rigorous standards apply across the board and quality is in no way compromised when it comes to selling souvenirs. The clothes and toys especially are well designed and will stand the test of time.

There is little point hunting for bargains. Prices are standardized and you will pay the same for a Disneyland T-shirt whichever shop you visit. While some items are unique to each shop, there is a good deal of crossover. This can be helpful if you cannot find a particular clothing-size in one shop and want to try elsewhere.

No single item is overpriced but there are so many from which to choose that a few small gifts soon add up. Before you know it, you have handed over a small fortune. Here are a few sample prices (subject to change):

Mickey jelly lollipop	10F
Mickey drinking glass	15F
Pirate toy telescope	20F
Mini cowboy pistol	25F
Satin purse	30F
Nestlé chocolates	30F
Cavalry dress-up hat	55F
Minnie Mouse rucksack	59F
Mickey Mouse pullover	89F

Top tips

▲ All receipts are headed Disneyland® Paris, not by their individual shop names. You will need to make a note of which receipt relates to which gift, as each itemized receipt can be hard to decipher unless you are familiar with shorthand French (e.g. *sacados mndots* = Minnie Mouse candy-filled mini rucksack).

▲ Although there is a good deal of crossover between stores, try to remember where you saw that favoured item as you can never be sure if it will turn up at the next shop.

▲ To avoid long queues, shop in the early morning and afternoon.

Where to eat

If as much imagination went into preparing the food as it has into making the Theme Park, Disneyland® Paris would be one of the gastronomic highlights of Europe. However, although there are over 60 places to eat, spread across the Theme Park, Disney® Village and the hotels, what you get – with a few exceptions – is standard US fare, of a fairly high quality. There is no call to be overly snooty about it, of course, as it is the kind of food kids eat by the bucketful without even a murmur of complaint.

Top tips

▲ If you are set on having lunch within the Theme Park, try to eat before midday or after 2.30pm to avoid the crush. If you have already seen the parade, eat while it is on, when the restaurants are likely to be emptier.

▲ The evening rush for dinner tends to be between 8pm and 9pm. Avoid it if you can.

▲ Some restaurants (marked in this chapter with an asterisk) may be closed off-peak on Mon and Tues, others on Wed and Thurs.

✿ Children's menus are available in all of the Theme Park's restaurants, as are bottle-warmers and highchairs for babies and toddlers.

Your best bet is to find a place where the queues are not too heavy and the food is reasonable. Regardless of each restaurant's ostensible theme (be it saloon, jazz club or pirate grotto) menus tend towards standard American fast-food fare, especially at the counter-service eateries. Unfortunately fast-food is not something at which Disney excel. This is surprising, considering how well they do everything else. If you are resigned to a quick-fix, fried-food fate, you will find children's fun meals are by far the best value and should satisfy the majority of grown-ups just as readily.

Best for breakfast

Few things can possibly be more fun for your kids than starting their day with a gigantic buffet breakfast accompanied by some classic Disney characters. They get to meet all their favourites, cuddle, kiss, collect their autographs and have keepsake snaps taken with them. Disneyland® Hotel guests can book a character breakfast in **Inventions Restaurant**; Hotel New York® guests can breakfast with their idols at the **Manhattan Restaurant**; while guests of the Davy Crockett Ranch® can attend **Crockett's Tavern**.

All other guests can currently pre-book a character breakfast at the **Los Angeles Bar & Grill** in Disney® Village, though venues tend to change seasonally.

Café Fantasia at the Disneyland® Hotel lives up to its name with a substantial buffet that will set you up for the entire day. The **Parkside Diner** at the Hotel New York® is a relaxed thirties Manahattan-style neighbourhood bistro offering an equally generous buffet spread.

On Main Street, USA, the **Cable Car Bake Shop** serves a continental breakfast, while **Plaza Gardens Restaurant** is a whimsical setting within the Theme Park which serves an ample buffet breakfast from 10am.

Best for lunch

You are not permitted to take your own food into the Theme Park, but there is a picnic site just outside the entrance, between the main car park and railway station. It is worth considering stashing a prepared picnic in one of the lockers just inside the main gate, but if you do head back outside for a picnic lunch, be sure to get your hand stamped so that you can get back in again.

When it comes to lunchtime menus, both the hotel and *à la carte* restaurants are somewhat variable and often rather expensive; the table service restaurants provide a budget three-course meal.

Chicken and chips at **Au Chalet de la Marionette*** (Fantasyland) is excellent for kids (and almost deserted at 3pm) as is the vast **Cowboy Cookout*** (Frontierland) which otherwise tends to be quite crowded. In Discoveryland **Café Hyperion*** offers a popular fast-food menu plus a show, though the food queues here are often far too long. **Buzz Lightyear's Pizza Planet*** (Discoveryland) offers your kids the chance to play safely and graze while you take a well-earned breather.

Market House Deli on Main Street, USA has classic American sandwiches such as hot pastrami on rye. An ice cream for dessert at neighbouring **Gibson Girl Ice Cream Parlour** is a fun treat.

For a quick and easy snack, there are mobile food carts (*chariots gourmands*)

Food for thought

- If the Theme Park placed every popcorn box sold in one year end to end, the trail would reach from Paris to Metz, a distance of some 300km.
- 60 tons of beef fillet are consumed every year – three times the weight of the Eiffel Tower.
- 283 tons of french fries are consumed each year. Laid end to end, they would cover the distance from Paris to Moscow.

dotted around serving popcorn, baked potatoes, ice creams, pretzels, pizzas, sandwiches, drinks and the like. The vendors only accept cash. Expect to pay upwards of 17F for a can of fizzy drink.

Best for dinner

For full service restaurants in the Theme Park you will pay a premium, yet the price reflects the quality both of the food and of the elaborate and imaginative décor. Their popularity makes it worthwhile booking a table in advance if you know you want to eat at a busy time.

The experience of eating in the **Blue Lagoon*** (Adventureland) is one you will never forget. You eat on the 'shore' of a Caribbean Pirate hideaway while the boats from Pirates of the Caribbean glide silently past, full of drooling guests. Snapper, swordfish and Caribbean delicacies cram the menu.

Auberge de Cendrillon* in Fantasyland is hosted by cast members wearing 17th-century costumes. In keeping with its Louis XIV theme, the restaurant serves classic French cuisine (the nearest you will get to a traditional meal in this corner of France).

Walt's*, on Main Street, USA, is also a superb restaurant offering fine American fare. If you are lucky, they will seat you so

Best for...

Fish & Chips
Toad Hall Restaurant (Fantasyland)

Hamburger & Fries
Annette's Diner (Disney® Village)
Planet Hollywood® (Disney® Village)

Ice Cream
Gibson Girl Ice Cream Parlour
(Main Street, USA)

Pasta
Manhattan Restaurant (Hotel New York®)
Los Angeles Bar & Grill (Disney® Village)

Pizza
Colonel Hathi's Pizza Outpost
(Adventureland)
Rock 'n' Roll America (Disney® Village)

Sandwiches
Market House Deli (Main Street, USA)
New York Style Sandwiches
(Disney® Village)

Steaks
Silver Spur Steakhouse (Frontierland)
Hunter's Grill (Sequoia Lodge®)

Seafood
Blue Lagoon Restaurant (Adventureland)
Yacht Club (Newport Bay Club Hotel®)

that you can watch the Main Street, USA parade in comfort from an upstairs window. The menu includes Veal Oscar, rack of lamb, crab cakes and stuffed Maine lobster.

If you choose to leave the Theme Park to eat, you will find the hotel restaurants become less expensive the further away they are from the main entrance. All are licensed to serve alcohol. In Disney® Village itself, a clutch of good eateries provides entertainment in novel surroundings.

Annette's Diner is highly recommended, as the queues outside will confirm. You are served by 1950s-style roller-skating waitresses against a chorus of memory-jerking hits. The menu is, essentially, hamburgers,

shakes and fries, but the quality is great and you can order a beer. **Planet Hollywood®** has established street-cred with kids while **The Steakhouse** is excellent, if a little pricey. Towards Lake Disney the giant **McDonald's®** has dependable price structures. The Audio-Animatronics® at the **Rainforest Café®** are a guaranteed thrill for first-timers.

Birthdays
You can celebrate a birthday by ordering a Disney chocolate cake for the end of your meal. These are available from the restaurants in Disney® Village and from all the hotels and restaurants in the Theme Park offering table service (including **Plaza Gardens Restaurant**). Try to give at least two hours notice either at the restaurant itself or at the information desk in your hotel.

Seasonal changes
All the Theme Park restaurants are open during July and August. During the winter months, however, several are closed all week, except during school holidays. Some may be closed on off-peak Mondays and Tuesdays, others on off-peak Wednesdays and Thursdays. You may also find that some of the hotel restaurants (especially those in hotels which boast more than one restaurant) are closed some days during the winter. None of the Disney® Village restaurants are seasonally affected.

Special diets
Vegetarian food is available at most Theme Park and hotel restaurants, but you may prefer to confirm this with staff before being seated. Typical vegetarian dishes include pizza, pasta, soups and salad. Kosher diets can be catered for with advance warning.

Where to sleep

To get the most from the Theme Park, you should try to stay there: then you can pop back to your hotel when the kids (and you) get weary, whilst continuing to immerse yourself in the Disney experience – just as much thought has gone into creating the hotels as into the Theme Park itself. The attention to detail is really quite impressive.

Disneyland® Paris reservations

✆ UK (08705) 030 303
✆ USA (1) 407 934 7639
✆ direct 01 60 30 60 53, 🖷 01 64 74 59 20
Disneyland Paris, Central Reservations Office,
BP 105, ✉ 77777, Marne-la-Vallée,
Cedex 4, France
www.disneylandparis.com

Accommodation off site

Staying off site can work out cheaper if you are prepared to seek out budget accommodation in or around Paris (for more details of accommodation in Paris, *see* pp.144–49). You can book cheap rooms through the Seine and Marne Tourist Information Office in the centre of Disney® Village. For a small fee, they will contact the hotel on your behalf and arrange the booking.

Accommodation on site

The resort has seven hotels, one of which is set a little way from the Theme Park. A free shuttle bus service runs every 12 minutes between the main hotels (though not Davy Crockett Ranch®) and the Theme Park and Disney® Village.

Staying in a Disneyland® Paris hotel means you are guaranteed entrance to the Theme Park (and are allowed in half an hour earlier in summer). What is more, you don't have to leave the magic behind when you exit the Theme Park gates.

While Disney would maintain that quality of service remains equal across the board, at the end of the day, you get what you pay for. Disneyland® Hotel, at the entrance of the Theme Park, is the most convenient and the most expensive. The Hotel Santa Fe® is best described as cheap and cheerful.

How they work

Most rooms accommodate up to four people, with twin double beds or one king-size bed, plus en-suite shower/bathroom. They have colour TV with satellite channels in several languages, plus, of course, a Disney movie channel and a number of in-house channels telling you about the Theme Park.

If you book a room independently you will be charged a one-off nightly rate: up to four guests and infants under the age of three can stay in one room inclusive, which can make booking direct with the hotel a good option. In peak season and at the weekends you will often need to pay for passports to the Theme Park at the same time as booking a room.

Hotel check-in is from 3pm, check-out before 11am; all of the hotels have luggage facilities. If you require express check-out (and you are paying by credit card) your bill can be hung on your door on the morning of your departure. As long as you agree with it, your bill will be automatically charged to your credit card.

All hotel residents are issued with a personal hotel ID card, allowing free access to

Staying on site

the hotel's leisure facilities, the car park and Hurricanes nightclub.

It is also worth using the special 'charge card' system: when you have checked in, you can give the receptionist your credit card details and are then able to use your ID card to charge most of your purchases in the park and in Disney® Village directly to your room account (except McDonald's®, the Gaumont Cineplex, Planet Hollywood® and the Rainforest Café®). Better still, all your shopping can be sent straight back to your hotel, so you don't have to carry it around with you. Of course this system is designed to make spending money even easier.

Each hotel has an information and/or concierge desk which will help you with reservations for meals, shows, golf and excursions, and other practical information.

For children

Each hotel has at least one themed restaurant featuring a children's menu (though beware long queues during peak periods, especially at the larger hotels). They also feature a pay-as-you-play video games room, and some form of supervised activity most days. There are also plenty of activities to look forward to in the evenings, and especially at weekends, during school holidays and when the park closes early in winter. While you are welcome to use other hotel restaurants, you are not entitled to use the leisure facilities at any hotels other than your own.

Top tips

▲ Cots need to be requested at the time of booking.

Disneyland® Hotel

✆ 01 60 45 65 41
✉ 01 60 45 65 33
1600–2450F per room, per night
478 'fairytale' rooms
(18 suites and 11 rooms for the disabled)
Rooms have mini-bar, telephone, radio, safe-deposit box, TV and air conditioning. 24hr room service. Dry cleaning service. Cots on request. Babysitting. Free valet parking. Currency exchange. Small indoor heated pool. Health club. Shop: Galerie Mickey.

This award-winning hotel is the smallest on site, but by far the most luxurious. Inspired by the sumptuous hotels built on the West Coast of Florida at the turn of the 20th century, its candy-pink turrets, dripping chandelier, majestic staircases and pastel décor are straight out of a fairy tale. Even if you don't get to stay here, pay at least one visit and soak up the atmosphere.

The hotel straddles the entrance to Disneyland® Paris: guests can enjoy panoramic views of the Theme Park, and smile smugly at the lines of day visitors queuing up outside the gates each morning.

The hotel's 50 best (Castle Club) rooms have an unforgettable view down Main Street, USA to Sleeping Beauty Castle, and their own direct access to the Theme Park, private lift, personalized check-in, private bar and complimentary breakfast.

Just for the kids

❁ Children's corner for 4–11-year-olds, supervized Fri–Sat afternoons: interactive CD-ROM, face-painting and other organized activities.

✿ Character breakfast each morning. Disney characters appear in the main hall every morning, and with Mary Poppins Wed–Sun.

✿ Video games room.

Dining and Bars

✿ Café Fantasia: classic movie-inspired café, ideal for breakfast.

✿ Inventions: buffet-style dining and character breakfasts.

✿ California Grill: West Coast cuisine, with an open kitchen so you can watch your food being prepared.

✿ Main Street Cocktail Lounge: piano bar overlooking Main Street, USA.

Hotel New York®

☎ 01 60 45 73 47
✉ 01 60 45 73 33
1000–1550F per room, per night
532 rooms
(31 suites and 13 rooms for the disabled)
Rooms have Minitel terminals, mini-bar, telephone, radio, safe-deposit box, TV and air conditioning. 24hr room service. Dry cleaning service. Cots on request. Babysitting. Car park with valet service (fee payable). Currency exchange. Indoor and outdoor heated pools. Health club. Two floodlit tennis courts (fee payable). Open-air skating rink (Oct–Mar, fee payable). Hair salon. Shop: New York Boutique. Free water taxi rides to the Newport Bay Club®.

After the Disneyland® Hotel, this hotel is the closest to the Theme Park (just 5–10 mins' walk), situated on Lake Disney® also within easy walking distance of Disney® Village. Based on the Manhattan skyline of brownstones and skyscrapers, it is a plush hotel with design touches from the roaring twenties. Its fountain even becomes an ice rink in winter.

The rooms are comfortable and spacious, but the hotel is sophisticated rather than fun. It's probably best suited to uptown couples: the extensive adjoining convention centre certainly attracts a lot of business. The best rooms have a lake view (supplement payable).

The best spot for families is the small children's play area adjoining the sprawling New York City Bar, where kids can play late into the evening while adults enjoy a drink or two. The Manhattan restaurant is marginally more expensive than the bustling Parkside Diner but it's well worth it (and worth reserving a table in advance to avoid the queues).

Just for the kids

✿ Roger Rabbit Corner near reception runs organized children's activities, interactive computer and Disney Channel TV Tues–Sat evenings.

✿ Goofy perfoms a rap with his friends in reception Sat and Sun mornings.

✿ Character breakfast each morning.

✿ Video games arcade.

Dining and Bars

✿ Parkside Diner: laid-back New York-style atmosphere.

✿ Manhattan Restaurant: Art Deco style, reminiscent of a 1930's club. Character breakfasts.

✿ New York City Bar: sprawling bar area with live evening entertainment.

Newport Bay Club®

✆ 01 60 45 55 11
✉ 01 60 45 55 33
870–1300F per room, per night
1077 rooms
(15 suites and 23 rooms for the disabled)
Rooms have mini-bar, telephone, radio, safe-deposit box, TV and air conditioning. Laundrette and dry cleaning service. Cots on request. Babysitting. Car park. No porters or trolleys. Currency exchange. Pool. Health club. Shop: Bay Boutique. Free water taxi to the Hotel New York®.

A stylish hotel themed on the elegant 19th-century resorts of New England and set on the southern shores of Lake Disney®, about 10 to 15minutes' walk from the Theme Park. Its towering lighthouse, rocking-chair-lined verandah, awnings and pergolas recreate the atmosphere of a vast sailing club. The light and airy blue and white décor adds to the nautical air. Most rooms sleep four, though there are a few family rooms for up to six guests. Try to secure a room with a lake view, or even consider paying the supplement to stay on the Admiral's Floor where you would benefit from a separate check-in area, porter service, concierge and 24hr room service.

Just for the kids

🌼 A children's club set in a pirate ship above the indoor pool, with face-painting, balloon-sculpting and colouring on selected days.

🌼 Disney characters appear in the main hall every morning.

🌼 Video games room.

Dining and Bars

🌼 Yacht Club: fish and shellfish.

🌼 Cape Cod: buffet.

🌼 Fisherman's Wharf: welcoming lounge bar with views over the lake.

🌼 Captain's Quarters: bar.

Sequoia Lodge®

✆ 01 60 45 51 34
✉ 01 60 45 51 33
760–1200F per room, per night
997 rooms
(14 suites and 21 rooms for the disabled)
Rooms have mini-bar, telephone, radio, TV and air conditioning. Laundrette and dry cleaning service. Cots on request. Babysitting. Car park. Currency exchange. Pool. Health club.
Shop: Northwest Passage.

Based on a Rocky Mountain hunters' lodge, this hotel is located beside Lake Disney® in the middle of 44,000m² of woodland, about 10 to 15 minutes' walk from the Theme Park. There are five timber and stone-built chalets (billed as hunting lodges) surrounding the main building, but it is more convenient to stay in the main lodge. Ask for a room with a lake view. The Sequoia Lodge® is a bit stark, although the roaring log fire in the lounge area makes a superb focal point in winter. The imaginative pool area is excellent.

Just for the kids

🌼 Children's corner with a variety of activities.

🌼 Disney characters visit every morning, and every evening except Friday.

- Outdoor playground.
- Video games room.

Dining and Bars

- Hunter's Grill: rôtisserie roast meats.
- Beaver Creek Tavern: international cuisine.
- Redwood Bar and Lounge.

Hotel Cheyenne®

☎ 01 60 45 63 14
✉ 01 60 45 62 33
545–990F per room, per night
1000 rooms
(21 rooms for the disabled)
Rooms have telephone, radio, TV, central heating, fan, one double bed and two bunk beds.
Laundrette. Cots on request. Babysitting. Car park.
No porter. Currency exchange. Shop: General Store.

Imaginatively themed as a Wild West town, with its rooms spread across 14 low-rise out-buildings on one side of a main street; you might easily find yourself sleeping above the bank or even the jailhouse. Covered wagons stud the way, and cast members roam Desperado Street in cowboy clobber. There's even the odd gunfight. Parents might find it a little too film-set flimsy, but it is the only hotel child centred enough to offer rooms with bunk beds, plus free pony rides during the warmer months. The rooms are adequate, though a bit of a squeeze for a family; over half are interconnecting.

The dining area is a cavernous barn with long trestle tables. The only real drawback is that there are no leisure facilities and the hotel is some 15–20mins' walk, from the Park, but there's a shuttle every 5 minutes.

Just for the kids

- Children's corner, with face-painting and colouring on certain days.
- Disney characters put in an appearance in reception every morning.
- Pony rides, weather permitting every morning.
- Log-built adventure playground, plus teepee-filled play area.
- Video games room.

Dining and Bars

- Chuck Wagon Café: nine themed, self-service Texan market food stalls.
- Red Garter Saloon: welcoming family atmosphere and live music.

Hotel Santa Fe®

☎ 01 60 45 78 27
✉ 01 60 45 78 33
444–850F per room, per night
1000 rooms
(21 rooms for the disabled)
Rooms with telephone, radio, TV and fan.
Laundrette. Cots on request. Babysitting. Car park. Currency exchange. Shop: Trading Post.

By far the cheapest hotel, with a New Mexico desert theme, complete with erupting volcano and dusty desert trails leading to 42 'pueblos'. The rooms are bright and well designed. It is 15–20mins' walk from the Theme Park, but there's a regular shuttle bus service.

Just for the kids

- A children's corner in reception, with face-painting, colouring, etc. on certain days.

- Disney characters appear every morning.
- Totem Circle children's playground.
- Video games room.

Dining and Bars

- La Cantina: self-service, American Tex-Mex.
- Rio Grande Bar: Mexican cocktails and live music.

Davy Crockett Ranch®

☎ 01 60 45 68 14
🖷 01 60 45 69 33
498 double-glazed cabins for 4 or 6 people
97 camping sites
Cabins feature bath, telephone, radio, TV, heating and housekeeping service on request. 4-person cabins have one double bed and a fold-away bed. 6-person cabins feature additional twin bunk beds. Towels and linen supplied. Heated comfort stations with toilets, showers and laundry. Bicycle, roller blade and minicar rentals (fee payable).
Shop: Alamo Trading Post.

About five miles (15mins' drive) from the Theme Park, the Ranch is billed as a wilderness hideaway. Situated in the heart of a 57 hectare forest, it is a resort in its own right.

The 4- or 6-person trailer 'log cabins' have luxurious self-catering facilities. Each cabin is spacious and well equipped, with microwave, refrigerator dishwasher and coffee-maker. At check-in, guests receive a 'welcome basket' packed with groceries. Outside there is a BBQ grill and a wooden table, with connectors for electricity and water for a caravan. At the heart of the ranch is a small western fort town complete with restaurant, store, pool complex, sports

facilities and play areas. The Blue Springs Pool, by far the best of the resort, is a large indoor heated pool with slides, waterfall, giant Jacuzzi, and a separate children's area. In addition there are two covered tennis courts and sports fields. Outdoor activities include jogging, mountain bike trails and archery. You could easily spend a couple of days here without even venturing out to the Theme Park at all.

The campsite

There are campsite facilities if you would prefer to bring your own tent but, despite first-rate facilities, it is quite expensive: around 400F per night for a small pitch with electrical hook-ups and dedicated water and drainage connections. It is better value for caravans and motorhomes.

Just for the kids

- Face-painting and mask-making workshops, outdoor playground, Indian camp with teepees, wild animal enclosure, small farm.
- Disney characters appear every evening in the village square.
- Supervised archery, bicycle obstacle course and treasure hunts.
- Pony rides, plus skates and mountain bike hire (fee payable).
- Video games room.

Dining and Bars

- Saloon: family lounge with country music and karaoke evenings.
- Crockett's Tavern: American fare. Character breakfasts available.

For ease of access, you can stay anywhere in central Paris (*see* pp.144–49 for hotel listings), near any métro station or the RER line. If you have a car, there are yet more options. Many of these hotels may be unexceptional in terms of their surroundings, but they all offer flexibility, freedom and good value for money. Most cater for children either for free, or for a nominal charge.

- The town of Bussy St Georges is just 4 miles (7km) from the Theme Park and one stop on the RER line. Take exit 12 from the A4 motorway, or RER station Bussy St Georges.

- Noisy le Grand is located halfway between Paris and the Theme Park, some 25 minutes' drive away. Take the A4 motorway, or use RER station Noisy-le-Grand-Mont-d'Est, six stops from the Park.

- Marne-la-Vallée and Collégien are just two rail stations from the Theme Park, or 10 minutes' drive by car. Take exit 12 (Val Bussy) from the A4 motorway.

- Lognes is 7 miles (11km) drive, or three stops by RER.

- Lesigny is 13 miles (21km) from the park. Take exit 18 (Lesigny Romaine) on the N104.

- Fontainebleau is about 20 miles (32km) from Disneyland® Paris; Melun is a little closer.

- Lagny is about 15 minutes' drive away, or 20 minutes by SNCF to Paris.

- For Ozoir-la-Ferrière, take the A4 towards Paris, exit towards Villeneuve-le-Comte, then follow directions for the Villeneuve-St-Denis. Turn right in the village for Ozoir.

Suggested hotels

Holiday Inn, Bussy
✆ 01 64 66 35 65

Sol Inn, Bussy St Georges
✆ 01 64 66 11 11

Novotel, Collégien
✆ 01 64 80 53 53

Château de Grande Romaine, Lesigny
✆ 01 64 43 16 00

Hotel le Révellion, Lesigny
✆ 01 60 02 25 26

Hotel Frantour, Lognes
✆ 01 64 80 02 50

Tulip Inn, Lognes
✆ 01 60 37 27 27

Novotel, Marne-la-Vallée
✆ 01 64 80 53 53

Ibis, Marne-la-Vallée
✆ 01 64 68 00 83

Hotel Premiere Classe, Marne-la-Vallée
✆ 01 60 17 30 19

Mercure, Noisy le Grand
✆ 01 45 92 47 47

Novotel Atria, Noisy le Grand
✆ 01 48 15 60 60

Au Pavillon Bleu, Ozoir-la-Ferrière
✆ 01 64 40 05 56

For alternative hotel information in the Disneyland® Paris vicinity contact

French Tourist Board
✆ UK (09068) 244 123
(calls cost 60 pence per minute)
www.paris.org/Hotels/Post/hotel.post.77000.html

As you might expect, plenty of thought has gone into catering for leisure time outside the Theme Park. If you have the energy after your thrill-seeking day, you will find that facilities for practising your favourite sports are first-rate. If spectator sports are more your style, head for the Sports Bar in Disney® Village, where uninterrupted coverage will keep you up to date with the latest scores, events and triumphs. Those with twitchy fingers can test their reflexes at a wealth of video simulator games and electronic amusements in the Disney® Village arcades, or at any one of the Disneyland® Paris hotel's games rooms.

Ball games

If they need to let off steam, there's plenty of space for you and your children to kick a ball around and try out at basketball, football and volley ball on the sports fields attached to the Davy Crockett Ranch®.

Boating

On the resort's man-made Lake Disney® you can rent out pedaloes and 'Toobies', miniature tyre-like motor boats built for two (*Toobies 50F per half-hour; pedaloes 60F per half-hour*). The service is not available during the winter.

Cycling

Rent a quadricycle and take a tour around Lake Disney® (*60F per half-hour*). Winding woodland trails have been laid out around Davy Crockett Ranch® for cycling and jogging. The campsite offers 24-hour bicycle rentals for guests (*40F per hour for adults; 20F per hour for children*). There are also special family deals (*two bikes 50F per hour, four bikes 70F per hour*).

Golf

The Theme Park has its own 27-hole championship-level golf course. Broken down into flexible 9-hole sections, it is open to golfers of all abilities who can test their skills among the lakes, hills, waterfalls and rivers of this huge 222-acre course. There are also 25 driving ranges (10 are covered), a 600m² putting green (in the shape of Mickey's head, of course), plus a pitching green and bunker. The three 9-hole courses conveniently begin and end in front of the Club House, offering drinks, snacks and a chance to freshen up and relax. Golfing equipment is on sale at Goofy's Pro Shop and lessons (not from Goofy, thankfully) are available.

Situated a few kilometres south of the main resort, and well signposted, the golf course is just outside the resort's Boulevard Circulaire between the hamlets of Magny-le-Hongre and Bailly-Romainvilliers. The course is open all year daily from 8.45am until sunset. Package rates and less expensive twilight green fees are also available.

Green fees

18 holes
160F during the week,
280F weekends and public holidays.

9 holes
120F during the week,
180F weekends and public holidays.
For information and bookings call
☎ 01 60 45 68 90.

Health clubs

The Disneyland® Hotel, Hotel New York®, Newport Bay Club® and Sequoia Lodge® all have their own health clubs with gyms attached. Their facilities are excellent, and include aerobics and exercise machines, Jacuzzi, massage, sauna, solarium and steam rooms.

Membership is free for the duration of your stay, though the solariums normally cost extra (but they're free at the Newport Bay Club®), while a massage session will set you back anything from 150F per hour (Newport Bay Club®) to 500F per hour (Disneyland® Hotel).

Ice-skating

Here is a winter treat that's not to be missed. The Rockerfeller Plaza ice rink at the Hotel New York® is framed by skyscrapers, just like the original back home in Manhattan. Only open from October through to March (and weather permitting), the cost for a two-hour session is 50F, with a small reduction if you bring along your own skates.

Swimming

Both indoor and outdoor pools can be found at the resort's hotels. There are heated indoor pools at the Disneyland® Hotel, Hotel New York®, the Newport Bay Club®, the Sequoia Lodge® and Davy Crockett Ranch®. At the Sequoia Lodge® the pool is specially landscaped in its own woodland chalet in keeping with the hotel's National Park theme. At Davy Crockett Ranch® the tropical pool area – Blue Springs – is enormous, complete with water slides, waterfall, a giant Jacuzzi concealed in a grotto and separate kid's pool. Both the Hotel New York® and Newport Bay Club® have good indoor pools with additional outdoor swimming areas.

If you have forgotten to pack your costume, you will find swimwear available at the Bay Boutique (Newport Bay Club®), Northwest Passage (Sequoia Lodge®), Alamo Trading Post (Davy Crockett Ranch®), and Team Mickey (Disney® Village).

Tennis

Four open-air hard courts are available: two flood-lit courts at Hotel New York, open from 7am–10pm (*100F per hour*) and two more at Davy Crockett Ranch, open 9am–9pm. There is no court fee if you are staying at one of the theme hotels. You can hire racquets (*30F*) and a box of balls (*50F*) on site, or purchase tennis gear from the Team Mickey Shop in Disney® Village. Advance reservations are recommended.

Visitors with special needs

Disneyland® Paris is designed to be as user-friendly as possible for all its guests. All the shops, restaurants and toilet blocks are accessible by wheelchair, and a *Disabled Guest Guide* is available at City Hall on Main Street, USA, at any information booth and at each of the hotel receptions. Note that cast members are not permitted to lift disabled guests in and out of wheelchairs.

For a free copy of the *Disabled Guest Guide*, call ✆ 0990 03 03 03 or write to:

Disneyland® Paris Guest Communications
PO Box 305
Watford
Herts WD1 8TP, England
or
BP 100
✉ 77777 Marne-la-Vallée
Cedex 4, France

Getting around

Special Services Parking is located near the entrance of the Visitor's Car Park close to the Disneyland® Hotel. All the hotel car parks have special areas reserved for guests with reduced mobility. Both wheelchair and stroller rentals are available from Town Square Terrace, just inside the main entrance. Specially adapted minibuses circulate between the hotels and the Theme Park.

Within the Theme Park

Disabled visitors get special access to most attractions and restaurants, and there are discounted day pass rates for wheelchair users and their companion. Priority is given for prime positions in Fantasyland and on Main Street, USA for the shows and parades. Ask a cast member for assistance.

There is a free facility for wheelchair users to collect any purchases they make in the Theme Park from one central location at the end of the day. A couple of shops feature specially designed dressing-rooms (Les Trésors de Schéhérazade and La Chaumière des Sept Nains). City Hall can issue you with a special card, which entitles you to use the designated entrance for special needs guests along with one companion. Disabled guests can remain in their wheelchairs throughout the following attractions:

Frontierland
The Chaparral Stage
Critter Corral
Rustler Roundup Shootin' Gallery
Thunder Mesa Riverboat Landing

Adventureland
Adventure Isle
Le Passage Enchanté d'Aladdin

Fantasyland
Alice's Curious Labyrinth
Castle Courtyard
Fantasy Festival Stage
La Galerie de la Belle au Bois Dormant
La Tanière du Dragon
Le Théâtre du Château

Discoveryland
Arcade de Jeux Vidéo
Les Mystères du Nautilus
Videopolis
Le Visionarium
La Voie Stellaire

The following attractions can accommodate guests able to leave their wheelchairs and walk a short distance unassisted:

Frontierland

Big Thunder Mountain

Phantom Manor

Adventureland

Indiana Jones™ et le Temple du Péril

Pirates of the Caribbean

Fantasyland

Casey Jr. le Petit Train du Cirque

It's a Small World

Le Pays des Contes de Fées

Peter Pan's Flight

Les Pirouettes du Vieux Moulin

Discoveryland

Space Mountain

On the following rides, disabled guests will require assistance from a companion:

Main Street, USA

Disneyland Railroad

Horse drawn streetcars and motor vehicles

Frontierland

River Rogue Keelboats

Fantasyland

Blanche-Neige et les Sept Nains

Le Carrousel de Lancelot

Dumbo the Flying Elephant

Mad Hatter's Tea Cups

Les Voyages de Pinocchio

Discoveryland

Autopia

Orbitron

Star Tours

Within Disney® Village

At Buffalo Bill's Wild West Show, special areas are reserved for guests in wheelchairs. The show is not recommended for anyone suffering from asthma or other respiratory allergies. At Hurricanes nightclub, an elevator is available for guests in wheel-

Top tips

▲ Despite Disney's best efforts, not all of the pathways around the Theme Park are completely wheelchair-friendly.

▲ Individuals with back or muscular problems should not ride Autopia, Star Tours or Big Thunder Mountain.

chairs. All the cinemas at the Gaumont Cineplex are wheelchair-friendly.

At the hotels

All seven theme hotels have bedrooms specially adapted for guests in wheelchairs. There are a limited number of wheelchairs available for rental from the reception desk.

Catering for specific needs

Sight impaired guests

City Hall provides portable tape players and audio cassettes which describe the attractions in detail, as well as special guide books in Braille. Braille maps of the Theme Park (in French or English) are provided free. Guide dogs are allowed into the Theme Park though they are not always permitted on the attractions which are recommended for sight impaired guests. At Planet Hollywood® menus in Braille are provided in French and English.

Hearing impaired guests

For groups of hearing impaired guests, guided tours in sign language can be arranged (allow a month's notice). The Gaumont Cineplex in Disney® Village is equipped with magnetic loops.

Visitors with learning difficulties

Many of the more startling attractions not recommended for young children may prove equally unsettling for visitors with learning difficulties (see **Restrictions**, p.185).

Entertainment

At Buffalo Bill's Wild West Show the daily drinks consumption is 750 litres of beer and 600 litres of Coca-Cola®, whilst there are some 83,000 dishes to wash every night.

Dusk signals the end of another day at the Theme Park. This is the green light for Disney® Village to begin gearing up for its nocturnal guests.

Clubbing

Billy Bob's Country & Western Saloon

Polish up your cowboy boots and head for Nashville. This place is a country-music fan's fantasy: at its heart is a stage with a live western band. This is the spot to nibble some nachos and do-si-do your partner to the sound of guitar, fiddle and drums.

Hurricanes

An unpretentious late-night club for teenagers and up. Free entry for on-site hotel guests, but an inflated 80F for anyone else.

Rock 'n' Roll America Café

Temple of rock 'n' roll with live music, dancing and karaoke in a 1950s setting.

On-screen entertainment

Gaumont Cinema

Its biggest theatre has a whacking 260m² screen and seating for 700.

The Sports Bar

Root for your favourite team on one of 10 giant TV screens in this lively theme bar.

Video Games Arcade

All the latest high-speed, high-tech games to satisfy die-hard gamers and beginners alike.

Live shows

Reserve tickets for these shows in advance. Call ✆ 01 60 45 71 00, or visit City Hall.

Crescend'O

Show lasts 1hr 30mins.
Tickets: adult 220F, child 150F

A guaranteed jaw-slackener, this exclusive, aquatic circus has been devised by Muriel Hermine, the Olympic synchronized swimming champion. As part of the unrivalled special effects, a pool containing almost 600,000 litres of water magically appears and disappears during the show. Stupefying acrobatics by an all-swimming, all-dancing cast make it look effortless. Aquatic ballerinas, trapeze artists, trampolinists as well as musicians, jugglers, ice-skaters, fire-eaters and a stunning white horse all make an appearance during this spellbinding show.

Buffalo Bill's Wild West Show

Tickets: adult 325F, child 195F, including meal, drinks and a souvenir cowboy-hat

A dynamic dinner show, comprising cowboys, Indians and real-live buffalo, horses and bison, relives the spirit of the Wild West. With plenty of audience participation you will find yourself cheering on your own team of trigger-happy heroes as they perform daring feats of acrobatic horsemanship and shooting displays. Inspired by La Légende de Buffalo Bill, which toured Europe at the end of the 19th century, this show provides non-stop laughter and thrills for the entire family. It is a good idea to arrive at least 45 minutes early so you can enjoy the raucous pre-show entertainment. The earlier you start queuing for your seats, the closer to the action you will be.

Because of the use of live animals and shifting dust in the arena, the show is not recommended for guests suffering from allergies or asthma.

Saving money

A holiday at Disneyland® Paris is not cheap, but neither need it be too expensive if you are sensible. Once you're in, you're in, so, apart from food and souvenirs, there is little to fork out on. And if you stay at one of the cheaper resort hotels, and don't go mad in the shops or the video arcades, then you won't need a second mortgage to make the most of your visit. Here are a few more money-saving tips:

✿ Visit mid-week when package prices are cheaper.

✿ Look out for special deals and promotions at certain times of the year, such as three nights for the price of two and Kids Go Free.

✿ Three-day passports are the best value for money, but be sure you can budget for that long a stay (taking hotel bills, meals and extras into account). Two days is enough time to experience the best of the Theme Park.

✿ Pack a warm pullover and raincoat and visit in the winter months when both entrance ticket prices and hotel rates are cheaper.

✿ Throughout the Theme Park there are food carts offering filling snacks at a reasonable price. Packing your own picnic costs even less.

✿ Keep your kids away from the pay-to-play arcades. They guzzle up 10F coins quicker than you can get them out of your pocket.

American Express

American Express card holders can enjoy special privileges whenever they use their card to book at Disneyland® Paris. 'Service Magique' is an exclusive treatment programme, which includes hotel upgrades, a free welcome pack on arrival, VIP access at certain restaurants and discounts on merchandise. Full terms and conditions are available upon request. Check with your local American Express travel office or contact the dedicated American Express booking line on ✆ UK (08705) 030 309.

Magic Kingdom Club

The Magic Kingdom Club is an ideal way for the family to enjoy any of the Disney Parks and stores worldwide at reduced rates. You can also get discounts with Disney's preferred travel companies. There used to be a European Magic Kingdom Club operation, but now everything is handled by the US office, which can be reached on ✆ US (1) 714 781 1550. Membership costs around $85 for two years (including subscription to the Disney magazine).

All sorts of additional benefits apply to holders of Magic Kingdom Club Gold Cards including discounts on the following:

✿ Theme Park passports.

✿ Purchases in all Disneyland® Paris, Disney® Village and resort hotel boutiques.

✿ Purchases at The Disney Stores (except in Germany).

✿ Room and package rates.

✿ Green fee at Golf Disneyland® Paris.

✿ Hertz® car rentals.

language

Also *see* **What to Eat**, pp.140–3, for help in deciphering a French menu.

numbers

one	*un*	thirteen	*treize*	fifty	*cinquante*
two	*deux*	fourteen	*quatorze*	sixty	*soixante*
three	*trois*	fifteen	*quinze*	seventy	*soixante-dix*
four	*quatre*	sixteen	*seize*	eighty	*quatre-vingts*
five	*cinq*	seventeen	*dix-sept*	ninety	*quatre-vingt-dix*
six	*six*	eighteen	*dix-huit*		
seven	*sept*	nineteen	*dix-neuf*	one hundred	*cent*
eight	*huit*	twenty	*vingt*	one hundred and one	*cent-et-un*
nine	*neuf*	twenty one	*vingt-et-un*		
ten	*dix*	twenty two	*vingt-deux*	one hundred and two	*cent-deux*
eleven	*onze*	thirty	*trente*	one thousand	*mille*
twelve	*douze*	forty	*quarante*		

days

Monday	*lundi*
Tuesday	*mardi*
Wednesday	*mercredi*
Thursday	*jeudi*
Friday	*vendredi*
Saturday	*samedi*
Sunday	*dimanche*

months

January	*janvier*	July	*juillet*
February	*février*	August	*août*
March	*mars*	September	*septembre*
April	*avril*	October	*octobre*
May	*mai*	November	*novembre*
June	*juin*	December	*décembre*

time

What time is it?	*Quelle heure est-il?*	evening	*le soir*
month	*un mois*	today	*aujourd'hui*
week	*une semaine*	yesterday	*hier*
day	*un jour/une journée*	tomorrow	*demain*
morning	*le matin*	soon	*bientôt*
afternoon	*l'après-midi*	later	*plus tard*

transport

airport	un aéroport	subway	le métro
bicycle	une bicyclette/un vélo	platform	un quai
bus stop	un arrêt d'autobus	car	une voiture
bus	un autobus	taxi	un taxi
railway station	une gare	ticket office	un guichet
train	un train	ticket	un billet

mealtime

bib	un bavoir	another	un/une autre
bottle	un biberon	small	petit
child's portion	une portion d'enfant	hot	chaud
spoon	une cuillère	cold	froid
fork	une fourchette	menu	la carte
knife	un couteau	fixed price menu	le menu
glass	un verre	highchair	une chaise haute
beaker	un gobelet	games	les jeux
cup	une tasse	crayon	un crayon
plate	une assiette	straw	une paille

bedtime

babysitting	le baby-sitting/la garde d'enfants	double room	une chambre pour deux personnes
blanket	une couverture	single room	une chambre pour une personne
bunk beds	les lits superposés	interconnecting rooms	les chambres communicantes
cot	un lit d'enfant		
room	un lit		
twin room	une chambre à deux lits		

general

baby	un bébé	entrance	l'entrée (f)
child	un enfant	exit	la sortie
boy	un garçon	hospital	un hôpital
girl	une fille	money	l'argent (m)
doctor	un médecin	policeman	un agent de police
medicine	le médicament	police station	un commissariat de police
nappy	une couche	post office	la poste
pharmacy	une pharmacie	shop	un magasin
pushchair	une poussette	supermarket	un supermarché
open	ouvert	tobacconist	un tabac
closed	fermé	WC	un WC/les toilettes
cheap	bon marché	men	hommes
expensive	cher	women	femmes
bank	une banque		

quiz answers

1

It's the Mona Lisa, the world's most famous painting, painted by Leonardo da Vinci between 1503 and 1506. It now hangs in the Louvre.

2

It was named after its inventor, Dr Joseph-Ignace Guillotin. His aim had been to create a more humane method of execution than the traditional axe which often took several blows to sever the victim's head from their body, resulting in a slow agonizing death. The good doctor's solution to this problem was to increase the force with which the blow was delivered. A razor sharp blade set between two greased wooden runners would, when released, fall with such force that it invariably severed the head at the first attempt. Not only was the guillotine more humane, it was also quicker than previous methods meaning more people could be executed per day than ever before.

3

France defeated Brazil 3-0.

4

Marseille. The National Anthem is called the *Marseillaise*. It was the song sung by revolutionaries from Marseille when they marched on Paris in 1792.

5

The métro.

6

The Empire State Building in New York which is a massive 381m (1,250ft) tall.

7

Strange as it may seem, the answer is c. Afer his defeat at the battle of Waterloo in 1815, Napoleon was exiled to the island of St Helena. He became a recluse spending most of his time indoors, and he was poisoned by the arsenic used to colour the walls green.

8

It's on the French 10F coin.

9

It was the cart used during the French Revolution to transport condemned prisoners from their cells to the guillotine.

10

The answer is a. The Hôtel-Dieu is Paris' oldest hospital. However, lack of medical knowledge meant that, until the last century, few patients who checked in ever checked out again.

11

It's the blue whale. You can see a skeleton of one of these huge beasts in the Musée National d'Histoire Naturelle. At over 30m (100ft) long and weighing over 150 tons, the blue whale is the largest creature that has ever lived, larger even than the dinosaurs.

12

It is called the Latin Quarter because until the early 19th century the university authorities insisted that everyone who lived there spoke only in Latin – and that meant everyone from the professors and students down to the kitchen staff.

13

Henri de Toulouse-Lautrec (1864–1901). You can see some of his paintings in the Musée d'Orsay.

14

A vineyard. The grape harvest is celebrated each year with a parade. The subsequent vintage is then sold for charity.

15

An abattoir. In the early 1900s, until the funding fell through, the government wanted to build a state-of-the-art carcass-cutter on this site. It's doubtful whether it would have attracted the same number of visitors as the Cité des Sciences et de l'Industrie...

16

The names of the four steam-powered locomotives are W. E. Cody, C. K. Holliday, G. Washington and Eureka.

17

The paddle boats actually run on rails beneath the water, so the rigmarole of mooring them is all for show.

18

Raiders of the Lost Ark, which was released three years before Indiana Jones™ and the Temple of Doom.

19

The answer is b. There are approximately 1,200 Audio-Animatronic® figures in the Theme Park.

20

Alec Guinness played Obi Wan Kenobi in the original Star Wars movie. His part was played by Ewan McGregor in the recent prequel, The Phantom Menace.

Index

Main page references are in **bold**

take the kids series

- the first series of its kind for parents
- lots of family holiday ideas
- expert advice on health, safety and budgets
- what to do if your child gets lost
- stress-busting games and toys for bored kids

titles 2000

- **Amsterdam**
- **England**
- **Ireland**
- **London**
- **Travelling**

CADOGAN

take the kids
London

Joseph Fullman

survive and enjoy!

Further information

Jo Taborn
Cadogan Guides
West End House
11 Hills Place
London
W1R 1AG
✆ (020) 7287 6555
✉ (020) 7734 1733
jo.taborn@morrispub.co.uk

Distribution in the UK

Grantham Book Services Ltd
Isaac Newton Way
Alma Park Industial Estate
Grantham
NG31 9SD
✆ (01476) 541080
✉ (01476) 541061

Distribution in the US

The Globe Pequot Press
246 Goose Lane
P.O. Box 480
Guilford
Connecticut 06437-0480
✆ (800) 243 0495
✉ (800) 820 2329